The
Complete
Guide
to Home
Business

The Complete Guide to Home Business

Choosing Your Business

Start-up Planning

Home-Business Space

Launch Funding

Fine Tuning

Growth

Exit Strategies

Robert Spiegel

AMACOM

American Management Association

New York • Atlanta • Boston • Chicago • Kansas City • San Francisco • Washington, D.C.
Brussels • Mexico City • Tokyo • Toronto

Special discounts on bulk quantities of AMACOM books are
available to corporations, professional associations, and other
organizations. For details, contact Special Sales Department,
AMACOM, an imprint of AMA Publications, a division of
American Management Association,
1601 Broadway, New York, NY 10019.
Tel.: 212-903-8316 Fax: 212-903-8083

This publication is designed to provide accurate and authoritative
information in regard to the subject matter covered. It is sold with
the understanding that the publisher is not engaged in rendering
legal, accounting, or other professional service. If legal advice or
other expert assistance is required, the services of a competent professional person should be sought.

Library of Congress Cataloging-in-Publication Data

Spiegel, Robert, 1950–
    The complete guide to home business / Robert Spiegel.
      p. cm.
    Includes bibliographical references and index.
    ISBN 0-8144-7043-2
    1. Home-based businesses—Management.   2. New business
enterprises—Management.   I. Title.
  HD62.38.S67   1999
  658'.041—dc21   99-43414
                                          CIP

Printing number

10   9   8   7   6   5   4   3   2   1

To
Dave Bedini,
my home-business musician friend,
for choosing the right wines and keeping me honest.

Contents

Preface

Your Complete Home-Business Resource Guide

Complete is a big word. The goal of *The Complete Guide to Home Business* is to help you launch and grow a profitable home enterprise. This can be broken down into a number of smaller goals:

1. To help you identify the questions that will come up as you choose a business and begin to drive it forward.
2. To provide answers to these questions.
3. To provide resources for the answers we can't provide.
4. And most importantly, to encourage you to believe that you will be successful, while at the same time preparing you to face some of the difficult realities of home-business ownership.

In order to make sure this book gives you the information you need, we include resources at the end of the book that direct you to further information on the various subjects of home-business management. Whether you need to find the regulations governing franchises and business opportunities or the sources for loans and investment capital, these resources will help you obtain the information necessary for launching your company.

Many of our resources are organizations, associations, books, government departments, and university offices. But we also include Web sites, online newsgroups, chat rooms, and other Internet opportunities since most entrepreneurs are online and eager to go directly to Internet sources. The Internet is the quickest and most efficient way to get the information you need to launch your business and to grow. If you're interested in registering your trade name or trademark, you can download the forms, fill them in electronically, and return them online, saving weeks of correspondence.

Because of this efficiency, we encourage you to get online, if you are not already there. Business owners are expected to have e-mail addresses now, plus there's plenty of free publicity and commerce opportunities online. Our resource section at the end of each chapter gives Internet sources, and Chapter 24 covers marketing on the Web. We also understand that there is plenty of flux on the Internet, so the sites we list as sources have been selected for their stability and their likelihood of existing at their current addresses for an extended length of time.

Many of you will dart in and out of this book as you need it; you don't need to read it cover to cover. However, you may find that, over the course of launching and growing your enterprise, you end up reading most of this book. This is your business reference text. If you need some quick marketing ideas, go straight for the chapters on marketing. If you need information on getting help to avoid cash-flow crunches, you can go right to the chapters that discuss ways to stabilize your business. Also check the resources at the end of the book.

We hope you'll keep this book as a desk reference and use it over and over as you build your business. You may spend the first years concentrating on choosing a business, funding, marketing, and publicity. You may spend later years exploring outsourcing and investors as well as purchasing additional enterprises. Through it all, *The Complete Guide to Home Business* is your resource for success.

Acknowledgments

A number of people made this book possible. First, I'd like to thank Deidre Knight for encouraging me to pursue this idea and for convincing AMACOM to take a chance with the book. I want to thank Jacquie Flynn for bringing it warmly into the AMACOM offices, and additional thanks to Florence Stone for helping me explore ways to develop the message of home business through the American Management Association.

On the personal side, I want to thank my children, Jesse, Mari, and Connie, for allowing me to "play" on the computer when I otherwise would have been "lion" on the floor.

Introduction

The Business World Has Changed Forever

When I started my first business in the mid-1980s, I was a one-man shop in a tiny office. Not quite a home business, but close. I worked hard to hide the fact that I didn't have a full staff and didn't even have a secretary or receptionist. Just those few years ago, your business was considered marginal if you were not fully outfitted with employees, equipment, and sizable quarters. I used an answering service that specialized in sounding as if they were staff members. They had an extensive client base of mini-businesses, all pretending they were full-fledged operations. Anything less was not viewed as a legitimate business.

By the time it became acceptable to run a home-based business, I had a staff of twenty and my business had become very inefficient. So why did I bother growing a staff? Back then it was an important goal. I wanted the company to gain the credibility of a fleshed-out business with bookkeeping, production, clerical, and sales. When I finally sold the company and launched a home business, in the mid 1990s, the one-person shop was held in esteem. Now it is cool to run your company from the spare bedroom and hold business meetings in the living room. What a change. And the change is here to stay.

How did such a drastic alteration in our business climate arrive so rapidly, in such a quick ten years? Some say it was downsizing that sent middle managers out on the street for the first time in American business history. Thousands of middle managers suddenly became consultants for the same type of corporations that had sent them packing. As consultants, they didn't need the backup of an uptown office, so they set up shop in their homes. They already had professional credibility, so they didn't need the facade of an outside office.

Others attribute the change to the personal computer, which allows highly technical professionals to do their work at home. Previously, technicians needed the bulky and expensive computers and equipment that were only affordable for corporations and large public institutions such as universities. Now these highly trained professionals can work in the den and either bring their results in on disk or download their files over the phone to the larger computer at the corporation or university.

Other theories include the widespread use of overnight delivery services and faxes, which allows workers to produce top professional work from small mountain communities. Still others claim the home-business movement was spawned by the growth of the Internet. Other technology also helped the home-business movement: cheap copiers, voice-mail, cellular phones, Kinko's, women managers who embraced a less autocratic and authoritarian workplace, and outsourcing. Management guru Peter Drucker predicted it in the 1970s when he claimed that information would become the primary business currency and that information professionals would call the shots on workplace politics, undermining the authority and dominance of traditional managers.

Drucker foresaw the time when those with information would supplant the position held by those with capital. He was dead right. All around the country, those who have the freshest information are grabbing the attention of those with capital. In 1999 the *Wall Street Journal* estimated that over 30 percent of all venture capital was flowing into start-up Internet companies. The winners in the race for investment dollars are not Ph.D.s. Instead, they are likely to be college dropouts in their early twenties working out of a home business in their parents' house. They can attract venture capital because they have a better grip on the online marketplace than corporations and engineers.

All of these circumstances contribute to the change that has made your spare bedroom a credible place to conduct business. It takes an accumulation of factors to create a business change as sweeping as the home working and home-business trends. In the late 1990s, the federal government estimated that 40 percent of American workers spend some of their workweek at home. The government predicts this figure will rise to 60 percent by 2002. In addition to the workers at home, the government also estimates that there are now over 16 million home enterprises. The Small Business Administration (SBA) counts an additional 1.5 million new home businesses added each year. The home workplace is here to stay.

All these reasons make home business acceptable. But it takes more than acceptance to make a trend succeed. The economics of a home business is an additional motivater. SBA statistics show that 40 percent of new companies launched outside the home will still be in business after five years. For home enterprises, 57 percent will still be in operation after five years. This is a huge argument for launching a business from your study. The low overhead of a home business greatly increases your likelihood for success. These statistics show that for many companies, launching from home will make the difference between success and failure.

The final reason for launching from home is simply that many people prefer working at home. A home enterprise is part of a great American tradition. Prior to the 1900s, most U.S. workers were employed in their homes. These included farmers, store owners who lived above or behind their stores, lawyers, and doctors who used their front rooms for client or patient consultation. Many doctors even operated in their front offices. Working outside the home is a relatively recent change for the American worker, and many Americans find it unpleasant. America is a country where people are accustomed to working on their own property.

The industrial revolution, for all its manufacturing wonders, was a stressful, dangerous, and destructive environment for its workers. Even as automation changed the workplace from factory to office, the politics of crowded offices became a psychologically smothering place for some freewheeling Americans. The corporate office produced mammoth inefficiencies and a culture of sabotage. Outsourcing has pared away at this wasteful environment. The on-your-own, in-your-home option breeds creativity and efficient independence. You will never hear a home-business person complain that she just isn't as efficient now that she works from home.

As you kick off your home business, resist any inclination to apologize for the fact that you are running a company from your domicile. Make it a point of pride. If you're a home-business owner, you have bragging rights. You're leading the charge in a major American transition. Mom and dad are back at home, working with the family; your kids will never have to ask you what you do all day. You're setting an example of American enterprise in action right there in your den. No more organization man. No more blind and useless conformity. Your success will depend on your ability to bring it all back home and to foster your own personal business creativity.

Part I

Choosing a Home Business

Whether you launch a company, buy a franchise, or purchase an existing enterprise, choosing a home business is not just a matter of finding a great idea that will generate profits and build value. Profits and value are high priorities, but some people thrive in retail, while others thrive in publishing. Some entrepreneurs can't wait to meet new people and turn on their persuasive charm, while others have a natural shyness that is not easily overcome. The difference is not just a matter of experience; it's a matter of personality. If you intend to succeed in your new enterprise, it will have to draw on your personal strengths.

In addition to preferences and personal strengths, the professional experience you bring to the enterprise also matters a great deal in your selection of the right business. You need to decide whether to buy an existing business or to start a business independently. If you choose to buy an existing business, you will have a choice as to whether to buy a franchise or a business opportunity or to participate in a network-marketing company. All of these options have their strengths and weaknesses. Some of the choices may be a good fit for you while providing an absolute disaster for someone else. A franchise, for example, is not intrinsically superior to network marketing; it depends on your goals, preferences, skills, personality, and resources.

This section covers the different types of enterprises that you can start or buy, and it notes their individual qualities. This section also explains the different questions you will have to ask yourself in the process of choosing the right home business. We even provide a test to help you see if you have the personality quirks of an entrepreneur. The search for the perfect home business is an examination of your skills, your personal qualities, and your expectations as much as it is a search for the right type of business. It will be hard to determine what business is right for you until you assess your needs, experience, resources, tolerance for risk, and other qualities. To get the right match, you need to get to know yourself.

At the end of the section, we review the state of the home-business market. What's working and what's not working in home enterprises? This is the business climate. Many entrepreneurs start with this question, but it really isn't as important as the earlier questions of personality, experience, and resources. It is best to examine what's doing well and what's struggling in home enterprises after you have a pretty good idea of whether you want to launch from scratch or purchase a franchise. It saves you the trouble of trying to fit a round peg in a square hole if you see a particularly convincing opportunity before you have fully weighed what type of business you really want.

Six Factors to Consider

1. The business type: franchise, business opportunity, network marketing, or from-scratch operation
2. The products and services involved
3. Your personal strengths and preferences
4. Your professional experience
5. Your resources
6. The business climate

When you choose a business after you fully consider all of these elements, you will greatly increase your likelihood for success. Many business failures could have been avoided if the owner had studied all of these questions and then launched the business, fully aware of what the business would demand in time and money and what it would likely provide for him. This process reduces risk, and any effort to reduce risk at the outset will put you in a better position to succeed. Put another way, this investigation is an example of winning entrepreneurial behavior.

Chapter 1

Home-Business Possibilities and an Aptitude Test

What kind of business can you run from home? Are there some businesses that have a better future than others? These are key questions as you select the right enterprise for your home. The widespread acceptance of home companies and telecommuting offers you a broad choice of potential companies. Here are just a few of the businesses you can launch from home to give you some idea of the range of opportunities.

Home-Business Possibilities

Medical billing. This is a home business classic. This is a stable, flexible, and lucrative business. It requires very little in start-up costs, and once you have a client base, your marketing efforts will be minimal.

Desktop publishing and word processing. This is another ringer for the home. The tools and software are relatively inexpensive, and the need for this service is continual. Once you have a few regular clients, there is not much ongoing need for marketing and sales.

Freelance writing, editing, copyediting, and proofreading. This job requires professional skills, but the start-up costs are minimal. This business requires a continual marketing effort, but once you develop a broad client base, your marketing effort will become less demanding.

Cleaning and janitorial services. This business requires cleaning equipment. The work is flexible, and once you establish a client base, advertising is minimal. A small yellow pages ad can keep you busy. Janitorial services for office buildings or restaurants can be done at night on a contract basis. Growth is possible since you can hire teams.

Newsletter writing and publishing. Real estate agents, banks, insurance representatives, and stock brokers all need newsletters. Once you acquire a few clients, this business requires little marketing. The work hours are very flexible.

Weekend retailing. This can include flea markets, craft shows, and specialty malls. Your retail hours are on the weekend, but you will spend time during the week selecting and buying your inventory. It requires investment in inventory and space rental.

Web writing and researching. There are growing opportunities online. It takes a bit of searching, but after a few days of poking around in job sites, you can usually find some Web-related writing and research work.

Web-store customer service. This may be the growth job of the next few years. With the explosion of Internet commerce, Web stores and bringing in online customer service reps to help with questions and problems. Most of these people work on contract at home on their personal computers.

Dessert production. Unless you live in a tiny town, there is always a need for desserts. Desserts can include cakes, pies, pastries, and homemade ice cream. Once you line up a few restaurants, you can produce desserts in the evening and deliver them two or three times a week.

Management consulting. This requires professional experience in solving common business challenges or knowledge of how to implement new technology. Before launching, make sure there is an ongoing market for your particular skills or knowledge base.

Household errands. Now that most families have two wage earners, jobs that used to be done by mom have become opportunities for a home business. Errands can include everything from grocery shopping to taking the dog to the groomer.

Freelance publicist. The publicist helps companies and professionals get press. This can include sending out press releases, scheduling talk-show appearances, and encouraging editors to use your clients as expert sources. It requires some work to build a client base.

Corporate meeting planner. With this job, you organize outside meetings for companies, corporations, and other organizations. Services can include booking travel and arranging for space and meals. This work is very detailed and requires knowledge of the travel and hospitality industries.

Playhouse/playground designing and building. Families can afford elaborate playgrounds, playhouses, and tree forts, but dad doesn't have the time and skills to build them. This creates opportunities for home companies. You can sell and construct prefab sets or design them from scratch.

Bookkeeping and payroll service. More small companies are outsourcing their bookkeeping and payroll to service companies. You can add pickup and delivery to be more competitive. This requires a good compatible software program and a thorough knowledge of small-business tax and reporting requirements.

Web-site design and management. This consists of designing and maintaining Web sites for clients. For some clients, you design the site and train the company's staff to maintain it; in other cases, you will maintain it yourself. There is considerable competition now, but the market will expand for quite a few more years.

Gift baskets. You can create gift baskets with a variety of treats, from specialty foods to fruit, candy, and nuts. You can work with a florist, sell at flea markets, or run your own yellow pages ad.

Lawn-care and fix-it service. As people get busier and busier, they become more willing to hire out some of their unwanted chores. Marketing for this job can include door hangers and flyers. In time, word of mouth will work.

Antique dealer. In this business, you buy antiques and resell them at weekend specialty mall spaces, in flea markets, or to a select group of clients such as interior designers. It requires a knowledge of antiques and some capital for buying inventory.

Business travel agent. This is similar to the traditional travel agent, except you work for a few regular clients from your home. Home agencies are replacing office-based agents who see their margin shrinking. The smaller margin is sufficient for a home operation, with its low overhead and lack of additional employees.

Graphic designer. This has become a popular home business because of the inexpensive graphics software and the increased demand for good computer artists. A small yellow pages ad and some minimal networking with marketing and advertising groups, can uncover plenty of work.

Kids' parties. Parents have more money than time these days. They want a special experience for their children, but they have neither the energy nor the time to do it right. Design parties that include a face-painting clown and a theme, and you'll get all the Saturday work you want.

Craft-fair manufacturer. With this business, you create crafts that can be sold at craft fairs or flea markets. You take samples to retailers; they take your products on consignment. This allows you to stay home and work while they sit at the booths.

Comic-book dealer. The trend is to run collectible businesses from home while running advertising in the yellow pages. In your ad, include your phone number, not your address. Then you build your business by making appointments with regular collectors. This way you can give the best deals and attract the best customers while avoiding the financial burden of a retail store and employees.

What Produces Home-Business Success?

Are you ready to start a home business? Do you have the right personal traits to go into business for yourself? I don't believe there is an entrepreneurial personality who would find success with any potential business. Nor do I believe there are people who are so unbusiness-minded they would fail at any venture. Each enterprise calls for different personality traits from its owner. I also believe successful businesspeople share certain qualities, all of which can be learned, developed, or nurtured.

Common Traits of Successful Entrepreneurs

- *Persistence and patience.* Perhaps the greatest truth in all business start-ups is that it takes longer than expected to turn the corner financially. Those who do not develop persistence will not stay in business long enough for success to come around its blind corner.

- *Resourcefulness.* You cannot line up everything you need to get your business going and expect your resources to be sufficient. No matter how well you prepare, unexpected turns will call for quick, effective scrambling.

- *Ability to motivate other people.* This is crucial even if you are a one-person shop. You will still need to motivate vendors to deliver excellent products and services, and you will need to persuade customers to purchase your products and services.

- *Focus.* You cannot build a business as one of a number of activities you have going. A business launch requires a concerted focus of mental effort and personal drive. To succeed, you will need to concentrate your energy on nurturing your enterprise.

- *Vision of a better future.* The dream of a better future is usually the motivation behind a business start-up. Keep this vision even when the prospects don't look promising. Most new companies go through bumpy periods. A vision for a better future can keep you going when the initial excitement wears off and the future begins to look dim.

- *Capacity for ongoing learning.* Even if you are successful, you will need to continually improve your products, services, and business practices. The necessity to study your customers' needs and to run a better business never goes away.

- *Willingness to change.* A successful business embraces change. Improvements mean change; growth means change. If you do not change positively, your business will move backwards.

Following are fifteen questions that will give you an idea how closely you match the profile of an entrepreneur. Successful entrepreneurs have some common characteristics. But if you do not score highly on this test, don't take it as a sign that your likelihood for success is diminished. The entrepreneur is just one of the small-business owner types. Here in the land of business dreams, we romanticize the entrepreneur. We often believe that an entrepreneur is somehow superior, brighter, or more the hero than the workaday business owner. But the entrepreneur is the gambler in the business crowd, the one who is willing to fail to achieve his goals, the swashbuckler.

Most business owners are not entrepreneurs. You won't find an entrepreneur running a franchise (she would fight with a franchise company over marketing strategies), and you won't find an entrepreneur putting in years building a local retail store. The entrepreneur has big dreams and wants action and activity. You may share few entrepreneur characteristics yet prosper as a business owner. Or you may share many of the characteristics of an entrepreneur and find it difficult to stabilize a business to make it produce wealth.

But then, you may score high on this test and go on to create the next wave of technological innovations.

The Home-Business Aptitude Test

1. How successful were you in school?

   ✓ A. I received high grades.
   B. I received average grades.
   C. Grades were up and down, depending on my interest.

2. What kind of child were you?

   A. I was cautious and careful.
   ✓ B. I was no more or less cautious than other kids.
   C. I was always falling out of trees and swimming out too far.

3. How concerned are you about how others view you?

    A. I am very concerned; I enjoy being well regarded.

    B. I try to gain the respect of others, but it's not everything to me.

    C. I really don't give it much thought.

4. Are you willing to borrow from others?

    A. No. "Borrow not and lend not" is my motto.

    B. I try to avoid borrowing from others.

    C. I don't mind borrowing because I always pay back more.

5. Are you an optimist?

    A. I consider myself a realist.

    B. I'm balanced, a cautious optimist.

    C. Every day things are getting better in every way.

6. Do you get bored easily?

    A. No. I can always entertain myself.

    B. I get bored in waiting rooms.

    C. Yes. I'm impatient, too.

7. Would you be willing to put all of your savings into a business you launch?

    A. No. I work too hard for my money.

    B. Only if I knew I had a very good chance for success.

    C. Absolutely. I'll just make sure I succeed.

8. Do you put your long-term goals and short-term goals in writing?

    A. No. I usually don't.

    B. I have a good idea of where I'm going, but I don't write it down.

    C. Yes. I write my goals down and review them regularly.

9. If your business failed, would you start another?

    A. No. I would focus on recovering.

    ✓B. Maybe, but I would take some time and think it over first.

    C. Yes. I would start the next day.

10. As a child, did you engage in money-making activities, such as lemonade stands or paper routes?

    A. No. School was my main focus.

    ✓B. Yes. Off and on I did.

    C. I always had my own source of income, ranging from babysitting to mowing lawns.

11. When you were young, did you prefer to be alone?

    A. I preferred being with friends.

    ✓B. I wasn't alone much, but I didn't mind it when I was.

    C. I used to enjoy playing alone.

12. When you complete a project, do you immediately start a new project?

    A. I try to take a break to refresh myself.

    B. It depends on the circumstances.

    ✓C. I like to have my next project lined up before my current project ends.

13. When you really get going at work, do you have a hard time stopping?

    A. I pace myself; I want to avoid burnout.

    B. Sometimes, but other times it is easy to set work aside.

    ✓C. I get excited about finishing, and the hours just disappear.

14. Were you a stubborn child?

    A. I was no more stubborn than any other child.

    B. I was stubborn about some things, but I wasn't a troublesome child.

    C. If I didn't get my way, I held my breath till I turned blue and fell right over.

15. Do you enjoy a workday with a variety of activities, or do you prefer a routine?

    A. I'm more productive in a routine.

    B. Routines don't bother me, but change is stimulating.

    C. If things are not changing all the time, I go stir-crazy.

Scoring the Home-Business Aptitude Test

For each question you answered with an A, score 0; give yourself 2 points for each B, and give yourself 3 points for each C.

0 to 20. You must be a government worker. I can't imagine how this book got into your hands.

21 to 29. If you choose to start a business, you will probably find a franchise more satisfying than the launch of a new business.

30 to 38. You have many of the qualities of an entrepreneur, but your natural caution may cause you to pull back just when you should push forward.

39 to 45. You're a natural entrepreneur. If you haven't started your first company yet, you will likely do it soon.

Chapter 2

Why Are You Choosing Your Home?

Deciding to locate your business at home is a very personal decision. It will affect the nature of your home life as well as the nature of the business you launch or buy. There are good reasons to keep your enterprise at home, and there are poor reasons. This chapter explores that choice and will help you decide whether your house is the right place for a business start-up. Making your home the launchpad will be more successful if you take a look at all the strengths and weaknesses of home enterprises before opening day.

Positive Reasons for Making Your Home a Business Site

- *Low overhead.* Home businesses have a higher success rate simply because you don't have to pay for rent and all the office trappings of outside space.

- *No commuting.* The average one-way commute to work is well over a half-hour. Some people travel a full ninety minutes to work each day and ninety minutes back home. Add it up, and you could be losing close to a full day of work each week. A home business ends this waste.

- *Easy ability to work late hours and off-hours.* There are many important work tasks that can be done in as little as fifteen or twenty minutes. If you work at home, you can pop into your office for a quick letter or phone call while the pizza bakes.

■ *Tax write-offs.* When you work at home, you can write off part of your mortgage payment or rent as a business expense. And don't worry about it flagging your tax return for an audit.

■ *Comfort and efficiency of home.* No office politics, no gossip, no water-cooler movie and sports reviews, no endless meetings—most people are far more productive at home without the distractions and unnecessary office stress.

■ *Ability to take care of kids while running a business.* Sometimes the whole reason for launching a home business is to create earnings while staying at home with children. This applies to both moms and dads.

However, not everything about a home business is great. There are some difficulties involved in having your business space cross lines with your personal space.

Drawbacks of Making Your Home a Business Site

■ *Loss of personal space.* For many home workers, it feels as if they are never away from the office. If you can't close the door on your business and go home, running a home enterprise can be a problem.

■ *Unprofessional presentation.* If your business depends on a stream of customers visiting your business, your home may not convey the proper business environment. This can also cause a problem for neighbors who object to strange cars parked in front of their houses.

■ *No meeting space.* If your business requires frequent business meetings and you do not have a large enough business space to accommodate gathering comfortably, a home business may not work.

■ *Family intrusions.* It can be hard to run a business meeting if your kids pass through or if your spouse comes in with household questions.

■ *Inappropriate space for employees.* The question of employees who report to your home is not fully answered. Many employees are not comfortable working in an employer's home.

■ *No room for growth.* A home enterprise offers little grow-ing room. If your business growth requires adding employees, additional work space, and office furniture, the house may not be your best location. You may choose to use your home just as the launchpad for your business.

■ *Difficulty with self-motivation.* In order to run a success-ful home business, you need to be able to make your own priori-ties, set your goals, and get going when the work bell rings, all without a boss or supervisor.

The following five considerations will help answer some of the questions about whether your home is the appropriate place to start your business. Consider these points and discuss them with your family before launching. After going through this list, you may come to the conclusion that it makes sense to launch from home with the intention of expanding out of the home once you have established the business. Moving out of the home when the business grows answers the question of whether you should bring employees into the home. Or you may be commit-ted to starting and keeping your business at home.

Five Factors to Consider

1. *The home business increases your chance for success.* Launching from home gives you a head start in making your busi-ness a success. The monthly expense of an outside office is far greater than your office expense at home. Because of the tax benefits of a home business, you may actually save money by working from your house. Overhead is the great killer for the emerging business; anything you can do to keep your overhead low will boost your chance to become profitable quickly. If you keep your company at home, the benefits will continue to help your business thrive, and all the savings in overhead will go di-rectly to the bottom line—and into your pocket.

2. *You need to create boundaries.* Ideally, you will set up your business in a room with a door that closes. You will have to develop very clear boundaries between home and business in order to run a home enterprise successfully over an extended time period. There are a number of limits that have to be estab-

lished: These include dividing lines between business and family, between work time and home time, and between business finances and family finances. If these lines are not specific, you can run into many problems with both your business and your family. When people have trouble integrating business and family, it is usually because the boundaries are not clear between the business and the home.

However, once you have gained the confidence and ability to work productively at home, you may wish to take advantage of the flexible options you have with your business. This can mean working around the children's schedule, or even working while they are home. Even though it is important to initially set boundaries when establishing a home-business environment, many home-business owners find that relaxing the boundaries can improve the quality of both business life and family life. But remember the analogy of the substitute teacher who walks into the classroom and writes "I'm strict!"on the blackboard, only to lighten up and get friendly once the class demonstrates order. It is easier to let up on the boundaries once they are established than it is to establish boundaries when your family is accustomed to your flexibility.

3. *Informal business is business.* Generally, business is much less formal than it was just a few years ago. Casual Fridays have become casual weeks in many companies. Sometimes this casual approach can translate into unprofessional appearance and inferior service. If you run a business from your home, you have to be strict in your ability to present your enterprise as a legitimate company. This means your phone manners, your correspondence, and your business meetings need to stay at a high professional level. If you let your home setting bring a lackadaisical attitude to your business practices, it can begin a deterioration that can make your business second-rate. You can avoid this by maintaining high professional standards even in the casual environment of your home.

4. *Do you want employees in the home?* Bringing workers into your home can be an easy, positive move forward, or it can be a disaster for the family. Usually problems arise when there isn't clear communication about the move to add employees.

Not all families welcome support staff in the home. The answer to this potential problem is to discuss whether or not there will be employees in the home when you begin planning the business. If everyone involved accepts that employees will be part of the natural growth of the company, feelings of imposition and resentment will be less of a problem.

But even if there is good communication, sometimes the experience of having workers show up early and stay late can be more troublesome than it seemed when you began your planning. For some home businesses, it just doesn't work out well. Be prepared to try an alternative, such as outsourcing the work or moving the business to an outside location. Don't take it for granted that your family is going to accept the addition of employees just because it's good for the business.

5. *Is your home a launchpad or a final destination?* This is a question that may be hard to answer during the beginning stage of your home business, but it should be considered. If you know from the outset that the home will be the incubator, with the goal of moving out of the home, then your decisions about balance between home business and family will be different because the home office is temporary. If your choice of home is permanent, then the balance of home business and family becomes paramount. Often, though, needs and priorities change once the business begins to thrive.

Home-business owners often come to a crossroads as the company grows. This usually happens when there is an opportunity for growth that would require a move out of the home. Some entrepreneurs get to this opportunity and gladly open an outside office to accommodate their company's growth and are delighted with the new direction.

Others find that a move outside the home erodes the pleasure and comfort of owning and running a business. In this case, it can be hard to get the genie back in the bottle. If you're tempted to expand to an outside office to follow your company's growth, give it the same serious consideration that you gave your launch. Not all business growth is positive, and not all growth is profitable. I've seen many companies become less profitable as they took on additional overhead to support growth. The home business has a magically low overhead. Give it a good hard look before you go to open an outside location.

As you choose to launch a business from home, remember to stay flexible. Approach the choice of a home enterprise as an experimental option. Until you are actually running the business, it will be hard to fully understand what the experience will be like. Home can be a very lonely place to work if you are accustomed to a busy office with plenty of social interaction. Some people thrive on teamwork; others have a hard time setting their own deadlines and priorities because they are used to a boss who delivers clear instructions. Yet others find they do their very best work on their own and in their home. Stay flexible so you can change if you find your home is not the best work environment for you.

It helps if you are clear about why you are launching a business in your home. Some people are very entrepreneurial and choose a home enterprise for the convenience and low overhead of the home. For these people, if home doesn't work out, they simply move the business to an inexpensive outside site. For others, staying home is a necessity, and the business launch is just a way of creating a job. For those persons, the stress of being self-employed may be unpleasant, in which case it may be better to seek employment with a company that will allow you to work from your home.

Chapter 3

Should You Build a Business or Buy a Business?

Whether to build or buy a business is a big question, and a fairly new one, for the home entrepreneur. Because of the rapid acceptance and proliferation of home companies, there is now a wide range of home businesses for sale. There are a growing number of franchises designed exclusively for the micro-business, and the business-opportunity world is also producing more and more options designed for the home. Just a few short years ago, if you wanted a business at home, you had to dream up your own idea. Now there are considerable resources to help you find an existing business concept you can run from home.

What's Your Best Chance for Success—to Launch or to Buy?

A business franchise has the lowest risk of all home enterprises. An independent business that you launch from home has a 57 percent chance for success; when you buy a franchise, the likelihood of your being in business five years later is well over 90 percent. The percentages vary from franchise to franchise, but the rates are far, far above that of the independent launch. This is the main lure of the franchise. Business opportunities offer similar low-risk companies. Buying an existing business greatly increases your likelihood for success because the enterprise has already been tested in the real world, and all the necessary adjustments have been made to ensure its viability.

However, if you have strong entrepreneurial ideas, the franchise or business opportunity may be too limiting for your taste. When you buy an existing business, you need to follow the system that makes the enterprise successful. To succeed in a franchise, you need to be able to follow directions and to apply the business system without questioning every aspect of its design. You don't have to be an entrepreneur in order to succeed as a franchise or business-opportunity owner, but you do have to be an entrepreneur to succeed with a self-created business.

Types of Companies to Launch From Home

The kind of business you can launch from home ranges from commercial carpet cleaning to management consultant. Many traditional businesses that could not be operated in a home setting just five or ten years ago are now thriving in the owner's house. This includes advertising professionals, real estate agents, and publishers. Computer software makes it possible for graphic artists and travel agents to easily operate from the spare bedroom. Now it is almost easier to try to identify the kind of business that can't be run from home than it is to list those that are being run successfully from someone's den.

A retail company is one of the few that is difficult to run from home, yet even this can be done. Many home companies derive revenue from setting up booths or tables at craft fairs or flea markets. Also, you can sell retail from a home business on the Internet. So retail has also become an option for the home enterprise. At this point, the greatest restriction on a home-based retailer is the flow of customers. The one kind of company that you can't reasonably operate from your spare bedroom is a business that requires a lot of traffic in and out of your home.

Types of Businesses to Buy

The kinds of companies you can purchase include franchises, business opportunities, and network-marketing systems. A franchise is an independently owned extension of the core business. McDonald's and Subway are good examples. When you open a franchise, you open under the name of the franchise and operate by the company's policies, offering uniform products and services. You receive the benefit of a known name that is promoted by the franchise company, but you have very little say in how to run your own business.

A business opportunity is similar to a franchise in that you get to market a known product or service, but you don't open your business as an extension of the franchise. A good example is Stride Rite children's shoes or Apple computers. When you sell Stride Rite or Apple products, you do not open a Stride Rite store or an Apple store, although you do get to use the product signs and logo in your window and in your advertising. You operate as your own company, offering the products provided by the business opportunity. You have much more leeway in your marketing and business operations, while still getting the support of national marketing. Some business opportunities even offer the whole business package, which gives you both a business plan and operations support.

The third form of business you can purchase is a multilevel marketing or network-marketing company. These companies are switching over to the term direct selling, since multilevel marketing and network marketing have acquired negative connotations. With these companies, you sell specific products provided by the company, but you receive very little production promotion from the company. You sell the goods based on your personal contacts rather than on the reputation of the merchandise. With direct selling, you also get an override on the sales of all the new people you bring into the distribution system. For many direct sellers, the real profits are in recruiting new direct sellers rather than selling products. This emphasis on building a network of new distributors can become a pyramid scheme, which is covered in more detail in Chapter 5.

Of these three types of businesses you can buy, the franchise is the most expensive, and it is also the most likely to succeed as a legitimate business. The franchise requires a franchise fee, start-up costs, and monthly royalties on your sales. You also receive considerable support and often get both a protected territory and an initial flow of customers. A business opportunity is less expensive. Some have no start-up fees, but you usually receive little support in getting the enterprise up and running. With direct selling, the buy-in is usually just a stock of inventory. There is little in the way of start-up costs, since there is no equipment, but you also receive no support in the way of protected territory, product promotion, or operations training.

What Are the Capital Differences Between Launch and Buy?

There is usually a direct relationship between the amount you risk and your chances for success. The company that is launched with $1.5 million in capital, with a strong business plan and a team of professionals, generally stands a better chance than the business launched with a $1,500 credit-card advance, with a fuzzy idea of both marketing and cash-flow management. The lion's share of home companies start out in the latter manner, with a hope and a prayer. A well-funded business launch stands a better chance for success than the business started out of your own wallet.

When you buy a franchise, you're closer to the well-funded example in which you are purchasing a known winner built by experts who have already developed effective marketing practices and cash-flow management systems. The investment required for a home-business franchise ranges from $5,000 to $50,000 and up. When you assess your financial capability for purchasing a franchise, break your capital into three pieces. The first piece is the franchise fee, which gives you both the right to operate as a franchise and the support system to encourage your success. The second chunk is needed to set up your business and to pay your bills until the company can pay your salary. The third part should be set aside for a second round of financing if it turns out that it will take the business longer than anticipated to begin cutting paychecks.

Although a franchise may seem expensive when you compare its start-up costs against the much smaller costs to launch an independent business, with a franchise you buy safety: You're purchasing the 90 percent likelihood of success. The total for a travel-agency franchise may be $35,000, while you can launch your own home travel agency for less than $15,000. The difference is that the franchise will give you a proven operating system, a name product, specific marketing techniques known to be effective, and coaching throughout your launch and growth. The franchise may also finance a portion (or all) of the franchise fee. For the additional dollars, you receive a team of professionals from the franchise company who will work to make sure you succeed.

What Are the Long-Term Prospects of Launch vs. Buy?

The long-term prospects of a launch are very much the same as those of buying a business. Once you have a franchise or an independent business up and going for about five years, the likelihood of continued success for the two is close to equal, with the franchise showing a slight advantage. In some retail businesses such as fast food, the franchise will always have a significant advantage, but with a business that lives on referrals, such as a travel agency, after the first few years the franchise won't give you as great an advantage. However, the franchise will always have an edge because of the franchise company's national marketing.

Launching a Company vs. Buying an Existing Business—Points to Consider

1. Launching a business is much riskier than buying a business. Part of the reason franchises stand a 90 percent or better chance of success is that they are already established as a business and already have customer acceptance.

2. There is a direct relationship between the amount of capital you can invest and your chances for success. Most business launches fail because they are underfunded.

3. Take your time in deciding whether to launch a business or to invest in a franchise or business opportunity. The more you research your options, the better your chances for success.

Chapter 4

How to Choose a Home-Business Franchise

The franchise world knows about the home-business revolution. They are watching you set up your den, and they are aware that thousands upon thousands of you are searching for business ideas. They have designed their franchises for the zero-staff company. They know what support you need and have a good idea of your start-up resources. They're at the trade shows waiting for you to come by their booths. You'll find their ads in all the home-business magazines; there are more than twelve of these publications.

There's an abundance of franchises available for the new business owner. Some will be just right for you, while others would be a complete disaster. A commercial landscaping service may fit your experience in landscaping, just as a management-consulting service may be a good match for someone with corporate training. Either one could be a nightmare if your skills and personality are not well matched with the requirements of the franchise. Maybe your skills and resources make you a better fit for a larger franchise that comes with all the bells, whistles, advertising, and specific product line.

There are five rules to help you choose the right home business. Ignore these rules, and you risk a squandered investment and lost time. Follow these rules, and you bring backbone and discipline to your selection of the dream home business.

Five Rules for Choosing a Home-Business Franchise

1. Assess Your Strengths and Weaknesses

Before choosing a franchise, you first need to know your strong suit. It also helps to know your areas of weakness. Some franchises require a large amount of direct contact with customers and prospects. If you are not accustomed to glad-handing, you may want to look for a franchise that allows you less contact. When you do your research on a franchise, talk to others who have this franchise to find out what their day-in, day-out activities are. The franchise may sound good on paper, but it also needs to be a good fit with your personality.

When you talk to those who have this franchise, choose some owners from the general list. The franchisor will likely try to steer you to the most successful franchisers, but you need to hear from the less-than-successful as well. Also, it helps to talk to some in your local area if possible. If they view you as competition, they may not be cooperative, but you can still learn quite a bit by simply observing their operation from a parking lot.

The closer the franchise is to your background and experience, the greater chance you will have for success. If your background is in business planning, you may want to consider a franchise for business-management consulting rather than a lawn- and tree-care franchise or disc-jockey service. There are hundreds of franchises available, so if you do a thorough search, you stand a good chance of finding a business that matches both your dream and your proven abilities.

2. Decide Whether You Want a Franchise or a From-Scratch Launch

Secondly, would a business opportunity suit you better than a franchise? A franchise isn't for everyone. You receive support and brand recognition, but you give up independence, since most franchisors retain control over the product and certain aspects of the service behind the product. A business opportunity is less restrictive and usually less expensive, but you don't receive the ongoing support and often don't receive the brand exposure.

A franchise is a full business concept that includes product, setting, marketing strategies, and identified customers. A business opportunity usually supplies a proven line of products with some national promotion, but you don't often receive a fully developed business with everything in place on opening day. Plus, you don't operate your business under the name of the business opportunity. A visit to a franchise and business-opportunity show will be quite an education on what's available on the market; it will also help you to see the differences between a franchise and a business opportunity. It isn't just price. The most expensive business opportunity will cost far more than the least expensive franchise. Once you get a good feel for the differences between the two, it will be clear which one is appropriate for you. A franchise show usually includes as many business opportunities as it does franchises.

3. Take Your Time and Do Your Research

This third rule is the fun part. Doing the research on possible franchises can be exhilarating. The first place to shop is in a magazine or directory of franchises. You can find these directories on most well-stocked magazine racks. Some include only franchises, while others contain franchises and business opportunities. The list of companies is categorized by business type, and it is presented in a way that makes it easy to do comparisons between companies.

Franchise shows are coming and going all the time. Three major companies present franchise shows around the country. At a franchise show, you can talk to the franchisors and get more information on the costs and potential return of the business. You can also ask for the Uniform Franchise Offering Circular (UFOC). Several states require franchisors to produce this document and deliver it to potential franchisees at least ten days before any agreement is signed. This document includes detailed financial information on the franchisor and its officers; it also lists all of the franchisees and former franchisees. Most franchise companies will qualify you before they give you this document since it contains detailed financial information about the franchise.

Before they hand out their UFOC, they want to be sure that you're not a competitor and that you're serious about buying. Call the current franchisees and the former franchisees, and ask them about their experience. People tend to be candid when they are asked about their franchise, although they may not reveal their earnings. A word of warning: When you attend a franchise show that presents both franchises and business opportunities, be aware that they operate by different disclosure rules. The franchise company is not allowed by law to estimate what you can earn from the franchise; it can't even quote what its present franchisees are earning. The business opportunities are not under this restriction and can quote you any potential earnings they want.

It is also a good idea to bring in an advisor during this research process, especially once you have identified a few companies that look like a good fit. An attorney with experience in franchises is ideal. The investment in professional help at this point can save you considerable time and money in the future. Throughout the research process, resist pressure from franchisors. A "chance of a lifetime" is always just as good next month or six months from now. If you do "lose your chance" because you resisted the pressure, don't be concerned; life is full of good opportunities. You shouldn't rush this decision. You will live with the consequences of your decision for many years, so take your time and make sure it's the right choice.

You can also learn by subscribing to one or more periodicals such as *Franchise Times,* the franchise publication by Crain's Publishing in Chicago, or *Successful Franchising,* which you can find at most franchise shows. One issue of *Franchise Times* listed a number of franchisors who were apparently generating more revenue from "churning" franchises than they were from selling products or services. Churning is the process of reselling franchises in an area after that same franchise has failed. The inherent problem is that it can become easier to resell a franchise than it is to make sure existing franchisees succeed. This kind of insider information can be invaluable.

4. Get Your Family on Your Side

The fourth rule, and an important part of buying a franchise and going into business, is making sure you have the support you need. If you're in business, your family is in business. Even if your family members don't work in the franchise, their lives will be directly affected by your enterprise. Starting a business can create cash-flow difficulties, particularly if you leave a regular paycheck to launch the franchise. Bring your family members into the decision-making process and their support will be much stronger. If your family actively participates in the business, it just increases your chances for success.

Try to get your family involved, both in the process of selecting a franchise and in the operation of the company. Owning a business, even a well-established franchise, means countless hours focused on the business. Whether or not you work from home, the obsession with the business can be very distracting to your family. If you work closely with your family, the problem will be easier to overcome.

5. Assess Your Resources and Your Ability to Defer Rewards

Lastly, taking the leap into owning a franchise takes financial resources, even if your financial resources are loans. That means risk. Starting a business also takes time, energy, and the ability to put off rewards for another day. All business owners learn to live with deferred compensation. For the first months or years, you work to establish a business. You will experience the pride of business ownership, but the financial return is usually delayed— your present financial security may even be affected.

This situation raises questions about your ability both to live with risk and to delay financial compensation. If your spouse plans to continue in a regular paying job, your ability to sustain a long building curve is enhanced. If you need your franchise to produce a strong income from the beginning, you are in a more difficult position. The ultimate goal is to give your franchise time to grow before you begin to take full compensation. The longer you can hold out, the greater your chances for success.

Following these five rules will help to ensure your success as a new business owner. If you ignore or treat any of these rules lightly, you hamper your ability to succeed. Thousands of people have created wealth from a franchise investment, and thousands of people have failed. The difference is often in the planning and research process. These five rules will help keep you on the right track. If you are diligent and committed to success, a franchise business can make your home business succeed.

The Association for Franchisees

There's an association representing the interests of franchisees: the American Association of Franchisees and Dealers (AAFD). Their address is P.O. Box 81887, San Diego, CA 93138-1887; their phone number is 619/235-2556. A membership in AAFD includes a subscription to *Franchise Times.* Membership is $100. It includes a guide, a service directory, a newsletter, and a free initial consultation with a lawyer, an accountant, and other professionals in the franchise business.

Pros and Cons of Buying a Franchise

The choice of purchasing a franchise comes with advantages and disadvantages. As with any major business decision, you need to examine and weigh the pros and cons. The disadvantages may seem minor compared with the opportunity to launch an enterprise with very little risk, but for independent entrepreneurs, the restrictions of a franchise agreement can be almost as stifling as reporting to a boss. Here are some of the good and not-so-good points of buying a franchise.

The good news about franchises is strong. For one, you don't have to be an entrepreneur to succeed with a franchise. You buy an entire package, which often includes a line of products or services and detailed guidance on how to sell those products or services. Once you buy in, and once the business is up and going, you still get support. This support is usually a mix of management and marketing. Your monthly fee often includes some national marketing that creates interest in your business. The quality of this marketing is usually far higher than any marketing you could produce as a fledgling enterprise. There was a time when a McDonald's franchise turned its owner into a millionaire after a modest investment. That franchise will still make you a millionaire, but now you have to be a millionaire to ante up. A fast-growing franchise can be a windfall for the franchisee—and it's a relatively safe way to go into business for yourself.

But there are some downsides to going the franchise route. Payment for a franchise usually includes an initial buy-in, and then continuing payments for marketing support, supplies, and products. In addition to the normal start-up and operations costs, you will also send monthly payments to your franchisor. Your mix of products, and even your customer service approach, may be controlled by your franchisor. This is fine if you have complete confidence in your franchisor. If you don't, these restrictions can be a burden. Many businesses have had to scramble to re-create themselves when their franchisor folds. If you don't have the business expertise to quickly adapt to an abrupt change, you could go down with your franchisor.

Selecting a Home-Based Franchise—Points to Consider

1. Search the full range of potential franchises. Don't rely solely on the companies you see at a franchise show. Check the handbooks and Internet listings.

2. When you focus on an individual franchise, check the references. Call some of the franchisees and former franchisees listed in the Uniform Franchise Offering Circular, not just the franchisees given to you as references by the franchise company.

3. When checking references, ask about the franchise company's ability to help the franchisee solve problems and ensure success. Go beyond the "How much can I make?" question and find out about the franchise company's management support for franchisees.

4. Consider hiring an expert to help you find the right franchise. Similar to real estate agents, many of them are compensated by the franchise company. Check your expert's references as well. You'll find experts' names in the back of franchise handbooks and at franchise shows.

Chapter 5

The Multilevel Marketing World

Multilevel marketing (MLM) has often been called network marketing; more recently it has also taken the name direct selling. With this type of business, you sell to friends, relatives, and acquaintances. Everyone you know or everyone you meet is a potential customer or associate. MLM is a business of passion and conviction, of sales pitches over coffee, of living-room demonstrations. It is also a business that lends itself to scams and wildly inaccurate claims. The false claims are often made about the value of the products and the earnings potential for the sellers. This business can be the "three-card monte" of home enterprises, a game for sleight-of-hand artists.

But when you participate in a legitimate direct-selling business and have the right personality for effective networking, this can be a very lucrative business with virtually no overhead. Some legitimate names stick out, including Mary Kay, Avon, Amway, Fuller Brush, and Tupperware. These companies have provided thousands of direct salespeople with independence and even wealth. For the right person, these companies can provide lucrative part-time income; for others, these companies have given their participants the opportunity to become millionaires. Tell you what: I wouldn't mind trading places with the driver of a Mary Kay pink Cadillac.

How Do You Tell a Con From a Legitimate Opportunity?

The key to telling the difference between the scam or pyramid and the legitimate network-marketing company is the inventory.

In a scam, nobody has to buy and use the inventory in order for the core business to succeed. If you spend all your time recruiting new network salespeople, or distributors, to work under you, you never have to sell any products to consumers. You continually recruit others to sell, and you train your new recruits to recruit new network salespeople. Each new distributor purchases the starting batch of inventory and goes off to find new recruits to buy into the program. Who needs consumers if you can generate a flow of new distributors?

If you succeed at selling the program, it doesn't matter what the products are. They sit dormant in garages all over town as you bring in more and more recruits through classified ads and free seminars on "How to Get Rich With Your Own Business." You receive a portion of the recruit's purchase, and you get paid for each of your recruit's new recruits. This is called building your downline; that's how you get rich. But is anyone actually selling products? Is anyone being trained to find repeat consumers who swear by the quality of the goods? Who cares? You're trained to find new recruits. That's where the money is.

You can see where this leads—it's a pyramid scheme. As long as you have a flow of new recruits, the products don't matter. Some of these companies offer a good line of products, even though they don't develop as companies that are designed to market the products. It usually takes a good line of products to drive the recruit-building effort. Companies can go on for years adding new recruits without ever developing a customer base who buy the products because they actually want them. The overwhelming percentage of products are purchased only by new recruits who buy the beginning inventory as the ante to get into the game.

Not all network-marketing companies are scams. Many create legitimate products that are well accepted, even loved by consumers. These companies have well-developed strategies for marketing and selling to consumers. Their plans include efforts to develop repeat buyers. They create new products to meet their customers' changing needs, just like any good manufacturer. These legitimate companies also offer opportunities to bring in recruits at a profit, but their core business is in the production and sale of excellent products.

Is Direct Selling for You?

Direct selling will work for you if you are enthusiastic about the products and you genuinely like to meet people. This is not a business for the shy. You need to be prepared to start a conversation about your products even in a grocery-store line, not because of your urge to sell but because you believe your products will have a positive effect on the people who use them. This is a business for the true believer who is convinced of the value of the products because they have had a positive effect on her life. If that's you, you can succeed in direct selling.

Other than a few sales techniques and pitches, you will receive little support from your MLM company. You won't get any national advertising, and you won't have a sales manager come to town to help you develop your marketing plan. You will receive products and some brochures; then you're pretty much on your own. A few MLM companies have gained word-of-mouth recognition, but it isn't always positive. Mention some of the big names in network marketing and many people will cringe, not because the products are substandard but because the name evokes images of a coworker at their kitchen table pressuring them to buy something they have no interest in whatsoever.

If you can sell in the face of the negative image of direct selling, and you have an excellent line of products from a reputable company, you can succeed. But as with any selling position, you will only be as successful as the time, effort, and creativity you bring to your job. Network marketers who do well are strong in the discipline of selling, which involves cold calling, giving talks, and following up, following up, and more following up. The direct sellers who do well make it look easy, but there is some heavy mining needed to bring in that direct-selling gold.

How's the Industry as a Whole?

The world of network marketing is growing, but it is hard to tell how much of the growth constitutes a healthy development of the industry. There are some good signs. Two associations, the

Direct Selling Association and the Multilevel Marketing International Association, work hard to set ethical standards and coordinate with government agencies to help the industry stay clear of unethical practices. These organizations attempt to bring self-regulation to the industry and clean up network marketing's negative image.

The number of people involved in direct selling has grown sharply during the 1990s. The decade started with less than 5 million people involved. By mid-decade, the number of people participating reached over 7 million, more than a 50 percent increase in just five years. The people involved range from downsized managers and professionals to stay-at-home moms, off-season construction workers, and military personnel. Total sales in direct selling exceed $16 billion. And there are no signs that this industry will slow down.

How Do You Evaluate a Direct-Selling Business?

The first consideration in evaluation is whether the direct sellers are actually selling products to consumers. If the answer is yes, the next question is, How many customers become repeat purchasers? Third, ask what method the seller uses to find customers and what method works effectively to encourage repeat sales. These are the core questions. Before signing up to be part of an MLM company, put these questions to a few of the sellers. If the company is legitimate, a seller will be proud to give you detailed answers to these questions. A legitimate MLM will have surefire methods for finding customers and turning them into repeat buyers. It is okay if recruitment is a major concern, but it shouldn't be the only concern.

Length of time in business is another sign. You should be wary of a company that doesn't have a long-term track record of producing products and supporting its direct-selling force. Unless you are very experienced in direct selling, you should only study companies that have been in business five or more years. Another consideration is trustworthiness. It helps greatly if you know someone in the organization you can trust. There are so many questionable companies in this industry that it can be a great relief to know you're with one that operates properly.

The final consideration is the line of products. In order to succeed with direct selling, you have to believe strongly in the products, and you have to be enthusiastic about the value of the products. Your excitement over the line of goods has to be sincere. You may be able to fake it for a short while, but you are not likely to be successful for long if you don't have a genuine belief in both the quality of the products and their value to customers. The best products are those that you use yourself to improve your own life.

What Are the Long-Term Prospects?

If you choose a stable, legitimate network-marketing company and have a strong belief in the company's products, your long-term prospects are very good. Efforts by the MLM associations may help clean up the industry and give it a more positive image. Even with MLM's tarnished reputation, total retail sales through direct selling continue to grow, which indicates there is a good foundation of consumer acceptance. Presently 3 percent of all American consumer sales come through direct sales. The future is promising for network marketing if you have confidence in the company you choose.

Once you get on your feet with an MLM, look at other opportunities to add new lines of products. You may wish to represent two or three noncompeting companies. If you choose complementary lines, you may be able to sell products from more than one line to your customers. Diet programs may fit very well with vitamins and nutritional supplements. Cosmetics also complement diet programs or nutritional products. The point is to make your marketing efforts do double duty by offering your customers a wider range of products.

For some home-business entrepreneurs, network marketing is the perfect enterprise. It offers freedom, flexibility, and virtually no overhead. There is no risk, and the business fits in well with other responsibilities such as child rearing. Many network professionals work presentations right in with their children's schedules, selling to fellow parents. One of the great advantages of network marketing is that you can sell to the people you meet socially, although some people see this as one of the disadvantages of direct selling—that every relationship gets tested as a potential sale.

Before Signing With a Network-Marketing Company—Points to Consider

1. Check references. You need to find out who buys the products and how many of the customers are repeat buyers. Don't be swayed by stories of how to bring in more sellers. If the participants are not actually selling products to customers, you may be looking at a pyramid scheme.

2. Check with one of the two multilevel marketing associations to find out if the company you're considering is legitimate. Also check with the Better Business Bureau to see if there are any outstanding complaints. The MLM industry preys on ignorance. If you do this basic research, you'll be fine.

3. Remember that it may take a combination of companies to create the right product mix. The same people who want weight-loss programs may also need a source for natural vitamins.

Chapter 6

Choose a Business That Draws on Your Strengths

The thirty-year mechanical engineer who decides to make a break and open a coffee bar or the state government bureaucrat who wants to start a consumer magazine about poker may find business difficult. As a new entrepreneur, you should thoroughly assess your personal talents and natural strengths. You should also appraise your weaknesses. To be successful, your business should lean heavily on your strengths and cover your weaknesses.

Sometimes you can balance your weaknesses with your spouse's involvement. I've seen many couples divide responsibilities naturally within a business. It's common to find that one partner is the expansive entrepreneur, who drives the company forward, while the other partner is the penny-pinching cop, who is less involved and lends a cool eye to all spending. This can be a great balance for a home business if both partners accept their roles comfortably. But if these roles create conflict, the business can run into problems.

Even though it is generally wise to find a business that matches your professional experience with your natural talents and strengths, there is something to be said for the transforming power that comes when you love your work. Take an accountant who leaves a top-eight firm after twenty years to begin breeding horses. You can say that he doesn't have the professional skills to expect success, and perhaps he doesn't even have the personal qualities to make this launch a sure thing. But his desire to make his living with horses may override all considerations. I have seen people develop the qualities they need for success simply because they want it badly enough.

What Are Your Skills? What Do You Love?

More often than not, people develop skills in the areas they love. I have seen many writers develop the talent they need because they are determined to be a writer. Usually people who are driven to write have some natural talent; the two go hand in hand. But this isn't always the case. Some people choose a profession that doesn't draw on their natural talents because a strong parent encouraged them in the path or because the path seemed to provide a stable source of income. Many of these people are the ones visiting franchise expos looking for a new career after a couple of decades doing work they don't like.

Your best chance for success will come if you can marry your professional skills with something you love. Short of that, it helps if you can match what you love with some natural albeit undeveloped talents. An example is the person who loves antiques and who has some underdeveloped aptitude for negotiating low purchase prices as well as a natural ability to sell in a retail setting. Skills such as purchase negotiations and retail-sales interactions can be learned if you have a natural aptitude and are strongly motivated. If your drive is strong enough, your ability to learn can be great.

How Do You Want to Spend Your Day?

Part of your decision in choosing the right home business is an evaluation of how you want to spend your day. This may seem simplistic, but your company is more likely to succeed if the business demands include activities that are naturally pleasant for you. Do you enjoy focusing for many hours at a time, alone, on a problem? This would work well for an architect, accountant, or writer. Do you prefer to be on the move, meeting new people or visiting different places? Perhaps a sales representative is appropriate, or a business teacher of computer skills to preschool groups. Other businesses, such as consulting, real estate, or meeting planning, offer a combination of periods of focus or concentration and times of movement or activity.

What's the Curve of Changing Roles?

With many companies, the role you have during the launch period changes as the business grows. This is less the case with a home business than for an outside business, but it still needs to be considered as you search for the right enterprise. With many companies, you start as a one-person shop doing a whole range of tasks, from drawing up ads to stocking inventory to making deliveries. You may go from batching envelopes for a direct-mail effort to selecting inventory for a craft fair booth. You spend your whole day jumping from one discipline to another. The one skill you may not have to develop is management; after all, you're doing everything yourself.

In time, as your business grows, you will begin to outsource more of the work so you can spend your time on the tasks only you can do, such as sales, planning, and product development. Bookkeeping may go to a service company, and you can hire a marketing company to take care of your advertising and direct mail. You may even hire part-time employees to take care of stocking inventory and making deliveries. These changes are common as a business grows. The owner delegates more work and concentrates on the tasks that cannot be delegated. More and more of his time is spent managing the work of others. In time, the owner's job has completely changed from what it was during the launch months.

Part of the success of your business will depend on your ability to effectively make these changes. The changes often involve learning new skills on the job. Many business owners have never hired or managed vendors or employees. All of a sudden the growth of your business depends on your ability to gain these skills and perform them well. Some business owners take classes and workshops on management to catch up; others call on mentors for advice. Some just rely on their instincts to carry them through a trial-and-error method for learning management.

Your company's ability to grow will depend on your ability to learn on the job, whether it's management, bookkeeping, inventory control, cash management, or contract negotiation. If you purchase a franchise, there will be less pressure to learn new disciplines. A franchise company anticipates these challenges and provides support that lets you grow a business without learning every single management skill. A franchise will also help you develop the skills that you must learn, such as staff and vendor management. But if you are on your own, you will have to learn some management practices on the job, and you will have to get very good at these skills very quickly. In order to make sure your business grows, you will have to develop a sharp learning curve.

The Peter Principle Is Alive and Well

The Peter Principle claims that we will all eventually be promoted to our level of incompetence. A good example is the excellent teacher who, based on superior teaching skills, gets promoted to administrator. This new administrator, who was selected for the position based on teaching skills, finds herself absolutely lost and ineffective in the management position. The job does not demand any of her natural aptitudes and instead requires skills she is lacking. The Peter Principle was identified when most of America worked for large organizations where a failed administrator who was a crack teacher had the option of returning to teaching.

For the business owner, the Peter Principle has its own special sting. When a growing business begins to demand new skills of its owner, the option to move back down to an earlier comfort level doesn't usually exist. If you're running a business and find that your company's growth has forced you into a position where your job is entirely management, you need to become a good manager to make sure your business thrives. It is hard to halt your company's growth while you hone your management skills.

To succeed, you have to defy the Peter Principle and make sure you don't reach a level of incompetence before your business is stable and profitable. Many businesses fail because the owner cannot make this adjustment. One of the ways to avoid this problem is to select a business that isn't likely to send you crashing into a brick wall of your own inexperience and ineptitude.

Build Your Strengths As You Grow

The overwhelming number of people who launch businesses expect to overcome the Peter Principle problem when they get to it. Blind confidence is certainly a hallmark of launch entrepreneurs. A friend of mine who was about to go into business asked an associate business owner what he could expect when he started a business. The associate said, "Owning your own business is not for the faint of heart." Unless you have previously owned a business and have already adjusted to the various changes and demands of ownership, you will probably come to these challenges unprepared. You'll have to grow on the job.

Your ability to weather the demands on a business owner will depend on your personal strengths. It certainly helps if you have management experience, but the skills you learn as an employee are always different than the skills you need as an owner. Be careful to select a business in which you can anticipate most of the challenges in advance, so they won't come as a surprise. Also, if you can anticipate the upcoming demands, this will help you determine whether you are really prepared to meet the challenges. You need to find a business that utilizes your personal strengths and aptitudes rather than one that forces you against the wall.

One of the best ways to determine the requirements of the business you want to launch is to pick the brain of a current owner. For the price of lunch, many owners are willing to reveal their challenges. Find a company that is similar to your dream business without being a direct competitor. Ask, What was it like for the first couple of years? What did you have to learn? What were the surprises? There are always surprises. If it isn't clear that you will be able to acquire the needed skills, consider purchasing a franchise instead. If you buy a franchise, the company will help you through the rough spots.

Look for a Business That Covers Your Weaknesses

Just as it's important to select a business that draws on your strengths, it is also important to find a business that covers your weaknesses. Personally, my Achilles' heel is staff management. After struggling with it in my own business for a few years, I asked the advice of a friend who managed the employees of his family restaurant chain. He started out managing a staff of twelve when he was in his early twenties. When I asked him how he coped with management, he said, "I've been managing people for over twenty years. I started with twelve. Now I manage twelve hundred. All I can say it that it doesn't get any easier. After twenty years, not a bit easier." Great.

If employee management is your weak area, you have two choices. You can select a business that will never require you to hire, manage, and sometimes fire people. Or you can commit yourself to learning the skills and getting good at it. Sometimes a willingness to overcome the weakness is a better solution than avoiding the weakness. In my case, I tried for years to overcome my weak area in management only to finally decide I simply had no aptitude for it. I never learned the trick of seeing clearly through management conflicts. I solved the problem by selling off the business and starting a new company that didn't require employees. As a business owner, you'll get to learn about those places in yourself.

As for my friend who managed 1,200 employees, I would guess that, over those twenty years, his management skills had improved. Management, like sales, is the kind of job that is a continual challenge even if you are improving. It is a discipline that can never be fully mastered; although its challenge is ongoing, we can get better and better at meeting the challenge even as the task continues to seem insurmountable. Some owners come to bite the bullet on management and say, "I don't like it one little bit, but I have to do it in order to run the kind of business I love."

What Type of Business to Launch or Buy—Points to Consider

1. Your best chances for success come when you choose a business in an industry you already understand. It is hard to learn the ins and outs of an entirely new industry while you're launching a new company.

2. Choose a business you love. The long hours will seem short if you enjoy your work and like your customers.

3. We all have weaknesses. Choose a business that draws on your strengths and minimizes your weak areas.

Chapter 7

What's Working in Home Business and What's Not?

Some businesses lend themselves to the home environment and others don't. An enterprise that requires a lot of traffic can become awkward for your family and your neighbors. Likewise, if you expect to hire employees, you may have a problem with zoning laws as well. Of the potential companies you can start in your home, you also have to identify which ones have a potential to produce the income you need, and you should find out which ones are likely to stay in business over the long run.

The home enterprises that look good now may be washed up five years from now, while a business you can't even imagine now may be the leader in five years. Who would have bet on a Web-site design business in 1992? Likewise, something may come along to drastically change the Web-site design business in the next few years. Even though it is hard to predict the future, there are some guidelines to help you determine if the business you are about to start is likely to have a future. Even with these guidelines, there may be some surprises along the way. Every businessperson, from Bill Gates to your next-door neighbor, needs to be prepared to change the business plan if things in the industry take an unfavorable turn.

There are some perennials in the home-business market. These enterprises have been successful for many years and look to have many good years ahead. In the professional field, there will always be a need for attorneys, accountants, and architects. These professionals have always been able to run small practices in their homes. In the nonprofessional field, small general contractors, plumbers, house and commercial painters, and electricians have all been good home-business bets; their future is also assured.

For the newer home business, some of the good long-term bets are companies that replace the services of former stay-at-home moms. Remember, mom was always busy with cleaning, laundry, errands, child care, child teaching, and dozens of other tasks. All of the chores that mom used to do still need to be done, but now most households have two wage earners, so there is nobody home to do those chores. A whole slew of new business opportunities—from house-cleaning services, to errand companies for seniors, to pickup and delivery services for laundry, to pet grooming—have come along to fill this need.

Another area of home-business growth is new technology. New opportunities include Web-site design, Internet advertising sales, cellular-phone sales, fax-broadcast services, computer-rescue services, and computer-network design. New technology companies emerge all the time. But be wary of these companies; not all new technology catches on. Just ask the people who invested heavily in books on CDs or interactive software stories for children. These products looked great when they were introduced, but they didn't find consumer acceptance and thus died on the vine.

The rule of thumb for determining whether a business has long-term potential is to simply give it the "needs" test. Does this service or product fill a need that is both ongoing and unlikely to be replaced anytime soon? Take computer repair. Chances are, more and more people will purchase computers, and very, very few will learn the skills to repair their own computers. Also, computers are hard to lug down to the shop. A visit-your-home computer-rescue business will be in demand for many years to come. Web-site design, however, may get easier and easier in time, so easy that it may cut out the professional Web designer. If the need you fill is a long-term need, your business will have long-term prospects.

Salespeople Will Tell You What You Want to Hear

Ask any of the booth attendees at a franchise and business-opportunity show what the long-term prospects are for their businesses, and they will tell you their opportunity has the best prospects of any business in the hall. You will not get a good feel for the business from the people who make a commission selling it to you. But you may get a very good idea of its business potential over the long run by asking some of the people who are making their living in the business. When you talk to a franchise or business-opportunity company, ask for a list of references. Call these people and ask how well the business has provided for them through the years.

When you call people who are running the same business you are about to launch, it is best if you can find a company that has weathered a recession. Some businesses get through economic downturns easily, while others see a significant drop in revenues and profits. It helps to get an idea of how your business will fare before you actually find yourself fighting a shrinking economy. Most of the business owners on the reference list will be willing to share a fair amount of information about their trials and their successes.

If you are not purchasing an existing franchise or business opportunity, you can still learn quite a bit about your future prospects by talking to owners of similar companies. Most business owners are willing to answer a few questions if you do not intend to be a direct competitor. If you are planning to open a cleaning service and can't find a noncompeting company to talk with, try calling a cleaner from another town. Find one that has weathered a recession. You may discover that residential cleaners experience a business drop during economic downturns, while commercial cleaners see no change at all. This kind of information may determine what type of company you choose to launch.

Home-Business Winners for Professionals

The traditional professions, such as lawyers, accountants, and architects, are always strong home enterprises. The new entries in the professional field are the technical and professional companies that used to require either larger computers or support staff. These include marketing consultants, graphic designers, publication producers, Web-site designers, computer consultants, and sales representatives. The big change for professionals is that high-powered personal computers and enhanced communications make it possible for many professional services to operate in the home, and the customers and clients of these services are comfortable with home businesses.

Home-Business Winners for Nonprofessionals

There is a range of new business opportunities for home-business nonprofessionals, which includes some of the traditional home enterprises such as residential cleaning, small construction contractors, and yard-maintenance companies. There is also a slew of new home businesses—such as travel agency; water-garden design; senior errand, pickup, and delivery service; day-care service; and home handyman—as well as numerous franchises and business opportunities. Just as with professional enterprises, the trade businesses are more accepted as home companies now. The growth area is in the tasks that used to be done by a stay-at-home mom, but even work such as fix-it services or heating and cooling changeovers are becoming good businesses, since dads are now strapped for time, too.

What's a Fad and What's a Trend?

Some business growth is for the long run, while other areas of business growth will show only fad-like, short-run results. A trend is a change in the business environment that expands over a long period. Consumer spending on the Internet is a trend that will probably continue to grow for many years, if not decades. The rental of videotape movies is a trend that has been steady for more than a decade, but the mom-and-pop video store was a fad-like phenomenon that only lasted a few years. Between the cheap grocery-store video rentals and the large-choice chain stores like Blockbuster, the mom-and-pop stores were squeezed out of business.

Many of the mom-and-pop video-store owners thought they

were on the cutting edge of a new technology that would carry them well into the future. They were, but other retailers moved in and offered consumers lower prices and more choices. The mom-and-pop shops couldn't compete. So even though they were on the forefront of a trend tied to new technology, their form of business was the equivalent of a fad. Just because you are involved in selling new technology doesn't mean you are safe from competitive forces. It is important to launch a business that is part of a trend, but even a trend doesn't ensure business success.

Yet starting a business that is part of a long-term trend is helpful, even if it doesn't guarantee success. Whatever you can do to increase the likelihood for success will be a plus as you choose a business. So look for trends and new technology developments, but keep in mind that although trends and new technology may be good indicators, they're not guarantees of business viability. Even if your business is initially successful, changes in the market can quickly turn consumers in a different direction.

Always Have an Eye on the Future

One of the good management practices of a successful entrepreneur is always keeping the future in view. Even the best entrepreneurs can miss a consumer turn. Microsoft is still kicking itself for missing the consumer lunge onto the Internet. The software giant had the lock on software for the personal computer, but it missed the boat on Internet access, which made it possible for America Online to take the leading role. The small entrepreneur faces the same challenge. Many of the mom-and-pop video-store owners jumped into other video-related businesses, such as video duplication of event video taping, which saved them from business collapse.

Change is natural and ongoing, and the pace of change has increased as competition drives new products and services into our lives. The business owner who is continually awake and watching for new opportunities will be able to change direction before the business grows rusty. Always ask yourself, What else do my customers need? This question put coffee in convenience stores, playgrounds in fast-food restaurants, and pickup and delivery into pet-grooming services.

The Business Climate—Points to Consider

1. When considering a particular company, think about how it will fare a few years down the line. Will the business survive a recession?

2. Keep long-term trends in mind. The growth of the Internet will have a significant impact on business over the next few years. Be wary of any enterprise that can be replaced by online services.

3. The two-worker home is here to stay, and so are the service companies that replace the stay-at-home mom. Even if there is a minor shift back to at-home child rearing, parents will be back at work as soon as the kids are in school.

Part II

Planning Your Start-Up— The Necessary Stuff

One of the great Yogi "Berra-isms" is, "If you don't have a plan, you could wind up someplace else." When you invest your time, energy, and money in a business, you don't want to "wind up someplace else." You want to wind up with a successful enterprise. Every business needs a plan. The plan should outline your goals and priorities, the steps you need to take to become successful, and the resources you need to take those steps. The plan should also have a timeline so you know when you will need your capital and when you can expect to see returns on your investment. Through the planning process, you will identify all the small but necessary tasks involved in becoming a business.

If you intend to get a loan or bring in investors, a formal plan is crucial, but a plan will also help you because it outlines everything necessary to get the business going. It gives you some milestones to help you measure whether the business is on track. One of the most valuable aspects of your plan is that it will let you know if you are off track before it's too late. Without a plan, if the business is not going in the right direction, you may be out of resources before you become fully aware of the problem. With a well-developed plan in place, you can usually tell when you need more capital weeks or months before the business begins to suffer. That can give you time to either round up some more capital or close down the business before you hit rock-bottom.

Business planning is not a mystery. There are standard ways to proceed, and all plans contain most of the same elements. Planning is tedious, frustrating, and boring, but it is not mysterious. It is not a special skill that belongs only to MBAs and accountants. You can buy detailed books on business start-up planning as well as software templates that walk you through the process, providing all of the necessary spreadsheets and the proper structure. These formal plans force you to think about who your competition is, what you can offer that improves on your competition, how you will market your products and services, and how much money you will need until the business becomes self-supporting and profitable. These books and software products are inexpensive and easy to find.

Most businesses start up without a plan. If you take the time to roll up your sleeves and create a plan, you increase your chances for business success. Like any of the preparations for your enterprise, planning alone won't ensure business survival, but the planning process adds to your chances. Planning is just one more effort you can make to help your new company get off to a good start and to guide you in the right direction as you push your business forward.

Chapter 8

What Is Your Business Goal—Equity or Income?

Some companies require continual capital investment without providing profits for years to come. These kinds of companies are often growth-oriented. All of the effort goes into creating more and more revenue without necessarily creating initial profits. Many of the Internet success stories follow this pattern, as do many media companies. When these enterprises finally become profitable, they can be wildly profitable, which justifies the continued investment.

These companies are often called equity companies since they build value before they provide profits. It is worth building a company that doesn't initially produce profits because the company has value that can be sold. The value, or equity, is sold as stock, or it (the company) can be sold outright. The Internet book retailer Amazon.com is a good example of a company that saw staggering increases in its stock prices and made many people wealthy long before it became profitable. Most home businesses tend to be income businesses rather than equity companies, since most home-business owners need early profits in order to create their own income.

An income company is one that creates more income than value or equity. A one-person legal practice is a good example. When an attorney begins her practice, she is usually profitable from the first client on. There are few start-up costs, and even advertising is minimal. But even though the company may be very profitable in its earliest stages, the business creates almost no equity. Attorneys don't sell stock in their private practices, and they cannot sell their company when they retire. When the attorney quits practicing, the business simply shuts down since there is nothing to sell except some office equipment. Most professional practices are income-based companies.

When you buy a franchise or business opportunity, you are buying a combination of equity and income. The franchise will generally create more to sell than a business opportunity, since with a franchise you are an extension of the core business. With a business opportunity, you may not have anything to sell at the end. When you participate in an MLM, you launch an income-only enterprise. As you choose among a franchise, a business opportunity, and a network-marketing company, your ability to resell the business is part of your consideration. A franchise may cost quite a bit more than a business opportunity or the initial product investment of an MLM, but you will probably get more than your investment back from a franchise even after it has supported you for many years. With a business opportunity or MLM, you are not as likely to have much to sell when you cash in your chips.

Choose Your Mix of Equity and Income

When you start your business, you will make a decision as to whether your company will be equity-based, income-based, or some combination of the two. Many business owners don't even realize they are making this decision. I launched a magazine company without any clear knowledge that the company I started was an even balance between equity and income. I had a pretty good idea that one day I could sell the business for a good return, and I expected to derive my income from the company, but my understanding of these principles was not clear.

The difference between equity and income can matter when you select a business. The question can be framed as, Are you buying a job or investing in an asset, or both? You may find that the answer to this question will help you decide which direction to go as you review your choices of potential enterprises. You may be more inclined to choose a franchise, with the knowledge that you are purchasing an asset and not merely creating a job for yourself. If you don't have much capital to invest in your business launch, it will cost you less to get a business opportunity going. You will generate income, but you are not as likely to have anything to sell at the end.

Write Your Plan Backwards

As you develop your business plan, it can help to plan backwards. In the end, what to you want out of a business? Many entrepreneurs choose a business that offers both income and equity growth because they want to sell the business down the road and use the equity return as a retirement nest egg. Be careful with this strategy. Any of the mom-and-pop video-store owners who thought they could sell their stores and get enough to retire on were sadly disappointed when the total value of their work to build a business was the price used videos brought. If you plan to use the sale of your business to retire, choose a business that is not subject to the rapid ups and downs of the consumer marketplace.

You will be wiser to plan for retirement independent of the potential sale value of your business. Even if your business has perennial strength, that doesn't mean you will fare well when it comes time to sell. For one thing, you may find that when it's time to retire, you are in a recession and can't get your asking price for the business. Or maybe your company sells at a good price, but you take the payout over time and the new owners fail. The business returns to you in default, but by then the company may be decimated. Many business owners have been unhappily yanked out of retirement and forced to revive a crumbling company.

There are many unknowns in any industry and with any potential buyer, so selling your business to gain your nest egg is very risky. Every day that your investment is in your business, your capital is at risk. If your business produces a good income, set aside some for retirement and let any sale proceeds be a bonus rather than a necessity. This will give you the economic freedom to wait out a recession if it's time to retire and the climate is lousy for a sale.

So as you develop your business plan, take into account whether you want to create income, equity, or both. Once you have this settled, you can determine what you want from your business as you grow it and what you want from your business when you leave it. Knowing this will help you with your planning. As you write your plan, you will begin to see whether the business you are about to launch will truly meet your needs. Some entrepreneurs discover, through the planning process, that the business they are about to embark on is not the one they really want. This is a valuable discovery to make before you launch.

Take Your Resources Into Account

As you choose your business and go through your planning, the process of plotting out your month-by-month pro forma (estimated expenses and revenue) will give you a good idea of how much you will really need to get started. Although it is hard to predict exactly when the business will become profitable, estimating the first twenty-four months of expenses will give you a ballpark idea of how much you will need. Most beginning business owners underestimate their expenses and overestimate their revenue, which creates a plan that shows a profit months before the business actually gets there. But there are some ways to get an accurate picture of what is likely to happen.

If you buy a franchise or business opportunity or if you participate in a network-marketing company, you can talk to some of your fellow business owners to get an indication of when you can expect to derive revenue above expenses. Most entrepreneurs do not do this valuable exercise. Instead, they try to figure it out themselves. Since most entrepreneurs are optimistic, they go off on a false road. Conversations with fellow owners can help you avoid this potentially dangerous mistake. It could be that the business that looks like it takes $35,000 in start-up capital may actually require $70,000. This common mistake, which sometimes leads to business failure, can often be avoided with a few conversations.

If you start a business from scratch, you won't have references to speak with, but you can call owners of noncompeting companies that are similar to yours. You can call a business in another state so the owner will not be reluctant to talk to a potential competitor. Another way to gain a realistic picture of your true start-up costs is to attend an industry conference. Most of these conferences present sessions on the financial needs of the business. These days almost every industry, from weekly shopping to publishing to commercial cleaning to day-care management, has these conferences.

Take the Company's Future Capital Needs Into Account

As you develop your business plan and evaluate your business's ability to create income, remember to take the company's future capital needs into account. You will probably plan to launch with the purchase of equipment for business operations and communication. Most of this equipment will have a specific length of use. After that period, the equipment will be either worn or obsolete. It will then need to be replaced if you are to improve your business or even just stay competitive. If your planning anticipates that you will take additional income in the third year to set aside for retirement, make sure you have accounted for equipment enhancement or replacement. This repeated investment could eat up your extra income.

Most experienced business owners put ongoing equipment purchases into their monthly and annual budgeting. They know this is a somewhat predictable expense that will go on for the length of the company. New owners often miss this consideration. This is the type of oversight that can put new owners behind their projections. As well as budgeting for replacement, you will also need to budget for repairs. If the repairs are necessary or your equipment can be upgraded instead of replaced, then the savings become a bonus. But don't plan on these savings.

Budget like a pessimist: Expect the worst and be pleasantly surprised when it is not so bad.

Also take growth into account. With some home enterprises, the owner knows he wants to eventually move to an outside office as the business grows. With other entrepreneurs, the goal is to remain at home, and all growth will be evaluated and guided with home-office capability in mind. If your goal is continual growth and expansion out of the home, your need for new money will have to be addressed again and again as the company swells. Ross Perot says that every time a company grows 30 percent, it needs a new source of capital. As you grow your business, your borrowing ability will also grow. Plus, as your business becomes profitable and promising, you can attract investors. The source of growth capital doesn't have to come out of your profits or personal assets.

If you plan to remain a home business, you will probably not need more than one or two rounds of financing unless you begin to flounder. If you have burned through two rounds of financing and are still not on your feet, then either you have a business idea that's questionable or you misjudged your start-up needs. If growth is not your highest priority and you plan to stay at home, you shouldn't need more than one or two rounds of adequate funding. Your business plan can reflect the fact that you will not require additional funding after the second year.

Take Your Future Income Needs Into Account

Just as your business has ongoing capital needs, so does your family. These needs should be considered as you plan your business. Many families live frugally during the company's start-up period. This is to be expected. But as the company begins to perform, there will be some needs that have to be addressed. Say you live on $40,000 per year right now. For the first couple of years in business, you may decide to gear down to $25,000 per year and live at a lower standard until the business stabilizes. This is wise and it's common, but it creates a pent-up need for things you went without during the start-up years.

Once the business produces income, your financial needs

will be higher than the $40,000 you originally judged adequate, since you now have to both pay off business loans and purchase the items you put off, which usually include all high-ticket products such as cars and large appliances. So after two years of scrimping, you will have to plan on producing an income of $50,000 or more per year just to begin to get back to the level you enjoyed before the business launch.

Another consideration is the stage of your family in the life cycle. Will you bring kids into your life once the business grows? Perhaps your kids are up and out, but you need to sock away money for retirement. Getting back to status quo is not always adequate to support your family's needs. Most commonly, the business needs to contribute to growing family needs as you move forward. If so, this should be part of your business plan. Holding a job would have meant promotions and continual raises. As part of your business goal, you will want to replicate this lost income. Take all this into account as you choose a business and write a plan.

All of these planning considerations will force you to examine whether the business you are about to buy or launch will meet your family's needs. The planning process forces you to match a business's prospects with your true needs. Many entrepreneurs forgo this rigorous evaluation and just make their launches, which is risky behavior that sometimes can have destructive results. Being in business is intrinsically risky. Anything you do to reduce that risk will give you a better chance of being in the 57 percent of home companies that succeed. Risky behavior will increase your likelihood of landing in the 43 percent that fail. Take it from one who has made some of these miscalculations.

Calculating Your Launch Investment and Your Returns—Points to Consider

1. As you examine business possibilities, look closely to see if your enterprise will create equity as well as income. When it comes time to pass your business on, will you have a company that can be sold? If so, this equity value is part of your overall return.

2. Remember, you may need a second round of financing after your launch. If your business is a quick grower, you may even need a third round of financing. Make sure you know where these funds will come from before you launch.

3. Don't forget to take your own growing needs into account when you select a business. Make sure the business you choose will help you reach your long-term personal financial needs, whether those include raising a family, saving for retirement, or both.

Chapter 9

You May Be at Home, But You're Still a Business

One of the major challenges of running a successful home enterprise is the business environment of the home space. You need to make sure your company's level of professionalism is as high as or higher than a public office. Many home-office salespeople who sell by phone dress up as though they will visit the client they're calling. This helps create a "dressed-up" sound to the phone conversation. The professional appearance helps to encourage a professional bearing. Use whatever tricks you need to make sure you run your business just as professionally at home as you would in a public setting.

There is danger in getting too lackadaisical or too lax. Some people have no problem with this at all. They always deliver quality work whether they work from home or from an employer's office. For others, working from home means everything is more casual, from their attire to the regularity of their business hours. If you are going to be a successful business owner, self-discipline is the order of the day. You have to deliver your goods and services just as professionally as any nonhome-based business that might be competing with you.

This doesn't have to be taken to the extreme. Business in general is becoming more casual. Many companies have instituted casual-dress Fridays, and once that genie is out of the bottle, it stays out. There is also a casual air to how people are introduced and in male/female etiquette. I was taught that a man should never offer his hand to a woman for a handshake, that he only takes the woman's hand if she offers it. Nowadays, I feel like some old relic from a prehistoric past. I think I'm the only guy left who remembers this rule. Likewise with the rule that the lower-level person is presented to the higher-level person during introductions. I can hear you thinking, "Huh?" But those considerations were once important. Learning these manners from a business mentor used to be part of the apprenticeship of business. Not anymore.

I maintain some of these old habits to this day for the same reason I'm careful to use the right spoon. Someone from the 1 or 2 percent of the population who know anything about these old manners may be sitting across from me, so I make sure I get it right, but it feels out of sync with today's ever-growing and widespread casual manner. Since working at home encourages a relaxed work environment, it pays to be extra careful to keep all of your business practices and general quality level higher than expectations. The big danger is that a customer may lose confidence in your product or service because it is produced in a home rather than in a "professional" environment.

Creating the Home-Business Environment

Even though it is important to present a high level of professionalism in your home business, many of your clients will be comfortable with a casual business setting. Don't match their casual level. Always stay with quality work and deliver it on time. Your clients will notice this and appreciate it even if they don't appear to demand it. They may be very relaxed with you in your home setting, and it may seem as if they don't particularly care how relaxed you might be about the work, but if they perceive that your work is less than professional because of your home environment, you could lose a customer without knowing why. Your clients may be judging your work critically even though they are casual in your presence.

Creating a New Professionalism

You will find that more and more of your clients and customers will be very accustomed to home businesses, and many are now running companies in their own homes. These people will be very adept at distinguishing between the business setting and the quality of your services or products. Many home professionals pride themselves on being able to deliver high-quality service from a home setting; they also pride themselves on the warmth and general humanness of their domicile enterprise.

I know a marketing consultant who holds client meetings in his living room. If his wife or children come home during the meeting, everyone gets introduced. His wife and kids visit with the clients for a few minutes before moving on to their own interests. When I first attended some of these meetings, I was concerned that his clients might be uncomfortable with this unprofessional intrusion on a business event. "They don't mind it," he said, laughing. "They come to me because my marketing programs work. Who cares if my son comes in while we're having a meeting." This is the key to balancing professionalism with a nonbusiness environment. Most clients and customers will buy based on your goods, not because of the formality of your work space.

The difference for this marketing professional was that he knew his clients and they knew his excellent work. He also had a strong reputation in the professional community. If you are just beginning to build your reputation, you may need to present a more formal image until you develop a strong working relationship with your customers and clients and gain a positive reputation for delivering outstanding products and services.

Creating an Outside Staff

One way to grow and improve your home business without moving to outside quarters is to line up vendors who do the work that would be done by staff employees in an outside company. In Chapter 19 on outsourcing, we go into considerable detail on methods for making an outside staff effective, but for planning purposes keep in mind that you can develop a very sophisticated home business by using outside experts. As you determine the full breadth of products and services your company can offer, remember that you don't have to do all the work yourself.

Some of the standard tasks you can send outside are book-keeping and accounting. You can also buy marketing expertise and advertising services. But some home-business owners get very inventive in what can be done by outside companies. There are now catalog companies and Web sites that sell hundreds of products without putting one item in inventory. All of the products are drop-shipped by the manufacturers. The catalog takes orders and sends them to the manufacturer with payment. The manufacturer sends the merchandise to the customer. All the catalog company does is create catalogs and process orders. The catalog itself is designed by an outside graphic designer, then printed and mailed by a specialty printer with a letter shop. Even the order taking and credit-card processing can be done by an outside service.

As you lay out the plans for your business, use some creativity to see if you can expand your company's products and services by using outside staff. The more different items and services you can sell to the same customers, the better chance you have of increasing your profits. If you are maintaining the grounds for an office building, why not also try to sell them on the idea of maintaining their indoor plants or adding an aquarium that you can place and maintain. Or perhaps you could sell them some water gardens, which you would design, build, and maintain. You can contract out the water-garden design and construction for a small profit, then take on the maintenance as part of your core business. All it takes is imagination.

Creating Water-Cooler Input

One of the great advantages of building a staff in an office or shop is the impromptu brainstorming you get if your employees are interested in the business. You don't have to give this up just because your company is in your home. Some home-business owners create brainstorming sessions by inviting outside people who have an interest in the company's success. These people can include your spouse, bookkeeper, accountant, attorney, marketing expert, printer—even your computer repair person. Most of these people will be willing to occasionally take an hour or two out of their schedule for some creative talk.

An effective way to do this is to invite a group of suppliers, vendors, and professionals to a happy hour session at a lounge with good after-work snacks. Send your group a note stating that you would like some input on a particular challenge. You can even name the subject in your note. Give them about two weeks' notice, then follow up three days ahead of time to remind them. Let them know that drinks are on you and there will be snacks. You'll be surprised by the positive turnout. Most people get this request very infrequently, so they are usually willing to take part. Besides, this is good networking for them as well. Remind them of that in the note.

Creating an Effective Advisory Committee

It helps to have some management input that is more formal than a brainstorming session. Since your business is likely to be a sole proprietorship or a limited-liability company, you are not likely to have a formal board of directors, but this shouldn't stop you from forming a board of advisors. As you did for the brainstorming group, you will want to hold this meeting after work, but in a more formal space than a lounge. If you are working with an attorney, accountant, or ad agency, one of these may have a conference room you can borrow.

Your advisory committee should include a group of well-experienced professionals. Meet with these people individually and ask them if they could participate. If you are turning a strong profit, you may want to offer them a small payment for their participation. If you are not in a good financial position, you can ask them to volunteer. Like those invited to the brainstorming sessions, these people do not commonly receive this request, so they are likely to say yes. You may get a few nos, but if you keep asking, you'll get your group. Most people are flattered by the request.

Your best setup is a group of five to seven people who can meet quarterly for a couple of hours after work. Include your accountant, your attorney, and a selection of professionals, which can include a marketing or advertising professional, a noncompeting home-business owner who is already successful, and a couple of professionals who have experience in your industry but who do not compete directly with you. Retired professionals from the Small Business Administration's SCORE program are very good candidates for participation.

The goal for an advisory committee is to get feedback on how you are managing your business. It is common to share financial reports with your committee so they can take a good look at your balance sheet and income statement. Seasoned businesspeople can look at these documents and quickly ascertain whether you are on the right track or not. They will also be able to tell you whether your expenses are out of line with your revenue, and they will probably be able to spot positive or negative trends in your company's performance.

Setting Up Shop—Points to Consider

1. In developing your home-business professionalism, it's best to begin with formal etiquette and loosen up as it seems appropriate with your clientele. No one will fault you for being too formal. You can always relax as you develop your business relationships.

2. You can create a very full and professional business organization by hiring the right vendors to be part of your business team. Choose your vendors carefully, though, as part of your team, they represent the quality of your business.

3. You can devise a creative environment for business ideas by gathering your team of vendors together for informal brainstorming on product extensions or service improvements.

Chapter 10

Your Formal Business Plan—Its Many Benefits

It's a rare business that launches without a loan or investors. The plan that you need to demonstrate credibility to your banker is not the same plan you need as your operating blueprint. The plan you use for yourself needs a great deal of detail. The one for an outsider should be a sketch that spends more time arguing your credentials and less time spelling out the week-by-week tasks. All your banker needs to see is the overview, the marketing plan, and some of the general goals and positive projections. You can leave out the month-by-month pro forma. The plan you prepare for a potential investor should be your complete proposal; investors usually want to see the full pro forma.

Planning Is Aiming—You're Lost Without It

Business planning is one of the few tasks that should never be delegated, no matter how dreary it may seem. It is important that the business owner roll up his sleeves and go through the rigorous process. The task forces you to eyeball every facet of your business, and it makes you extrapolate the future from your good use of resources. Ideally, you should complete a full plan annually and review the pro forma monthly. You should review the plan in more detail quarterly to see where your projections were correct and where they were inaccurate.

If you discipline yourself to develop a plan every year, after a few years your projections will begin to get very accurate. After five years of running a publishing business, I was able to develop plans that were effectively projections of expenses and revenue, all allocated by expense category and revenue type. My plans took the form of charts and spreadsheets instead of the written text of the first year's plan. After five years, I no longer needed to explain the position the company held in its market. All those thoughts had become second nature. Everyone in the company knew exactly where we stood compared to our competitors.

The projections grew accurate after a few years. I learned how much money I had to leave in the company to foster new growth and how much I could take out for my family. I had also learned how much it cost to generate a new customer and how much it cost to retain a customer. I could project how much it would cost to find and keep a customer over a five-year period, and I could predict within 3 to 5 percent how much that customer would spend with us during that time. In addition, I could determine how much it would cost to provide that customer with products over the same period. Using these figures, I could determine both how many customers I needed to break even and how much profit I could create with a 20 percent increase in new customers.

Sounds like fancy accounting, but I actually had no background or experience in accounting or in spreadsheet projections. All I had was the knowledge a business owner gains after years of finding and serving customers. I learned to develop projections by running a business sixty hours per week for years. I learned it through overspending and getting in trouble and through trying unorthodox ways of reaching customers inexpensively. After a few years of keeping the eye on the ball and changing unsuccessful practices, it became clear. But it only became clear because I tracked all of the numbers and continued to plan and review those plans regularly.

Even an Informal Business Needs a Formal Plan

You may think that since your business is a tiny home company, planning is an empty gesture. But even an informal business benefits from a plan. For one thing, you want to be able to predict when your business is going to turn a profit, and you want to know how large that profit might be. You also need to be able to compare expenses to revenue as your business grows. Your plan provides two important functions: It gives you a tool for prediction, and it gives you the ability to measure the financial elements of your business. These two functions are crucial, whether your business is formal or casual.

The ability to predict will help you determine if you have enough capital to launch your business and grow it to the point of profit. One of the reasons to continue to revise the plan is to get it to be a better and better predictor of capital needs. The measurement quality will help you determine if your investment in marketing and product development is productive. Some businesses fold when they are just a couple of quarters from turning a good profit because they didn't have a device to show they were close to breaking even. Other companies fold two quarters later than they should have when a good plan would have revealed the problem months earlier. A well-written plan that is continually revised can help you understand the sometimes mysterious finances of a business.

Set Your Goals and Plan Backwards

The best way to make your way through a plan is to start with your desired outcome and work backwards. If you want to create a specific income and build your business to a particular level of equity, use that as the starting point and determine what milestones your business needs to reach in the preceding years in order to attain your goals. Most people plan in the other direction, writing down the things they think they should do to make the business succeed, while hoping the outcome will be pleasant. If you start with your goals first and then determine all the steps that will be necessary to reach those goals, your plan will become a road map that leads to your goals rather than a list of nice things to do to launch a business.

As you set your goals and work out the steps it will take to realize your goals, you will begin to see some of the specific tasks and investments that are required to get you there. As you develop your plan, you will also get a clear idea of the requisite time and resources you need to succeed. It is hard to determine the exact resources you will need if you don't know what your desired outcome looks like. Planning backwards forces you to assess the investment you need and how long it will take. It also spells out each milestone.

Create Monthly, Quarterly, and Annual Goals and Milestones

As you build your plan from the back forward, break your milestones down into measurable periods. Start with your annual goal, showing your total expenses, your total revenue, and your resulting profit (or loss) for the year. Then break it down by quarters, and break your quarters into months. Create a plan that covers a three- to five-year period. Once you're done, you will have the guidelines to show you how close or far away you are from your expected path. Within a few short months of operation, you will have a good idea if you're going in the right direction.

These monthly, quarterly, and annual projections will help you determine if you are going to hit your income goals. To measure your progress toward equity goals, there is a rule of thumb you can use. Like any rule, it is not particularly accurate, but it works as a barometer. Ask yourself the question, Can someone else with business aptitude step in and run this business? If you are a management consultant with twenty years of corporate experience, the answer is no. If you run a commercial cleaning business with two crews, the answer is yes. Then take your income (or profit), after deducting an average salary for your management position, and multiply that income by five. This is roughly the potential asking price for your enterprise.

Every industry has its own multiples; if you know these multiples, you can get a more accurate picture of your company's value. The state of the economy also affects these multiples. I've seen the magazine industry's multiples fluctuate from four to ten in just two quick years because of the economy. Five times is a safe average for the sake of ballpark equity growth. In figuring your own salary, use the amount it would cost you to hire a manager to run your company. Most business owners pay themselves an inflated salary if they can, rewarding themselves for creating a profitable business. Don't use this salary; use the amount you would pay someone else.

Alter Your Plans As You Learn and Grow

As you gain a track record and measure that record against your plan, it won't take more than a few months before you will see how accurate your forecasting method is. If you have considerable business experience, you may be close to your forecast; but for most new business owners, the plan is usually far from reality. Your expenses will almost always be underestimated and your revenue will be overestimated. At this point, rewrite all of your forecasts, and continue to rewrite and reforecast every quarter until your forecasting is within a few small percentage points of reality.

It may take six to eighteen months before you develop an ability to accurately predict your business future, but once this materializes, you will have an invaluable business skill—the ability to see your future business destiny coolly and clearly. The feeling of power you get when this begins to happen is justified. Being able to chart your destiny is pretty close to being in charge of your destiny. There will always be mitigating factors, such as economic downturns, changes in your competition, and trends in your customers' habits, but in time you will be able to adjust for these variables as well. Learning good planning skills is like giving yourself a steering wheel for an out-of-control car.

There are a number of resources to help you create your business plan. Software packages are particularly helpful because they prompt you through the process of writing the plan. The books on business planning are able to show you examples of actual plans. You will also find some help on the Internet. Many small-business sites offer examples of business plans and articles on how to write business plans. These services are usually free at sites such as America Online's Business Know How or the small-business area on the American Express site, www. americanexpress.com.

Sample Business Plan

Here is a sample business plan. This is based on an actual business plan that was effective in gaining the interest of a venture capitalist. When the venture capitalist showed interest, he requested a pro forma. Specifically, he wanted to see a projection of the expenses and revenue on a month-to-month basis over twenty-four months.

Complete Home-Business Web-Site—Business Plan

Contents

Overview
Target Customers
Competition
Revenue and Profitability
Management Team
Funding and Income

Overview

The overall goal of the Complete Home-Business Web Site is to become the leading commercial source of information for the home-business market online. Unlike most Web sites, which provide their owners with a public-relations and customer-service vehicle, the Complete Home Business Web Site is designed to be profitable. All the decisions in the development of the site will be made with revenue and profit in mind. We are monitoring the Internet market for advances in marketing and product-fulfillment technology to glean the most successful programs to bring to our site. All of the programs will be selected for their ability to reach customers and create revenue.

Services of the Complete Home-Business Web Site

- Business supplies and equipment catalog
- Business books and tapes catalog
- Chat rooms
- Networking opportunities for visitors to find loans and investors
- Networking opportunities for visitors to find business opportunities and franchises
- Networking opportunities for visitors to find vendors such as Web designers
- Services to help entrepreneurs draft and present proposals to venture capitalists
- Bulletin boards
- A wide range of archived information on launching and running a small business
- A regular electronic newsletter offering articles and information on our services
- E-mail
- A small-business/home-business newsgroup
- A push-technology service to give customers a stream of custom-selected information through e-mail

Revenue Streams of the Web Site

- *The Complete Home-Business Web Site product catalog.* This virtual online catalog will offer a full range of office products, formed in association with a major online business-supply retailer such as Office Max.

- *Business books, audiotapes, and videotapes.* This will be a virtual online catalog of all the relevant books in print on business, formed with a major online book retailer such as Amazon. com or Barnesandnoble.com.

- *Business-opportunity matchmaking.* We will set up a network for visitors to learn about business opportunities and multilevel marketing companies. We will receive commissions when customers consummate deals.

■ *Franchise matchmaking.* We will set up an opportunity for visitors to learn about available franchises. We will receive commissions when customers consummate deals.

In order to create the traffic that will make these revenue streams productive, we will promote ourselves as the one-stop site for the entrepreneur. We will provide information, networking, and education. We will offer a wider range of business services than any other business site on the Internet. This will include an information push-technology service that will let us send preselected information by e-mail to customers who request it. A customer will be able to request all information on, say, service-business franchise opportunities with an initial investment of less than $10,000. We will be able to supply that information directly to the customer by e-mail as we obtain it.

We have identified a national production company that can deliver the technical services of designing and implementing the site. This company is also adept at tying the site to the search engines to ensure that our site comes up when browsers search for home business and other related keywords.

Target Customers

The target audience of the Complete Home-Business Web Site includes the following three groups:

1. *Active entrepreneurs.* These are people who already own their own businesses but need assistance to continue and to grow. The services this group needs include additional capital (investors and loans), office equipment and supplies, and networking opportunities.

2. *Launch entrepreneurs.* These are people who are about to start a business. These individuals need capital (investors and loans), business opportunities/franchises, education, and networking, as well as business supplies, equipment, and books.

3. *Armchair entrepreneurs.* These are the tire kickers, people who would love to launch a business but for one reason or another will not actually take the leap. These people are still very interested and will become customers of our site for a number of services, including books, education, and networking.

We will reach our audience in a number of ways. We will of course work hard to gain traffic from online browsers, those who are already online looking for information on small business. To reach this audience, we will use state-of-the-art techniques to get in the top of the search-engine results. The production company we have chosen is particularly effective in this area of technology.

However, these online visitors may not be the cream of our potential customers. Internet history, short as it may be, indicates the best online customers are the ones who are reached offline and encouraged to go online to visit a site. The Complete Home-Business Web Site, with its varied ways of reaching potential customers offline, may ultimately be our greatest source for online customers. We will reach customers offline through books, the radio show, articles, publicity, and public appearances.

The depth of the brand ensures us a steady flow of new potential customers reached through print, broadcasts, and appearances. This will also help us outmaneuver our competitors since most online business sites rely entirely on the visitors they find online. As we already stated, these online visitors are lower-quality prospects than those we can entice to go online through offline contact. Our offline customers will also not have the full knowledge of online business sites and will thus rely on our Web site for more services. Since we will provide the full range of available online business services, our customers will not have to shop around to obtain all the products and services they need.

Competition

There is a variety of competition in the small-business/home-business market. Most of the services we plan to offer are already available on a number of sites, but no site offers the full array of services that will be available on the Complete Home-Business Web Site. Plus, our site will have a number of services that cannot be found anywhere else on the Internet, such as the matchmaking and proposal draft and presentation services.

Most business sites are informational, providing archived information, newsletters, and links to other sites. Most of these sites sell banner ads as their sole source of revenue. Few of them are sophisticated in their information or design. No other business information Web site offers comprehensive business supplies and equipment (except the Office Max site, but it exists only as an online catalog and provides no information services that would draw our target audience, and Amazon.com offers the full range of in-print business books but also doesn't draw our target customers).

We will be the only site offering the comprehensive matchmaking services. One site, BizWiz, offers limited matchmaking for business opportunities, but that is just a small portion of the full offering of the shoestring site. Entreworld.org and Home Business.com offer information and a small selection of products, but these sites present only a small fraction of the shoestring services. There are countless entrepreneurial sites that are sales vehicles for individual business opportunities and multilevel marketing companies, but these sites tend to present generic business information in an unsophisticated manner.

The Complete Home-Business Web Site will occupy the top market position for its comprehensive set of services and for the quality of its information. It will also be the only site with a variety of revenue streams. We believe this ensures its success for rising above the competition and for drawing and keeping customers.

Revenue and Profitability

Most Web sites operate with the primary purpose of public relations or customer service. Sites designed entirely to generate revenue have just started to appear in the past twelve to eighteen months. The Complete Home Business Web Site is primarily designed to be a revenue-generating venture, so we have taken a number of lessons from profitable sites to develop our combination of revenue streams.

For one, we have designed a one-stop site so our customers can return over and over, using the shoestring site as their portal into the Internet. Secondly, we have identified our customers' major needs (both one-time and ongoing) and provided access to these items and services through the site. By affiliating with major suppliers, we will provide these products at competitive prices and make them easy to acquire online. These services will put us at the forefront of the world of profitable Web sites.

But the Complete Home Business Web Site will go further: We have created additional services with our matchmaking network. These services will be new to our customers. Previously, entrepreneurs who wanted to shop for business opportunities or franchises had to search high and low to find the appropriate providers. Now they will be able to search for any of these items online through our site. This will be the major feature to put our site out in front of all the competition.

Details of the Web Site's Revenue Streams

■ *The Complete Home-Business Web Site product catalog.* This virtual online catalog will offer a full range of office products including software, computers and accessories, office supplies, and furniture. We will accomplish this ambitious goal by forming an association with a major business-supply retailer, such as Office Max, and putting its full online catalog on our site under our name. This will save us the burden and risk of creating inventory and running a fulfillment operation. Our revenue will come through a negotiated margin. We will take the credit card order and pass it directly to the catalog company, retaining our margin. The catalog company will also provide the customer-service operation.

■ *Business books, audiotapes, and videotapes.* This will be a virtual online catalog of all the relevant books in print on business, formed with a major online book retailer such as Amazon.com or Barnes and Noble.com. This arrangement will allow us to offer every book or tape in print without inventory or fulfillment investment or overhead. We will be able to work out an arrangement with one of these providers to place its search software on our site and to give us a percentage of all sales that come from our customers.

■ *Business-opportunity matchmaking.* We will set up a network for visitors to learn about business opportunities and multilevel marketing companies. We will receive a commission if one of our customers consummates a deal. The business-opportunity customers will provide their information in a format designed by us for easy use by our customers. Our customers will be tagged so we will know if they invest with the business opportunity. We will set a standard percentage with the business opportunity. This system of not charging the business opportunity unless it makes a sale will ensure wide participation in this market of companies.

■ *Franchise matchmaking.* We will set up an opportunity for visitors to learn about available franchises. We will receive a commission if one of our customers consummates a deal. This system will work exactly like the business-opportunity system.

We are not sure which of these revenue streams will be the most fruitful, but all of them involve services that are widely needed among entrepreneurs. Many of them are ongoing needs, so we have the opportunity to create repeat customers.

These revenue streams are also unique, which gives our site some media appeal. It will be easy to gain publicity for our site simply because we will offer services that have not previously been available through the Internet or in any other way.

Management Team

The management team for this project will be Jim Shoe and Henry Younger. Shoe will be very involved in the strategy, writing, public speaking, content design, sponsorship, and affiliation development for the shoestring brand. Younger will be involved in the strategy, management, marketing, production, publicity, and sponsorship development for the site.

- *Jim Shoe.* Shoe has the promotional background to get the word out about the Complete Home Business Web Site. Shoe has lent his services to Younger's projects, and Younger has delivered work for a number of Shoe's projects. The core of the working relationship is mutual respect and trust, as well as a shared interest in business strategy, marketing, and publicity.

- *Henry Younger.* Spiegel has worked closely with Henry Younger for fifteen years. Younger launched Younger Communications in 1988. The company provides marketing, public relations, and production services for a variety of clients. The company also provides the full range of ad-agency services as well as event and broadcast production. Younger brings proven skills in creative direction, strategic market planning, public relations, product rollout, and event promotion. He has won regional and national awards as a creative director, writer, voice talent, and film/video director. Younger will manage the production and development of the Web site.

Funding and Income

It will require an investment of $200,000 to get the Web site up and running. Since Shoe and Younger will work on the site from their homes, the company will not require an outside office until it is producing enough income to need an outside customer-service center. When we reach that stage, we may choose to simply outsource customer service.

Approximately $100,000 of the start-up funds will go toward getting the site up and working right. The remaining $100,000 will go directly to advertising and promoting the site. Shoe and Younger will participate without salary until the site is producing enough revenue to create market-level salaries.

We expect to create enough revenue to cover expenses within nine to twelve months. At that point, salaries will be paid to Shoe and Younger. It will likely take another six to twelve months to begin producing profits beyond salaries and the recurring costs of customer service.

Once we reach this point, first-year income will be in the range of $100,000 to $200,000. Beyond that, we expect income to increase 10 to 20 percent per year.

Creating Your Business Plan—Points to Consider

1. It is important to develop a written plan even if you don't need one to convince lenders or investors that your business is likely to succeed. Writing a plan will help you create a focus and direction for your enterprise.

2. Always set the goals first, then plan backwards. Determine the revenue and income levels you need to reach, and map out when you need to reach each level. Then your plan becomes an outline of the steps you need to take to meet these specific goals.

3. Set monthly, quarterly,and annual goals. Review these goals monthly as your business gets going; then adjust your goals as you learn your business well enough to determine which goals are realistic.

Chapter 11

Licenses, Permits, and Zoning—Getting Permission

Every business, and every community, has its own set of specifics for business licenses, permits, and zoning. If you don't follow the regulations in proper detail, you could find yourself inadvertently and unnecessarily out of business. Make a list of the licenses and permits you need and the order in which they should be obtained. There is always an order. You may not be able to get your state tax number until you have a business license. If you don't know what you need, you can learn a great deal by calling your local Small Business Administration, your state business regulation office, and your city zoning office.

As you make these calls, ask around about what other offices you need to contact to start a business. Most people will be helpful, giving you ideas. If you are working with an attorney to set up or purchase your business, ask her what licenses you will need. Most business lawyers are well versed in the documents and regulations of launching an enterprise. But you don't need an attorney to plow through the paperwork. Most of the procedures are simple enough to get through without the expense of an attorney. The one area that may be tricky is filing to be a corporation or limited-liability company. But even these tasks can be done without an attorney if you're brave. I've done it, so anyone can.

You will also find some help at your local bookstore. There

are a couple of book series on how to start a business state by state. If you go to a well-stocked bookstore, such as Border Books or Barnes and Noble, you will find these books in the business section. You will also find a number of other books that will walk you through the steps of opening a business. The state books will contain most of the state and federal procedures, but you will likely be on your own to discover the city and county procedures. Call the zoning office and business license office for your local specifics.

Check Your Residential Zoning

Zoning regulations are a patchwork of laws and covenants that can date back 100 years, and they are in constant flux. Don't look too closely into this quagmire; you'll begin to find contradictory restrictions. Most cities have a number of zoning types, from fully commercial zones to residential zones that have big restrictions on commerce. In between, you will find hybrid zones that allow certain types of commerce and disallow others. The rise of the home-worker movement has made all of these regulations very confusing. Sometimes it's best not to ask too many questions. Just apply for a business license and hope for the best.

There is a rule of thumb: If your business does not make excessive noise and you do not have customer traffic and dangerous equipment, your neighbors will not care if your business is in your home. Keep in mind as you apply for your license that the triggers that will alert your bureaucrats include any activity that will bother the neighbors. If your business requires heavy trucks, construction equipment, a number of company vehicles parked on the street, or other unpleasant signs of business, you may be challenged. If you are running a consulting business out of your den, nobody will notice and nobody will care.

Get Your Licenses and Permits

Some home enterprises require more than a business license from your county or city office. For contracting work, such as electric and plumbing, you will need state licenses. Many other professionals require permits or licenses. In some states, you can provide massage therapy in your home without a permit or license, while other states require certification, which includes graduation from accredited schools and ongoing professional education.

There are rarely any spot checks to make sure a business has all its licenses, permits, and certifications. Usually this only comes up if there is some complaint about the business. It doesn't take much of a complaint—just one customer who believes he got a raw deal and officials could come over to check all your paperwork. If there are any holes in your set of permits, licenses, and certifications, you could be instantly shut down until you are in compliance, even if you were right in the disagreement with your customer.

Seek Professional Associations and Credentials

Credibility and networking are important in all types of business. You can gain these by joining professional and trade associations and groups. Some trade groups provide credentials that are essential to gaining credibility in your profession or trade. Others will provide contacts that will be important for continuing education in business and in your profession. Many groups and associations also offer networking opportunities that will help you reach potential customers and clients. Some groups will be very helpful and others will be of no help at all. Often you can't tell how beneficial an organization might be until you join and attend a few meetings.

There is a range of potential groups to join. Most major local newspapers carry weekly lists of business-group meetings. Business groups are usually happy to let you attend a meeting or two before you join so you can sample the value of their programs and also meet some of their members. A couple of visits will usually give you a good idea whether their programs or membership will help you in your business. Groups that can help your business include the local chamber of commerce, the state chapter of your professional or trade association, and tips groups.

The chamber of commerce usually offers good how-to business education on everything from taxes to publicity. Chambers generally offer education seminars free to paid members. Chambers of commerce are also a good source for discounted rates on group health insurance and HMOs. Your professional or trade association is a good place to stay abreast of the evolution of your profession, trade, or industry, although this is not usually a good place to meet potential clients and customers since you are surrounded by your competition. Tips or leads groups are small gatherings that usually meet weekly over breakfast, at lunch, or after work. A selection of noncompeting members share tips and leads on new businesses that need your services or products.

Consider Your Neighbors

Good home-business companies need to be good neighbors. Home companies are now widely accepted, but if you tread on your neighbors' peace, quiet, and parking spaces, you may find your home enterprise is not so acceptable to the residents on your street. Usually the most difficult business to run from a home is a retail company that requires a stream of customers through the neighborhood and across the lawns. Everyone accepts the occasional garage sale, but if it becomes a regular enterprise, you can run into trouble. Most residential zoning excludes retail, so your neighbors will have some official support if they find your business objectionable.

Another bone of contention for homeowners is parking. If your own company vehicles or the cars of employees interfere with your neighbors' parking spaces, you will likely have trouble. Even with the current high tolerance for home companies, your neighbors will find some backing if they go to officials with complaints. If your neighbors do complain, try hard to settle any disputes before your neighbors start making phone calls and writing letters to city, county, or state agencies and offices. If you want a happy home business, keep your neighbors happy.

Take Growth Into Account

I know a Mexican food manufacturer who runs a company with annual revenues of $10 million out of his living room, with no employees. Not all growth means you have to get an outside office. When he started, his company was generating $250,000 in sales. When he hit the $500,000 level, he felt he needed to hire staff and move into rented space. He was miserable for two years running a regular office (although the company continued to grow), so he went back home and farmed out all of his office work. He produces over thirty Mexican food items that are stocked in more than 200 grocery stores in twenty states. He spends most of the day on the phone and computer, sitting on his couch. His business keeps growing; he is a master of outsourcing. He spends a few months each year on a boat off the coast of New Orleans, getting his calls forwarded to the deck.

More and more home-business owners are beginning to discover that growth doesn't have to force them out of the den. With some creativity and imagination, you can find ways to accommodate your growth while staying at home. You may have to develop the skills of outsourcing, but many home entrepreneurs find outsourcing to be much easier on the nerves than hiring and managing employees. And your bottom line will love it if you can stay at home. Rented space is always more expensive than home space, plus an outside business always has more expenses than a home business—and that's not even counting the tax breaks from writing off some of your mortgage.

Doing the Local Groundwork—Points to Consider

1. Check all of your local regulations before you launch your business. If you need licenses and certificates before you open your doors, it is best to get these taken care of well in advance of your opening date. Otherwise, you could experience business interruptions.

2. As part of your preparations to start a business, check in with your neighbors. Give them the courtesy of letting them know you will be running a company next door. Show them the bright side of having someone in the neighborhood watching the streets.

3. Don't let your own growth catch you by surprise. If your business is likely to change through the months, make sure you know what steps to take to accommodate business expansion.

Chapter 12

Taxes and Legalities— Getting Legit

What's your best bet for legal status? Sole proprietor? Limited-liability partnership? Subchapter S corporation? dba? Huh? These questions are very important, but they don't require high-priced lawyers. Some legwork on your part, and a quick legal lookover, can save you major dollars while giving you the education you will eventually need anyway. Here is a quick sketch of the differences between types of businesses. Each business form has its own qualities, some of which are positive and some of which are not. You can find books that cover the subject of business legalities in depth. You can find additional information on the Internet.

Choice of Your Business Organization

One way or another, you will have to choose a business organization. If you choose none at all, you are really choosing a sole proprietorship, which just means you are running a business as yourself, using your personal Social Security number as your tax identification number. Whatever you choose, do it carefully because it is not always easy to switch back and forth; the tax authorities are not always pleased if you move back and forth to dodge taxes, although there are some very sophisticated ways of legally doing just that.

This is one area where it helps to get some advice from an

attorney or a tax accountant. Most certified public accountants (CPAs) can help you with this question. Depending on your tax situation, the question can get very complicated. Most attorneys and CPAs will be able to help you choose an appropriate business organization without running up high fees. Once you decide on the right organization, it isn't that hard to file, so you won't need to accrue additional accounting and legal fees to go through the process. But since this is an important decision with a number of potential tax consequences, it really is best to study up on the subject before deciding which direction is right for you.

Sole Proprietorship vs. Incorporation

A sole proprietorship means you are in business as yourself. This is also referred to as a dba, which is short for "doing business as." I run my freelancing as Spiegel Enterprises, but I am a sole proprietor, so I am actually Robert Spiegel dba Spiegel Enterprises, which means Spiegel Enterprises is just me, from a tax and legal point of view. I have owned corporations in the past. Corporations are separate entities that issue stock and maintain a board of directors. When I first incorporated, I did it thinking it offered protection. If something went wrong with the business, I didn't want anyone to be able to come directly at me and my personal assets.

It was a false security. Owning a corporation did almost nothing to protect me from corporate debt or liability. Sometimes even attorneys don't fully understand how the world works. I had an attorney agree that the corporate structure would offer some protection if the company took on more debt or liability than I could weather. I found out the truth the first time I applied for a bank loan. My company was humming right along, and I qualified for a corporate line of credit. As the papers were being drawn up, my bank officer said, "You are willing to back up this loan personally, right?"

"Back it up personally?"

"Yes, with your personal assets."

"Well, I thought my company's assets covered your exposure."

"Yes," he nodded, "they do, but it's our policy to also get collateralized by the owner." I didn't argue. I wanted the loan and I wanted it that day. But as the corporate years went on, I learned that vendors and lenders always seek to put the corporate president on the line even if the corporation can cover the exposure. There are instances when corporate protection really does exist, and I have benefited from these odd instances, but they tend to be outside normal business operations. In the day-to-day routine of running a company, a corporation doesn't usually protect its owner from the consequences of the company's behavior.

Limited-Liability Corporation and S Corporation

The limited-liability corporation (LLC) and the subchapter S corporation are business organizational structures developed with small and very small companies in mind. These organizational structures offer some of the protections and legal advantages of a corporation without as many of the reporting and other legal burdens of a full C corporation. These entities come with their own particulars that require some real study or the help of an attorney or tax accountant to determine if they are right for your particular needs. I would get legal or accounting advice before embarking on the formation of one of these hybrid corporations.

Keep in mind that even though these forms of business organizations present the image of protecting you personally from some of the troubles your business might get you into, the protective wall is thin and uneven. The attempt to distance yourself from your own enterprise may be just faulty enough to make all the additional effort of setting up an LLC or subchapter S corporation more work than the benefits warrant. Before jumping into one of these organizations, quiz your attorney about the real benefits of this type of organization. If you start hearing about how it will protect you from liability, take it with a grain of salt. If you hear that given your particular tax position, this form of business will give you considerable tax advantages, listen earnestly.

Finally, you may get the argument that this form of business will make it easier to bring in partners and investors down the road. Ask yourself, How far down the road? If you're looking for participation now, then you should probably form as an LLC or subchapter S. The same goes if you're anticipating participation at some specific point in the future. But if it is just a consideration you may have at some undefined future point, you don't need to launch as a corporation. You can switch to an LLC or subchapter S down the road if you need to change; the switch isn't very difficult.

Partnership

Watch out for the P word. Here's the problem with business partnerships: Most people launch a business because they want to control their own destiny. When you go 50/50 with a friend, relative, or business associate, you lose control of your destiny. Don't tell me how well you get along with your partner. Unless you are very special or very lucky, a 50/50 partnership can erode good relationships. The operative word in business is control. If your partner has less than 50 percent, you have control. You may still use the word partner, but your associate is really just an investor in the company you control.

A 50/50 partnership is a two-headed beast that will try to walk in two different directions someday. This presents a problem when both partners are heavily invested emotionally and financially in the outcome of the company, and neither one wishes to get bought out and walk away. The pulling in two different directions can tear the company in two, leaving both sides bleeding and perhaps dying. As silly and mundane as it may sound, all it takes to destroy a 50/50 partnership is for the spouse of one partner to begin to mistrust the other partner. That's usually how the destruction begins. We're all human, so don't be too quick to pride yourself on being above these possibilities because of the quality of your relationship with and trust of your partner.

One large exception to the above rule is side ventures. If you're running your own successful enterprise or career and see an opportunity to partner with someone else who also sees an opportunity to prosper with a side enterprise, a 50/50 deal can be successful and satisfactory. The major difference is that neither partner views the side company as the key to her destiny. If one partner begins to take a keen interest in the enterprise, the other can either take a happy backseat or take a buyout. It is uncommon that both partners grab for the reins at the same moment, so usually one partner defers and everyone's happy. Either that or neither one ever views it as more than a side venture.

Taxes and the Home Business

There used to be a big fear that if you deducted any home space for business purposes, you would get audited. Many people believed home-space deductions were a red flag that put the tax return in the audit pile. I have no idea whether this is based on truth or whether it is one of those urban myths like alligators in the sewer system. I'm hesitant to say it's hogwash because surely if I say such a thing, the next day I would see a former IRS audit boss claiming home-space deductions are consistently red-flagged for review. I know a handful of home-business entrepreneurs who went for years without taking their legitimate deductions because they were convinced it would spark an audit.

Whatever may have happened in the past, you really are safe taking the deduction today. We're seeing an explosion of home workers springing up all over the country. Over 1.5 million home companies are launched each year, and that doesn't count the home workers who can also take some of the home-space deduction. Even if the IRS wanted to tag all home enterprises for audits, there are simply too many for this to be possible.

Choosing a Legal Status—Points to Consider

1. Give careful thought to your business organization. Although you can switch your legal status after you launch, it can be awkward and expensive. Think of your needs over the coming years and choose a legal status that will serve you over a long period of time.

2. If you are considering a partnership, organize it carefully. Partnerships can present problems as the business grows and changes. Make sure you devise a buyout clause that will make a split-up as simple and nondisruptive as possible.

3. Your company's least expensive legal bills will be the ones you pay to set your company up correctly. Paying an attorney three years later to untangle an organizational mess that resulted because you launched without legal advice isn't cost-efficient.

Chapter 13

Insurance—The Nonproductive but Necessary Expense

The last thing a budding new entrepreneur wants to spend money on is insurance. Yet a good insurance policy has kept many a business alive after a calamity. Assuming your resources are not unlimited, you can pick and choose your way through the insurance world, adding coverage as you can afford it. You can measure your risk against your resources to get catastrophic coverage at the onset and additional coverage when your cash flow improves. You don't have to put your entire insurance package together before you launch your enterprise.

Business Insurance—Protection for Your Investment

A good business policy can come in handy if someone gets hurt while visiting your home on business or if a libel charge is brought against your company. I have seen both of these surprises come to unsuspecting home-business owners. Both times the owner had adequate coverage to keep the business from devastation. If you don't have insurance when you are shocked with a sudden insurance need, it can destroy your company. If your enterprise grows in value over the years, keep an eye on your insurance to make sure it is upgraded to remain sufficient to protect you.

Many new entrepreneurs resist insurance. They purchase it reluctantly, if at all. One home-business owner told me, "When you buy insurance, you're betting against yourself, and the insurance company is betting on you." That's one way to view it. Another way to see it is that you are about to devote a great amount of money and energy to an enterprise; you may also contribute many years to building your business. You do not want that investment to be vulnerable to a quick accident or an ill-perceived slight that you have no control over whatsoever. If you could control the world, you wouldn't need insurance—but you can't control the world.

Check with your household insurance agent to see how easy and inexpensive it might be to cover your business belongings through your household policy. Many insurance companies can work with home-business owners to create a policy that covers their business without drafting an entirely new policy. There are often ways to include property under the household policy while adding a stripped-down business policy that covers libel only. This can result in yet another savings in home-business overhead that keeps it lower than that of an outside office.

Health Coverage—An Indispensable Expense

Most people understand the importance of health coverage. This is not a business expense you can avoid any more than your rent or mortgage payment. Its monthly costs may be more than rent would be if you had an outside office; this expense is often the biggest shock when a home-business owner leaves the protective bosom of a good job. Health coverage may be your largest monthly bill during your first few years. Wouldn't it be wonderful to do without it? But you can't.

Although health coverage is a high expense, you can make sure you don't pay any more than absolutely necessary. Don't go shopping by yourself. Calling around town to ask for quotes on individual coverage will bring you some very discouraging sticker shock. Find a group that offers health coverage options, and review their prices before joining. Groups can include your chamber of commerce, some of the fraternal groups, and professional or trade associations.

Don't be embarrassed about asking health coverage questions right off the bat when approaching groups. Their membership people know your needs, and the group added group health coverage as an incentive to gain members. They will be just as happy to get you as a member even if the only reason you're joining is for the health coverage discount. As you do your comparison shopping, just add in the monthly membership dues and measure the cost of your health coverage. Balance it with the value of the membership to your business. You may end up in a group that has no business value but offers great health coverage rates.

Life Insurance—The "After You Die" Answers

Life insurance is more than just a way to help your family in the event of your untimely passing. Life insurance can be a way to secure a loan from family and friends. Adding enough insurance to make sure your debtors or their heirs get reimbursed can give some reassurance that you may not be able to provide through collateral. As long as you keep up your life insurance payments, you can provide this protection to selected debtors even if your business fails.

Life insurance can also be handy if you have whole life or universal life since you can borrow against the policy's assets. This surprised me once when I needed a new source of capital. I was aware I could borrow against a universal life policy I had kept for a number of years. So I called my agent to ask what my borrowing limits were, and I was surprised at how much credit was there waiting for my signature. Keep in mind, though, that if you are using your policy to protect debtors, the outstanding loan balances are subtracted from your death benefit. If you borrow heavily from your policy, you may have to add coverage to make sure all your post-passing needs are covered.

Disability Insurance—The Unplugged Hole

What happens if you are not able to work, but you're still alive and need care? This is one form of insurance that many business-people feel is truly expendable. I'm certainly sympathetic with that view. In the back of your mind, you may realize the importance of disability insurance, but you may also figure you'll pick it up when the business cash flow improves. At different times in my business, I've gone years without disability coverage. But this is important protection, especially if you have people depending on your income. Don't ignore this insurance just because you can. You are best off to commit a small part of your basic monthly overhead to this coverage.

Insurance needs don't go away. When you are struggling to get your business up and going, these are frustrating expenses because, like taxes, they are unproductive. Insurance payments can feel like capital stripped away before it can provide any forward movement for the company. But these are necessary costs, even if they seem less than crucial when you are struggling. View these expenses as irreducible overhead, part of the ante you pay to be in business. If you cannot cover your monthly insurance needs, then perhaps you simply don't have the capital necessary to be in business.

Getting the Right Insurance for Your New Enterprise—Points to Consider

1. Business insurance is a reasonable expense even if it's an unproductive cost. You need to make sure an unexpected event doesn't abruptly end your company. If your business is worth the investment of your time and money, it's worth protecting.

2. Health coverage may be one of your biggest overhead expenses unless you have a spouse with a regular job. You can reduce your costs by joining a business organization that offers discounted medical coverage.

3. Life insurance may seem like a luxury when you make a list of your start-up costs, but in time it can become an asset and even a foundation for your retirement.

4. Disability insurance may seem the most ridiculous insurance of all, but a simple accident could leave you unable to run your business or meet your obligations.

Part III

Your Very Own Business Space

Now we're getting to the fun stuff. What will your business nest look like? What tools will you include as the instruments in the cockpit of your enterprising rocket? What boundaries will you create so that you can focus hour upon hour on driving your company forward? These are the fun questions. This section covers the contents of your home office. Will it be in the spare bedroom, the living room, or the den? Perhaps you're the garage type. There are adjustments that need to be made with your family and your friends, as well as with time management. If you take well to these changes, having your business at home can be very rewarding, both financially and personally.

Setting up your home office is more than putting a desk and phone in the corner of the guest room. Besides setting up the equipment and furnishings you need, you will also have to adjust to being your own boss. This change will affect how you spend your time and whether you keep a regular schedule. You will probably share your work space and even some of your work hours with your spouse and children. No matter how strict you try to keep the boundaries between work and home, some family impositions are inevitable. In time, you'll find that the solution may be a compromise. Certainly your time is important, but when it comes to deciding who stays home with the sick child, the home worker is usually going to bite the bullet.

But the sword cuts both ways. The home-office owner gets

to make up the lost hours by going into the business space after dinner and staying there till bedtime (or beyond), skipping homework duty. These adjustments will affect your entire family. Some of it will be great: no rush hour, no commute, work at your own intensity level, captain of your own destiny. Some of it will be less than great: running household errands, attending school meetings, dealing with plumber visits, picking up relatives from the airport. These demands are not gender-specific in most households. But as the family makes the transition, most entrepreneurs find the change is positive overall. Most home-business owners readily accept the inconveniences because there are so many positives to working at home, especially the enormous overhead savings.

Chapter 14

Family and Friends—
Whose Space or Schedule
Is This, Anyway?

One of the biggest changes when you work at home is that family members and friends don't have to go through a receptionist to talk to you. Neither is your boss going to get angry if you have to drop everything to pick up your sick daughter at school. This accessibility may be part of the reason you want a business at home, but it can also be a nightmare when you have a deadline. You have to create boundaries to make sure you have time to do your work, but you also have to accept the fact that part of the value of running a home business is the flexibility. Sometimes that flexibility will be called to order.

When you first launch your home enterprise, you will probably be very protective of your time. After a while, though, you will find that your home business will be much more successful if you surrender some of your business time to family urgencies. This can help build harmony in the family, and it's easier to run a home business surrounded by family harmony than it is to run a home enterprise if you are continually emphasizing your boundaries. Total flexibility doesn't work if you have appointments, but when it can work, accessibility is usually part of what the home-business owner gives back to the family for using the house to run a business.

And what does the business owner get back for holding down some of the daily domestic responsibility? The ability to take family time to walk back into the den for a few hours in the evening. Some people think a home business works best when you bring strict discipline to the enterprise, but it usually works best when your business activities are integrated with household requirements. When you approach your business duties with a rigid schedule, it becomes an imposition on the home life rather than a natural part of the household. Most successful home entrepreneurs work off and on during all their waking hours, moving back and forth between home and work duties.

Sometimes the best way to view your home company is to think back on the traditional home enterprises of the 1800s, when most Americans made their living at home with their families. Sometimes the kids were in the house with mom, sometimes they were out with dad, and other times they were in school. When it was time to go to town for supplies, some of the supplies related to work and some related to home, but there wasn't a great deal of division between work and home life. Work was home life and home life was work. The idea of compartmentalizing or setting boundaries between work and home was ludicrous.

This may not be entirely possible today, but it is worth striving for. To run a business, you will need periods of time when you are available for meetings and when you can concentrate without interruption, but there are also tasks that need almost no concentration at all. I remember sitting in front of the television with my wife and son, putting together a small direct mailing. I can search and retrieve information from the Internet on my laptop in the living room while my young daughters play, each one taking turns climbing onto my lap.

After years of running my own companies, I treasure these interactions, and I like the idea that my kids see me working. None of my children will ever have to ask me, "What do you do at work, Daddy?" They see me. They hear my telephone conversations. They're in the living room when a client drops off a package of work. I have plenty of time to spend on private meetings with clients, but there is also time when it just doesn't matter if the person I'm talking to can hear a child in the background. Ultimately, I know that my business will succeed or fail based on the quality of my work and my ability to deliver it on time. The rest is just the way I choose to live.

Business Hours—Opening Your Shop When the World's Open

The schedule you develop for your business will depend greatly on the type of business you run and the needs of your customers. If you run a house-cleaning business that also does commercial cleaning in the evening, your hours can run all day and half the evening. Then again, you may hire crews to do the work while you sell contracts, so you spend your daytime hours calling on potential customers. If you are a management consultant, you may spend your time out of town at your client's facility. Your time back home may be spent writing reports and marketing to companies to get future work, in which case your time at the home office will be very flexible.

Your hours should be set by the needs of your business and by the needs of your customers. Some home-business owners like the structure of specific hours, and they often choose a business, such as house cleaning, that requires specific work hours. Those who prefer a more flexible schedule usually choose a business based on deadlines rather than a schedule and blend their work with home responsibilities. As you choose your business, these work considerations become important. Do you thrive on flexibility, or do you thrive on a schedule? The answer to this will help you decide which type of business will bring out the best in you.

Some businesses are by nature deadline-oriented: freelance writing, public relations, consulting, and tax accounting. These professions require very intensive work leading up to the due date, followed by a more leisurely pace after delivery. For some professionals, the buildup to the deadline generates an intensity that is very productive and creative. For others, the pressure of a deadline brings stress and inefficiency. Personally, I like deadlines. I'm willing to work long hours going into the deadline, and I equally enjoy a less demanding schedule after a deadline has passed. I find a rigid schedule uncomfortable and confining.

Part of home-business success comes from matching the enterprise you choose with your work style. If you choose a company that complements your natural style, you stand a much greater chance for success, since the business requirements will come much easier to you. Your business hours will always be set to accommodate your customers. So the balance between scheduled hours and a more flexible working arrangement comes from the type of customers or clients you serve. If you open a home-cleaning business, your customers will expect to be able to reach you during standard business hours. If you are not there and don't return messages quickly, they will lose confidence in your business. Being the boss of a cleaning business may offer little flexibility with your schedule.

If you are a management consultant, your clients will expect you to return calls in a reasonable manner, but that may be within one or two days, not within the next hour. However, your clients will also expect you to show up when you are scheduled to be at their facility, and they will also want you to deliver your reports on time. As long as you meet these expectations, it doesn't matter how you spend your day. You can send out proposals and write reports in the evenings while taking care of kids during the day. You may only work a regular workday when you are on-site at a client's office.

Usually difficulties in home-business schedules arise when the business owner makes an inappropriate match between the company's needs and his own inclinations. Take the tax accountant who puts in an eight-to-five day and has a hard time adjusting to the additional hours demanded at tax deadline time, or the house-cleaning business owner who likes to take an occasional Thursday off but doesn't mind working on the weekend. If you find yourself in this predicament, it may seem like your business owns you, but you may be able to make the adjustment with hired assistance. If not, you might find business ownership to be an unpleasant experience, all because your choice of enterprise didn't match your natural work style.

More Business Hours—Tinkering at the Computer After Dinner

Here is the most common complaint that goes with home-business ownership: "I don't mind it that you're running your business from our home. In fact, I kind of like it that you're here all day. But what really bothers me is when you go in that room to check your e-mail and you don't come back out for the rest of the evening.'' This is not a gender-specific objection. Sometime during the first few months, you will hear this plea. If it isn't resolved, it can become a regular argument that can be a family-splitting source of resentment. Remember, you need your family's support, even if it seems as if your family has no idea what pressures you're facing.

There are countless ways for families to resolve this problem, and it is the rare family that doesn't have to face this issue when there's an enterprise cooking in the household. As you launch a business, it almost always needs more attention than you can give it in a normal business week, whatever schedule you develop. And the company's need for more effort almost always comes before you have the cash flow to support outside assistance. This can cause constant pressure, and it is usually only relieved when the business owner sneaks back into the home office during family time.

This situation is so common and so predictable, I think it's a physical law. A seasoned business owner who has pushed past this awkward period in a company's life usually understands some of the required solutions. One answer is to simply realize that you can only give so many hours to the business, and that the business will have to develop at a pace that matches your ability to contribute effort. So you won't meet this year's goals, but you will keep your family intact. This can be a hard conclusion to reach, especially when you're under pressure. But it often works. Anyway, sometimes the extra hours you put in do more to relieve your fear of failing than they do to further the business.

One great solution is to bring your family in on the tasks. If your spouse likes the work, this solution can be magic. It helps the business and it often brings the family together. All of a sudden, instead of you-against-the-world, it becomes us-against-the-world. Putting the burden on more than one set of shoulders can greatly relieve the pressure while also giving your spouse a peek into the difficulties you're facing. This can give your spouse a much deeper understanding and appreciation of your endeavor. It also gives your spouse the chance to share in the adventure. When you succeed, you can turn to each other and say, "We did it together." This type of energy is a large reason immigrant families are often successful when they launch family enterprises.

Other solutions include compromises. One is to view long hours as a temporary situation. You and your family can decide that you need to work eighty hours per week for the next few months. When that time is over, you will either hire assistance or reconsider whether the business is worth the trouble and strife. If you choose this solution, be aware that it only works if you are truly prepared to make a major change if the period of time given to long hours doesn't get your business over the hump. The other compromise solution is to plan for this period of difficulty and commit funds or borrow cash to hire help before the business can really afford it. If you set aside the second-round financing discussed earlier, this is the time to use it.

Most business launches run into this problem and will require some solution. If you ignore the situation, you may cause larger problems in your family, your business, or both. This issue usually won't go away by itself. Most successful business owners face this problem and overcome it one way or another. This happens with almost all business start-ups, but it is particularly troublesome with the home business because the work space is just a few steps away from family space. Heed the warnings, make the adjustments, and explore the solutions. Ignoring this problem can bring an end to your business, your family, or both.

The Telephone—"Mommy, I think It's for You"

Who answers the phone in your home business? Yes, I have called some home enterprises only to have a child or other family member answer the phone. Some business owners see this as a disaster, while others see this as no problem at all. Whether this is appropriate or not depends on the nature of your business and the training your child has with the telephone. To offer a blanket "No, this is never appropriate" is simply not practical. In some companies, there is nothing wrong with your child answering the phone. It depends on the nature of your business, the nature of your clients, and your child's ability to take a coherent message.

In this day of voice mail, e-mail, and cellular phones, it isn't that important to have a live person answer the phone. The solution for most companies is to have a separate line for business and to instruct your children not to answer your business line. This works especially well if you know you can return your messages in a timely manner. If you know your clients will not be perturbed by a child answering the phone, and your child has demonstrated a professional manner and an ability to take reliable messages, it can be handy to have your child answer the phone if you're busy on another line or somewhere around the corner.

The problem with family members taking messages is when you are receiving a call from a new client and your child yells out, "It's for you, Mom." This will not make a very positive first impression. If there is a chance that the person calling is contacting your business for the first time, voice mail will make a more professional first impression than a family member, especially a child. Since voice mail has become prevalent, this problem is not as great as it used to be. If there is any question at all about the professional level of the person who grabs your business line, let voice mail take the call.

Time Management—Your New Boss Is Watching All the Time

By now, you are probably aware that the biggest time-management problem for the new home-business owner isn't self-motivation. Most people who have a home business are plenty motivated. The problem comes with focus and with punching out. Once you have a schedule worked out that accommodates your clients and customers, and after you have worked out your hours with your family, you still may have some fine-tuning to do in the time-management area. The final time-management challenge is developing the discipline to make sure you do the right tasks during the limited time you have to work on your business.

There are a number of books that deal exclusively with this subject. There are even time-management systems, such as Day-timer, that are devised to help you spend the right amount of time on the tasks that are most important. This discipline applies to employees as well as business owners, but it is especially crucial for business owners because there is more freedom to stray from the important tasks that need to be done when there is no boss standing around waiting for your output. This problem ultimately comes down to setting priorities and sticking to the priorities once you establish them.

One of the first things I discovered during the early months of starting my first business was that I was never able to get everything done on my to-do list. I didn't have this experience when I was an employee. If I couldn't get everything done on my list, I simply met with my supervisor and explained what I could get done and asked her to hone my list down to the tasks that were important. I came away from these meetings with a set of tasks that I knew I could deliver. Nobody was disappointed, and I was able to meet all my deadlines.

As a business owner, my list of tasks just grew longer and longer. Within a few months, it became obvious I would never get all the way through the list. At the end of each week, there were a considerable number of tasks undone. What I didn't realize at the time is that this situation was not temporary. As long as I owned this business or any other, the list of tasks would always be longer than my ability to check off the items. I came to realize that creating a priority list was more complicated than simply listing which tasks needed to be done first and which ones could be done later. Now, I had to decide which tasks fall into the category of never getting done.

Setting priorities became a matter of creating categories of tasks that were absolutely crucial for today and which ones could be put off to another day. Then I decided which tasks absolutely had to be done that week and which ones could be put off to another week. If you go on and on with this process, you will collect a number of tasks that will never be on the critical list. Then you have to decide what the consequences will be if you never get to these items.

You may find you have to designate some of these tasks as

crucial because they may never become urgent but are so important that your business will falter if they are eliminated from the list altogether. A good example of this is marketing. You can get so wrapped up in completing work for existing clients that you don't do the work necessary to line up future work. This oversight can result in some awkward gaps in business income. So even though some tasks don't seem critical at the moment, they may become critical if they are ignored, and they may become critical when it's too late.

Most time-management systems ask you to rank your tasks in the following four categories:

1. Urgent and critical
2. Urgent but not critical
3. Not urgent but critical
4. Not urgent and not critical

Once you have all of your tasks separated into these four categories, you do the tasks in group 1, you do some of the tasks in group 2, and you do some tasks in group 3 but you make sure that you do not do so many of the tasks in group 2 that you don't also do some of the tasks in group 3. You never do any of the tasks in group 4 unless there is a reason to move one of these tasks to another group.

This simple system is very effective. It forces you to quit doing unimportant tasks because they are on your list or because you particularly enjoy them. Most business owners have pet jobs they enjoy. Once you set your priorities, you will begin to see whether some of your pet tasks are preventing you from doing more important work. You may keep some of your pet tasks anyway because they make your day more pleasant, but at least you will be aware of their standing in the priority scale.

As a business owner, I always reserved the chore of getting the mail from the P.O. box myself because I enjoyed it so much, but I was aware this was a pet indulgence that could easily be delegated. I kept it because it was an enjoyable break that didn't take too much away from my ability to complete more important jobs, but I knew it was on the list of tasks I could strike from my list. Sometimes these departures from your scheme of priorities are necessary to balance your day, but having them in perspective is crucial even if you choose to keep them on your list.

Working Out Your Home-Business Schedule—Points to Consider

1. When you first launch, it's best to keep regular hours that are predictable for your family, your vendors, and your customers. Once you establish your credibility, you can become more flexible.

2. The biggest danger for most beginning home companies is that the entrepreneur can't pull away from the business. You may have to schedule time when you don't allow yourself to work.

3. If you are accustomed to having a strong supervisor set your priorities, goals, and schedule, you will probably benefit from a formal time-management system. These are readily available in bookstores and office-supply stores.

Chapter 15

Humble Space, Magnificent Communications

A business in the home used to mean unsophisticated equipment, but computers and telecommunications have become so inexpensive that you can run state-of-the-art communications out of your den. Your ability to compete as a home business often comes from your ability to match the technical equipment of large corporations. Most home-based graphic artists can run the same software used by the largest magazines. The low prices of sophisticated software make it possible for the home company to offer the same products and services of large corporations at lower rates. As recently as the early 1990s, it wasn't possible for a home business to compete directly with a large enterprise.

Breakthroughs in communications will help your business even if you don't compete with large organizations. The cellular phone lets a carpet-cleaning business owner respond to a request for a quote instantly even if she is on a job. The owner can also move crews around town instantly by talking with crew managers while they're on the job. There are costs involved with cellular phones, but the expenses are small compared to the savings that come from quick responses to your customers and clients. Most home companies benefit greatly from the falling costs of improved technology.

In fact, improved technology makes many of the new home-business categories possible. More and more successful Web sites are launched by home entrepreneurs on a personal computer that can be purchased on a $100-per-month lease. You can purchase state-of-the-art equipment just by using the savings you get by setting up business in your home instead of renting an outside office. The same goes for many consulting opportunities that used to require very powerful computers and software that previously were only affordable to large organizations. Marketing-research consultants can now offer their clients the latest modeling and database services from a home computer.

Clerical support is another area where home-business owners are making a big savings. The proliferation and acceptance of voice mail frees the home entrepreneur from having to hire a receptionist or telephone answering service. Customers and clients don't expect to get a live voice, even from large corporations. Because of inexpensive cellular phones, you may be more likely to get a home-business person on the phone than you are to reach a company worker. Just a few years ago, the opposite was true. This is just one more way the home-business owner can beat the large organization.

You can also do without a secretary these days. When home companies first began to appear, many of them hired word-processing companies to take the place of a secretary, but most owners no longer need this service. With a laptop computer, you can send or fax letters whenever you want, even if you're on the road. E-mail has replaced a large portion of business correspondence and is easy to produce from a laptop on the road. You can draft your proposals on your laptop as you fly to your client, then forward the proposal to your partner over e-mail for revision when you get to your hotel. After dinner, you get your revised proposal, take it to Kinko's or to the hotel business center, and make twenty copies for the mid-morning presentation in the client's office. Who needs a secretary?

The Telephone—Your Business Lifeline

The telephone is still the most predominant tool for business communication. E-mail is replacing some phone calls, especially since an e-mail often gets answered more quickly than a voice message, but e-mail is replacing more correspondence than phone calls. The falling rates for cellular phones are making the phone an even better business tool. The cell phone allows you to make calls and return calls while out on errands or on the way to an appointment, thus saving your precious office time for other work. The cell phone's ability to make travel time productive has made home-business people more efficient, especially real estate agents and salespeople who spend hours each day in their cars.

The predominance of voice mail, though, has changed the nature of business telephone communication. It wasn't long ago that when you called, you reached the person's receptionist or assistant. Besides leaving a message, you could find out the time of the person's return and other information, such as whether the person you are calling is really the person you need to speak with about your concern. The assistant often saved you time as you worked to connect with the right person in an organization. With voice mail, you usually go directly to the person's extension without talking to a receptionist or assistant. This can slow down your ability to make sure you're talking to the right person.

You can get around this by leaving the right voice message. You can give the person the option of passing along your message to the appropriate person; by giving out your e-mail address in addition to your phone number, it hastens a response. This can help greatly in getting where you need to go over the phone. When you leave a voice message, don't just ask to be called back. Your phone message will be most effective if you explain exactly why you're calling, state the question or two you want to have answered, and give your phone number and e-mail address. Often you will get a response by e-mail with the answers to your questions. You can ask follow-up questions over e-mail, and you very likely will be able to complete the communication.

The alternative to leaving detailed voice messages is that your call may not be returned. We all receive so many unsolicited calls each day that we no longer believe we have an obligation to return a call when the caller doesn't state his intention. Not long ago, it was considered impolite to neglect returning calls. But telephone salespeople have destroyed this courtesy. Now people don't think twice about ignoring messages from callers who are not completely forthcoming about their intentions. Many people now refuse to answer their calls, letting voice messaging screen out calls from salespeople. All it takes is about five interruptions in a day before a person begins to ignore the phone.

If you develop a style of being very explicit in your phone messages, you can accomplish a great deal without ever talking with a human being. You can ask your questions and get them answered, or you can find out who the appropriate person is for this communication. I have initiated calls using voice messaging, located the right person to talk with, explained my inquiry, received an appropriate response by e-mail, followed up the e-mail with more detailed questions, and completed all the necessary communication without once talking to a live person in the organization. It is a matter of learning how to use the phone effectively in our new media-busy world.

In setting up your phone to receive messages, you should also work to encourage your caller to be clear about what is needed. In your recorded message, ask your caller to give the reason for the call and also ask for a return phone number. You can try leaving your fax number and e-mail address in the message to see if it encourages your callers to try alternate ways to communicate with you. Be careful, though, about how long your message gets to be; if it's too long, it becomes annoying.

Computers—A Whole Business in a Box

The personal computer may be the single biggest reason people can now work from their homes. Computers have had a very democratic influence on the business world. The greatest business machine of all time can be in the hands of a home-business owner just as easily as in the hands of those with tremendous capital. Peter Drucker was correct two decades ago when he predicted that information would become the capital of the future, and that those with the best information would be the leaders, as opposed to those with the most capital. We have reached that place now, and Microsoft is the perfect example of a company that became dominant through the effective use of information, not by great capital.

Bill Gates didn't build the biggest and most expensive factory. He didn't corner the market on steel, nor did he build the railways to haul material from one end of the country to the other. All he did was design and promote the most efficient way to store, access, and deliver information. He also did it in a way that made it affordable to the greatest number of people. If he had built a system that worked only on the large computers of the past, his name would not be known outside a small circle of information professionals in large organizations. Instead, he built a system that worked on a computer that was small enough and inexpensive enough to be available to virtually anyone who wanted one.

This shift from a capital-based economy to an information-based economy is a big part of what lets you compete with large corporations from your den. The tools of accounting, research, marketing, publishing, communications, arts, and even movie editing are no longer just in the hands of those with access to large amounts of money. The personal computer, with its relatively inexpensive software, allows millions of Americans to work from home and even launch their own independent companies at a very low cost. Give this potential to a country of people who are, by their nature, independent and inclined to believe they can forge their own destiny, and you get the entrepreneurial explosion that has hit America.

You can set up your state-of-the-art, high-tech office for just $2,000 or $3,000. You can lease all of this equipment for about $200 per month, far less than the cost of a tiny rented office. Upgrades to this equipment, to keep you at your highest efficiency and most competitive, are equally affordable. As you choose your computer equipment, keep efficiency in mind. Don't take any savings that will cost you in time or energy; the cost of faster and more efficient computers will pay for itself very quickly by saving you time and keeping you competitive.

The Internet—Your Worldwide Connection

The Internet has also become an extraordinary business tool. Like the personal computer, the Internet allows a tiny home business to compete with large corporations. You can now run a Web site that presents a business catalog of products that are owned and stored by other manufacturers. As you receive your orders, they are immediately forwarded to the manufacturer, which sends the product to your customer. You can set up a system that will let you deliver hundreds of products without ever stocking one piece of merchandise. By developing and marketing an online catalog of products that are drop-shipped by manufacturers, you can create a Web catalog that generates millions of dollars in business, all from a home office in New Hampshire.

Until very recently, the Internet was slow to produce e-commerce. This changed during the Christmas season of 1998 when consumers finally got up the nerve to type their credit-card numbers into Web sites for online purchasing. Online consumer spending rose to $4.8 billion in consumer retail sales. Business-to-business sales hit $8 million that same year. Forrester Research projects that consumer retail spending will hit $17.2 billion by 2002. But brace yourself for the real news, Forrester Research projects $327 billion in business-to-business e-commerce by 2002. International Data Corp. is even more optimistic, forecasting business-to-business sales exceeding $500 billion by 2002.

If reality is anywhere close to these staggering projections, those who are positioned to take advantage of any of this growth will prosper. Some of this business will be companies buying from their regular suppliers online, but not all these changes will be neutral. Some of this commerce will go in the direction of clever entrepreneurs who can offer products and sales strategies that are superior to their big-business competition. All it will take to slice off a chunk of this monster business will be the knowledge of what the purchasing agents need and knowledge of how to get it to them more efficiently and less expensively than anyone else.

It isn't a wild prediction to say that the Internet sales growth will turn thousands of bright e-commerce entrepreneurs into millionaires between now and 2002. And certainly this growth will continue beyond 2002. There are some business-opportunity packages that are designed to help new business owners participate in some of this growing market, but few of these opportunities have proved fruitful for their buyers. Most of the home-business Internet success stories come from those who are launching their own companies. This may change in time, but the change is not yet on the horizon.

Copiers, Faxes, and E-Mail—Your Robot Clerical Staff

Inexpensive and efficient business tools end your need to hire clerical support to help your business run and grow. You may have to learn to type, but copiers, faxes, and e-mail make a great deal of paper and mail unnecessary. The business-equipment world is also making these items better and less expensive than ever. You can buy a fax that doubles as a copier, and most computers come with fax capabilities, so you don't need separate pieces of equipment to outfit your home with a computer, fax, copier, and phone system. You also don't need the highest-tech copier to get by. Most home-business owners use a small copier, then pop over to Kinko's when they need a dozen reports collated and bound.

Since this office equipment is inexpensive, most people you do business with will expect that you have all of these capabilities. Customers and clients will ask for your fax number and e-mail address. These items are almost as basic as a phone number. If you do not have a fax number and e-mail address, some clients and customers may wonder if you are running a professional operation. Make sure you are well equipped with these time-saving and money-saving devices when you launch your business. Most of these items will last for a few years, so the expense doesn't come often and it isn't very high.

Furnishings—Your Entrepreneurial Platform

What do you need to be both efficient and frugal? What furnishings do you need to run a thriving business? I started with used government metal desks, the ones that weigh more than a tank; I moved up to wood desks as my business grew. Now, with the home-business wildfire, home-furnishing companies and office-furniture companies have developed furniture especially designed for the home office. One of the major new pieces is a computer desk that closes into a piece of furniture resembling a large cabinet, so you can put your home-business desk in the dining room, then close it at the end of the business day and use the same room as family space.

These new contraptions may or may not fit your needs, but it shows that there are enough home-office workers to warrant the attention of the major furniture manufacturers. The problem with this furniture is that it isn't really an improvement on traditional computer desks. When it tries to serve two purposes, it serves neither purpose very efficiently. For one thing, I strongly recommend that you carve out some home space that is for your office alone. You can't realistically pack up all your work at the end of each day. You will also want more furnishings than a computer desk nearby. You will need filing space; stands for your printer, fax, and copier; and shelf space for books and stack of folders that are part of your current projects.

Getting the Right Communications Equipment—Points to Consider

1. If you spend considerable time in your car, get a cell phone. It will pay for itself. Get reliable voice messaging that can be easily accessed for a distance. Make all your telephone decisions based on the economic impact on your business.

2. Good computers don't cost much, especially if you finance them. A new computer can put your production right up at the level of a large company for most services. A computer can replace a fax machine, copier, and secretary.

3. Get on the Internet. Business communications online can be much quicker and more effective than phones or mail. You may even find your entire market moves online over the next few years.

Part IV

Funding and Cash Management

This section covers the details of operating the money side of your business. Once you have furnished your space, set up your furnishings and communications equipment, and bought your business license, it's time to prime the revenue pumps. It takes money to make money, so here are the chapters on getting the seed capital you need to launch your home enterprise. This section also covers other financial concerns, such as cash management and use of outsourcing as an effective way to avoid hiring employees. Running a business is all about raising funds; creating revenue; managing expenses; correcting errors; managing resources, employees, and vendors; and often raising more funds. This section attempts to give you a picture of all the details involved in mastering your money.

As a home entrepreneur, you have one of the greatest business advantages: a low overhead. This is the reason so many home enterprises succeed. With a low overhead, you can launch with less capital and stay alive with a lower level of income. Most outside companies need thousands of dollars more per month than you will need to launch. You already have your phone, electricity, heat, rent, and furnishings to get going. Even if you invest in office furniture and communications equipment, it is a one-time expense and is low compared with an outside office. The biggest overhead item for most companies is payroll. Since you're working at home, you are probably anticipating a business that either will need no support staff or will need employees only after the business can reasonably support them. This gives you a huge head start toward success.

Even though you will not need as much seed capital as an outside business, you will still need some to fund equipment and marketing and to cover the salary or wages you are giving up to go into business for yourself. You may have to live without a paycheck for six to eighteen months. A large part of the funding needed to start a home business goes to cover the owner's missing income. This is yet another advantage you have over an outside business. For a business that launches with an office or warehouse, the missing salary may be the smallest part of the pie the owner has to provide. You don't have to be part of the large number of entrepreneurs who forgo a paycheck while they cover the wages of employees.

Once you get your business rolling and it begins to pay your salary, you have to learn the rules of cash management. It is hard to learn good cash management when you are struggling to survive, but it becomes necessary once you are able to make ends meet. For one thing, you need to make sure your new-found flow of cash doesn't fuel new spending. During those first few months, you will become a master of pinching pennies. This is a trait you want to keep as your business grows, for every penny you save goes right into your pocket. There are ways of taking your frugality and making it your standard business practice so the pressure to spend is curbed by strong cash-management practices.

Finally, as your company grows, you will need help both to keep your business operating smoothly and to relieve you of the long work hours you will undoubtedly develop. Outsource as much as you can so you are not tempted to move your business outside your home. The same business that may provide a strong income as a home enterprise can become a money loser once you venture out and incur a pile of new overhead. The way to stay in your home while still growing and getting help is to use vendors to do some of your tasks, such as bookkeeping, production, even marketing and selling.

Once you master all of these elements, from finding start-up funds and creating sales to managing your cash and utilizing vendors, you can keep a business profitable for many years. You will have to keep current with developments in your field or industry, and you will have to continually replace customers or clients who leave, but these skills can also be mastered. Once you have all of these areas under control, there is no reason you will ever have to work for someone else again. That is the goal most entrepreneurs have when they set out on the road to run their own business.

Chapter 16

Financing—Funding Your First Step

There are countless ways to finance your business. Personal savings is the easiest, but most beginning entrepreneurs don't have adequate personal savings to fund a business start-up, even a home one. If you don't have cash on hand, there are dozens of places to get help for borrowing or to find investors. You can turn to family and friends, get a bank loan, take out a home-equity line of credit, refinance your home, or take some cash advances on your credit cards. Using credit cards to launch a business is the least wise, since credit-card money is the most expensive money you can borrow. Yet credit-card advances now hold the top position in the list of most commonly used sources for start-up funding. Common as it may be, launching a business with credit-card advances is dangerously close to gambling.

It is best to find less expensive and more substantial sources for your start-funds. This chapter directs you to some of these sources and also explains the advantages and disadvantages of each potential source for funding your entrepreneurial dream. There is no perfect source of capital; each one is a compromise in one way or another. Generally, the money that is easy to obtain (such as credit-card advances) is very expensive, and the money that is harder to obtain (such as a bank line of credit) is more difficult to get. You can seek investment rather than borrowing, and you won't have to pay back the funding, but then someone else will own part of your dream. In order to find the right funding mix, you have to weigh all of these considerations and determine which source is the best fit for your endeavor.

Using Personal Savings

This seems like a no-brainer. If you have money set aside, you use it instead of borrowing or rounding up investors. But there are some reasons to keep your personal savings in place and borrow to launch your business. For some, the personal savings constitute money set aside for emergencies or for retirement. Rather than dipping into this family cushion, many home-business owners use the stash as collateral and borrow against it at a low interest rate. Why not just use the savings? Because we are much more likely to make a monthly loan payment than we are to pay back our savings, so the loan ensures that the personal savings will remain intact.

Borrowing From Family and Friends

In most cases, it is easier to obtain funding from family and friends, but it is easier to ask a bank. When you go to a bank, you're asking for a loan from people who give out loans professionally. The procedure is very businesslike and impersonal. We may complain about the impersonality, but it serves both the lender and the borrower to keep the discussion friendly and businesslike. When you go to family or friends to borrow, it is often accompanied by the feeling that you are imposing.

Even if they intend to pay back the loan at a fair interest rate and back it up with some security, people often feel like they're standing with their hand out when they approach family or friends. For this reason alone, many new entrepreneurs prefer going to the bank. Another danger in using family and friends as your source for start-up capital is that if things go wrong, you don't have to see your banker year after year. When you borrow from relatives and friends, you risk putting strain on your relationship; even if they forgive your inability to pay back the loan, you may not get over the discomfort.

Using Your Home Value for the Home Launch

For most Americans, the home is their greatest financial asset, and so it is commonly used to finance a business launch. There are a number of ways to use your home. For one, you can use your house as collateral for a bank loan. This may allow you to qualify for a lower interest rate than you would otherwise receive. You can also take a home-equity loan or a line of credit on the equity in your home. Some home-equity programs are so aggressive that you can even borrow beyond the actual equity you have. These aggressive loans tend to have a higher interest rate than the more conservative loans. The difference comes on the limit the company is willing to loan against your equity. Banks will usually only loan up to 80 percent of your home value, but their interest rates are low.

The final way to use your home to borrow seed money is to refinance your home and take the additional money for funding. This process is greatly simplified if you complete your refinance before you quit your day job to launch. If you quit your job first, you may not qualify for the low-interest mortgage that makes refinancing advantageous. Another plus in refinancing is that you can write off the interest on the loan since it's a home mortgage, thus putting you in the position of gaining a considerable tax savings. If you expect to use a home-equity loan to launch your business, check to see if a refinance might give you a better rate for your loan.

Utilizing Credit-Card Advances

Even though this is the leading source for start-up funding, it is the most expensive. In spite of the fact that I discredit it as a reasonable way to raise capital, I admit to having used this source of funds to help out my own companies during times when cash stretched thin. This type of borrowing comes with a couple of problems. One of the difficulties is that it is easy to forget to pay yourself back. When the bill comes, it is too easy to simply make the minimum payment, so your outstanding balance from your first draw may still be there when you decide to go for another draw. Over a period of years, the balance can just grow and grow.

The other problem with credit-card loans is that they come with the highest interest rates of any conventional borrowing. Even the cards that advertise a low interest rate usually only offer the lower rate for the first six months. After that time, the interest pops right up to the high mark. Although I have never seen a study on the success rate of companies that are financed by credit cards, I believe it is safe to say that these companies have a much higher failure rate than companies launched with more favorable sources of capital. For one, the credit-card advance is usually the final alternative for an entrepreneur. For those who qualify for better loans, the credit-card advance is only an option if things get rough. For those who start up with credit cards, there may be no borrowing power left if the business hits a rough patch.

If credit-card advances are your only source for launch money, I would advise putting off your business start-up. There are certainly stories of very successful companies that were started with credit cards, but we don't hear the stories of the failures of credit-card launches, which undoubtedly outnumber the success stories by a large percentage. Save your credit-card balances for business emergencies, and get yourself in a stronger financial position before starting your business.

Having Family and Friends as Investors

Relatives and people you know need less assurances and are more open to your ideas than professional investors. Your relatives and friends are often inclined to support you and when they see your plan, they're hoping it will give them reason to invest. Professional investors take the opposite approach. As they read your plan, they're looking for the faults; they want to find reasons to pass your opportunity by. For this reason, relatives and friends will always be your best bet as investors.

Another of the strong advantages of having family and friends as investors is that they will usually be patient if your business takes longer than expected to get off the ground. Professional investors will be pounding on your door if you fall off schedule. The disadvantage of using family and friends as investors is the same as when using them as lenders. For many entrepreneurs, it feels as if they're asking for a handout even if they're offering an opportunity. Also, if things go poorly, you will still have to see these people in the future. With strangers, if things go wrong, you don't have to face them for the rest of your life.

Using Angels and Venture Capitalists

Angels are private investors interested in making more on their capital than they can make through mutual funds or publicly traded stocks. Often they have most of their wealth in secure investments and want to take a portion to speculate in a higher-risk venture that may produce a larger-than-ordinary return. Venture capitalists are professional investors who may be in charge of a large pool of capital gathered from a range of sources. The venture capitalists are entrusted to invest in high-risk, high-return businesses. Most angels and venture capitalists do not invest in home enterprises, but they will if it's the right business.

There was a time when it was out of the question for a home business to bring in investors. In the past, there was no way a home business could grow large enough to interest investors while staying small enough to remain in a home. That is changing. I watched a Mexican food manufacturer build his business to a value of $10 million while staying in home without one employee other than himself. Steve Dawson, founder of Hatch Chile and MP Foods, produced over thirty supermarket items, from salsa to taco shells, all from his phone in the living room.

Dawson launched his home business by raising over $350,000 in a limited public offering. He then grew the business to a multimillion-dollar enterprise with products on shelves in over twenty states. Ten years later, he sold his business for $10 million to one of the country's largest food producers. At one point, about three years into his launch, he set up a small outside office with two employees. He disliked the lifestyle and moved back home, sending his employees to their own homes to continue providing their services as vendors. For a few months each year, he lived on a boat on the Gulf off the coast of New Orleans, having his calls forwarded to his mobile phone on the deck.

This is a very unusual story for a food manufacturer with thirty items on the shelves in grocery stores in twenty states, but the idea of a significant enterprise being run from a home is becoming more and more common with Internet companies, since much of the work can be done by team members in their homes all over the country. Plus, venture capitalists have gone nuts for Internet companies. In 1999, more than 30 percent of all venture capital went to new online enterprises, many of which are run from the homes of the cyberspace entrepreneurs. Venture capitalists are more concerned with finding the next Amazon.com or eBay than they are about pretty offices.

If you decide to pitch to angels or venture capitalists, make sure you learn the ropes. Even though they may be relaxed about your business setting, they are very particular about how you present your business idea. They expect a formal plan with a full two- or three-year, month-by-month pro forma showing how much capital you will need, how it will be spent, and when you expect to turn a profit. There is an odd thing about the Internet, though: Profit isn't everything. Many venture capitalists get their return when the online company goes public after three or four years and the value of the company skyrockets. It can explode in value without showing a profit.

Investment dollars are not out of the question for a home business, but it isn't a likely situation unless your business has the potential to gain significant stock value. This also means that your company will need to be larger than just an extension of yourself. To attract investors, you will have to make the case that the business could be sold at some point to another person or company that could pick up where you left off and continue to grow the business. If this is the case with your enterprise, you might consider going through the pain to gain investors, but be prepared to learn how the system works before you send off proposals. At the end of this book, you'll find resources to learn the process of pitching to angels and venture capitalists.

Finding a Franchise or Business Opportunity to Fund Your Business Purchase

If you are considering the purchase of a franchise or business opportunity, you may find that your best financing source is the franchise company itself. Most franchise companies will help you find appropriate start-up dollars. Many will actually finance part of your purchase while also helping you find funding to keep you going during the first year of operation. When you buy a franchise, you will need funds for the franchise fee, funds to launch the business, and some funding in reserve. The franchise companies commonly help by financing the franchise fee itself.

The franchise companies' willingness to finance their fee is one of the ways these businesses compete with each other. Some of the companies will finance the fee at low interest, or no interest at all, while others will finance some of your product purchases as well. Many of these companies also help you locate financing from a third party. The advantage of seeking a franchise company to help you with financing is the low interest and favorable terms. Most of these companies still require qualifications similar to those for a conventional bank loan. One significant variation is that the franchise company will be comfortable with the fact that you are about to quit your day job.

Another major advantage of receiving financing from a franchise company is that you will have a cooperative partner if you run into trouble with your payments. If you run into difficulties, the franchise company will be motivated to help you solve the problem rather than just putting pressure on you. As opposed to a financial institution, the franchise will be on your side if the going gets rough. It will likely also have some understanding of the nature of your difficulties and some useful suggestions to solve the problem.

Although most franchise companies will help you obtain financing to cover their fee, this fee is just a portion of the capital you will need to get your business going. You will also have all the usual expenses of launching a business. Many franchise companies will guide you to sources for these needs, but few of them will offer loans that go beyond covering the franchise fee and some beginning inventory of their products. However, their guidance will be helpful, since they will point you to financial institutions that are familiar with the particulars of lending to franchise start-ups.

Putting Your Finance Package Together—Points to Consider

1. Personal savings are always the best source of start-up funds, especially if the funds are not designated as kids' college money or retirement savings.

2. Loans are usually preferable to investment dollars unless your enterprise fails. If you succeed, the loan will someday be paid back; the equity you give up for investment dollars will never come back to you.

3. Pick your investors carefully. Venture capitalists will want to come in and take over if they don't like your performance.

Chapter 17

Government Resources—Checking Big Brother's Purse

Much as we may complain about the federal government, it offers some help to entrepreneurs. There are federal government programs designed to help small-business people find funding, and there is a vast amount of information available to help new business owners learn about business regulations, tax-reporting obligations, and even management strategies. The Small Business Administration (SBA) puts a wealth of information online, providing a user-friendly Web site at www.sba.gov. You can also connect with government information for small business at www.business.com, which is the U.S. Business Advisor, an online clearinghouse for small business. You can get help over the phone by calling 800/827-5722, which puts your call right through to the SBA.

The federal government is much easier to deal with online than over the phone. Its phone operators seem to have limited awareness of individual programs that help small-business owners, but the government online sites are very user-friendly and are usually set up with good search mechanisms. Its Web sites are very good for discovering which programs may be able to help you launch, and you can usually find all the forms you need online as well, whether it is an application for a loan or the paperwork required to protect your trade name.

The SBA has a number of loan programs for new entrepreneurs. Many of these are set up to encourage specific types of owners or those who are launching in specific geographic areas. The SBA doesn't actually make loans; it sets guidelines with participating banks that make the loans. The SBA guarantees a certain percentage of the loan value, which encourages banks to make the loans. Even though the SBA guarantees the loan, you still have to qualify to borrow. The SBA essentially gives you a boost in the qualifying process. Even though you still have to qualify for the loans, the SBA programs help make loans available to you that you wouldn't ordinarily be able to get without the SBA.

Programs Provided by the SBA

SBA Loans

The SBA offers a variety of loans. Most of these loans come with guidelines that help the small-business owner who can qualify. There is the LowDoc loan program, which minimizes the amount of paperwork you have to prepare as long as you are borrowing less than $100,000. The LowDoc program serves both the bank and the borrower, since its application process is quicker for both your bank and you. Usually a LowDoc application only takes two or three days to process and approve.

The SBA also offers a number of loans under the CAPLines program. These loans are for short-term borrowing and can come in the form of lines of credit or revolving credit. These are mostly for existing companies that can demonstrate ongoing cash flow. Both the LowDoc and the CAPLine programs are easier to get if you are not a start-up, since much of the qualification process is determined by how well your business is already performing. This doesn't entirely leave out potential funding for start-ups, but it is best to consult the SBA directly or the SBA officer at your bank to find out if your launch needs can be met by these programs.

Minority and Women-Owned Set-Asides and Enterprise Zones

The SBA offers programs to encourage minority and women entrepreneurs and to nudge small-business owners into geographic areas that have particular employment needs. Check with your local SBA office (or the SBA online) to find out if you meet the qualifications for these programs. These programs are designed to help you qualify for loans that you would not otherwise be able to get. As with most SBA loans, these are easier to get if you are already up and going and can provide some financial history. Your history doesn't have to be unblemished, but you have to be able to show that your future looks strong enough to suggest you will be able to pay the loan back.

Small Business Investment Companies

These are privately owned venture-capital companies that receive low-interest loans from the government to invest in companies the government is tagging for encouragement. The government's role here is similar to that of the loan programs except that these venture-capital companies purchase equity for their funding instead of offering loans. Like most venture capitalists, these individual companies have their own preferred industries and business types. Government involvement just gives you an extra chance to get the attention of investment companies that otherwise would not be likely to fund your venture.

The 8(a) Programs

This is a program that helps the right small enterprises gain access to government programs and management assistance based on minority status or size of the business. Many government agencies are required to purchase a specific percentage of their goods and services from companies that meet the 8(a) qualifications, which include minorities, women-owned enterprises, and small businesses. Search the SBA Web site or call the SBA directly to get the details on whether your business qualifies for 8(a) set-asides.

Dealing With the Federal Government

Many entrepreneurs are independent spirits who abhor the bureaucratic aspects of the federal government, so they are not likely to explore the programs and information that are available through the SBA. Other entrepreneurs are continually seeking any advantage that might make the difference between success and failure and view the government as a large benign entity that can be utilized to gain services and contracts. Some clever entrepreneurs scour the government regulations to find the support they need to launch their business. They research all of the programs and discover what type of business will receive the most helpful government support, then configure their companies to meet the qualifications.

Whether you take the road of avoiding all contact with the federal government or create a business designed to extract loans and contracts from the government, keep in mind that the government, especially the SBA, has vast sources of information that can help you with your business. If you need statistics on the likelihood of your business idea in order to strengthen your argument with a venture capitalist, try the SBA. If you want to show a potential investor what government contracts are available for your enterprise, look through the SBA Web site to search out your information. The federal government provides a vast amount of free data to small business. Even if you detest working with the government, you can still access a wealth of business information through the SBA Web site.

Getting Help From the Federal Government—Points to Consider

1. The Small Business Administration is a worthy source of start-up loans, particularly for women-owned and minority businesses.

2. The federal government in general, and the Small Business Administration in particular, are good sources for business information. If you need data and statistics to beef up your business plan and proposal, go to the SBA.

Chapter 18

Financial Management—An Eye on the Bottom Line

There is a wide range of tools to help the fledging business with financial management. This is a crucial area of concern for the new entrepreneur; it can be difficult for a new business owner to comprehend the realities of financial management. The dream of business ownership is so strong that your vision can get clouded. When your business runs into trouble, the first reaction is to try harder. If your sales strategies are not successful, you increase them. There is a huge temptation to do more of the same thing if your efforts are not successful. Putting in long hours is another common response to a business that is not producing enough revenue to support its expenses and its owner.

When you first start a business, it can be very hard to tell if the difficulty is a matter of giving the business time to get off the ground or if the business idea in its present form will just not work. The sooner you can tell the difference between these two realities, the better chance you will have to make adjustments, renew your faith in your present course, or shut the business down. If you are running a franchise or business opportunity, you can measure your performance against the track record of similar companies to see if you are going in the right direction. If you have launched an independent business, it is more difficult to tell if your problem is with the business concept or whether the company will turn around, given time.

This is when your business plan and financial pro forma come in handy. These tools will help you see how far off track you are and how long you can suffer before your resources run dry. If you provided for a second round of financing, you now have to decide whether this will be a matter of throwing good money after bad or whether investing further is a wise choice that will give you that final push over the top and into the black. You will have to review your numbers closely to see if your company is improving or is stuck in a cycle of loss.

If there is any question in your mind at all, get some professional advice. The Small Business Administration has a service that can be very helpful to the budding entrepreneur: SCORE. SCORE stands for the Service Corps of Retired Executives. The SBA provides a clearinghouse to match up entrepreneurs with the appropriate volunteers. There is no charge for the consulting you receive from SCORE personnel. These are experienced businesspeople who may be able to help you define your business problems and find the appropriate solutions.

Some seasoned entrepreneurs develop a very useful philosophy for dealing with rough patches. Here is the thinking: If you find that you cannot create the right level of sales, change your product or service, or change your marketing strategies, until you are successful because all business is simply a matter of making adjustments until you reach the right level of profit. This way of viewing business problems is fine as long as you have the resources to keep trying until you get things right. If you run out of resources before your boat quits leaking, you're out of business.

Ultimately, you need to set up the kind of financial controls that will give you the best possible information to help you see your business clearly. These controls include a good bookkeeping system, a designated person to help you monitor your expenses (if you have a tendency to overspend), a good accountant who can help you analyze your financial statements, and one or more advisors who are familiar with your type of business and your industry. The trick is to create a team of interested people who can make sure your decisions are clear and reasonable. Without this team, you run the risk of making your decisions under pressure and in fear. When you buy a franchise or business opportunity, this team usually comes with your purchase as part of the support system. For an independent company, you have to create this team.

Designating a Company Cop

Your company cop is the person who oversees all expenses. For many entrepreneurs, the perfect company cop is the spouse of the owner, since the spouse is a principal even if this person isn't involved in managing the company. Also, because of the way marriages work when they're successful, it may be very natural for the spouse to counterbalance any excesses of the entrepreneur. In many situations, it is the risk-taking, adventurous, and optimistic one in the marriage who launches the company, so the more realistic and conservative spouse is often perfect for watching the expenses.

I remember visiting with an entrepreneur friend of mine shortly after he and his wife separated. During the previous four years before the separation, they had launched a successful advertising agency. The couple comanaged the enterprise. During the four years they worked together, they built the agency into one of their community's premier agencies. I asked how the business was doing with the separation. He said that his wife was running it on her own. "It won't be successful, though," he added.

I asked why, and he told me she was a big spender. He explained that he had managed to curb her inclination to spend, but since he was now out of the picture, nobody would have the authority to govern her spending. "I'm sure the business will continue to bring in revenue," he said, "but with the spending out of control, the agency won't last long." Sure enough, within six months the agency ceased operation.

The beauty of having your spouse as the company cop is that your spouse is the one person in the world who has an equal interest in the company's success. Your spouse is also the only person who has equal authority. In order for this relationship to work, you have to have a strong marriage. Otherwise, the oversight may provide conflict, defensiveness, and resentment. But if the two partners have trust in and experience with each other, and if the entrepreneur views the spouse's involvement as a commitment to success, the arrangement can be a powerful way to ensure that the enterprise succeeds.

It is difficult to designate a company cop who is not your spouse. For one thing, there is nobody else who brings the same authority to your enterprise. If you have investors, they will certainly have an interest, and they may even have authority over your company, but they usually will not be involved in daily operations. However, if your investors have a controlling interest and they lose faith in your ability to manage the business effectively, they may simply take over the financial management of the company rather than appointing someone to act as a company cop.

Setting Up Your Books

If you buy a franchise or business opportunity, your bookkeeping system may be part of your purchase, in which case you simply plug your numbers into the system and it creates your reports and balances. If you create your own business, you're on your own for setting up your books. This can be easy or this can be a nightmare, depending on how much direction you obtain and whether you get the right advice. There are a few guidelines to keep you from getting into too much trouble with your bookkeeping system.

First, you should get a widely used software system that will be familiar to you, your bookkeeper, and your accountant. Depending on how much bookkeeping is necessary, you may be able to do your books yourself at first, which is helpful for getting to know your business and how its numbers work. You should first select a good accountant who is familiar with both small business and start-ups. It is particularly helpful if your accountant is also well versed in your business type and industry. Once you have the right accountant, ask for a software recommendation. You want a program that is well used so it will be easy to transfer to an outside bookkeeper when the time comes to outsource your books.

You also need a program that is easy to use and creates the

appropriate forms and reports for creating financials and for sending in your tax deposits. Ideally, your software will prepare all of the monthly and quarterly reports so that all you will need your accountant for is the yearly tax return. There are now a wide number of inexpensive programs for small business; most of them will create all the reports you need. Many of these programs will also walk you through the steps it takes to set up the books. At this initial stage, though, it does help to be working with an accountant who knows your software and who will be available for phone consultation if you run into glitches.

Your accountant will also be able to make sure that your books are set up so they can accommodate changes in the future. So, if you use a software package that your accountant knows, it will be easier to make adjustments as you grow. Take it from someone who had to change some bookkeeping and reporting procedures after two years of using an inadequate bookkeeping system that was a mystery to my accountant: I had the choice of buying a new bookkeeping program and re-inputting two years' worth of entries or spending a considerable amount of money to have my accountant study my software package.

Bookkeeping—Inside or Out?

Should you have a bookkeeping company manage your books, or should you do it yourself? In most cases, I recommend that you do your own books for a few months, until you feel very proficient with your system and gain a strong financial knowledge of your business. If you start right out with a bookkeeping service that sets up your books in conjunction with your accountant, the number crunching for your enterprise may always be a mystery to you. It is best if you know all your numbers intimately. This knowledge is one more tool you have to take the temperature of your company. Your awareness of your company's financial health will help you make adjustments before a wrong turn does too much damage.

Once you have a thorough understanding of your company's numbers, you will probably be happy to shift the tedium of account entry to an outsider. Sometimes the best person for this task is the company cop/spouse. It is very common for the wife of a carpet-cleaning owner to do the company's books in the evening and on weekends. This is an equally common situation for the husband of the corporate consultant. This keeps the numbers close at hand and makes sure both people are well aware of the financial condition of the enterprise at all times. This can also give the company cop the appropriate oversight tool.

If it isn't desirable to get your spouse to do your books, there are many bookkeeping services that take care of the books for small companies. Some of them will even swing by your home on a weekly basis to pick up your numbers and drop off financial reports. With these companies, you get very professional service for only a fraction of the cost of hiring an employee. You also get experience and efficiency that are beyond what you could expect from an employee. These service companies are very accustomed to working with accountants when it comes time to provide the appropriate reports and files. Likewise, bookkeeping services usually work with programs that are widely compatible, and they are well versed in the efficiencies of these programs.

Accounting and Taxes—Inside or Out?

If you don't start out using a professional accountant, you will end up hiring one as your business grows. With the constant changes in federal, state, county, and city tax laws and regulations, you will need someone who keeps up with the changes for a living. You do not necessarily need a certified public accountant (CPA) as long as you are confident that your accountant keeps up on tax-law changes; non-CPAs are much less expensive per hour than CPAs. It helps to find an accountant who is familiar with companies of your size and who is also familiar with the particulars of your industry.

Accounting for Growth

All your decisions on bookkeeping and accounting should take the future into consideration. If you expect to move from your home to an outside office and eventually hire an in-house book-keeper, this anticipation will affect the type of bookkeeping system you purchase and the type of bookkeeping service you use in the meantime, since you know there will come a time when you will need to load your files into your own computer. You certainly don't want to go through the nightmare of reentering four years' worth of entries because your bookkeeping service used a software program that is no longer available.

Also, if you anticipate a change in the structure of your business as you grow, this can have a bearing on whom you hire as an accountant. If you plan to bring in investors a few years down the road, it helps if you choose an accountant who has performed accounting for the type of company you expect to become in the future. These considerations early on can save you considerable strife and expense down the road.

Managing Your Company's Finances—Points to Consider

1. Name a company cop. It helps if you have a concerned (and conservative) person, preferably a family member, looking over your financial shoulder. For some reason, entrepreneurs are usually expansive and optimistic and often partner with conservative and cautious personalities, the perfect company cops.

2. It helps to get a professional to set up your books, even if you plan to keep them yourself once you get going. It's less expensive to hire a professional for a small amount of work at the outset than it is to hire an expert later on to straighten out your mess.

3. If bookkeeping is not your forte, outsource it and concentrate on skills, such as marketing, that will make your company great. Good marketers, not good bookkeepers, grow companies.

Chapter 19

Outsourcing—Your Outside Staff

Outsourcing comes with some impressive promises: You can buy better services than you can hire; you only pay for what you need; and you can add production capability and wider services without increasing your overhead. For a home business, outsourcing is the way to grow your business without moving out and hiring employees. Need a bookkeeper? Add a bookkeeping service. You can expand your company by adding whole new departments and bringing in as many employees as you need, all the while working in your quiet home office. But outsourcing is not as easy as looking in the yellow pages for service companies. It can be difficult to solve problems when you can't walk down the hall and talk to your sales manager. Your outside sales team may be in place, but the fit may not be there.

It's trickier than it looks. Outsourcing takes special management techniques. You can't just set it up and sit back. Done correctly, it gives your business much more power per dollar than employees do. Done ineffectively, it can gut your company's ability to compete. The good news is that it's here to stay. That means we'll all get used to it, and effective ways to make it work will become part of our new business culture. Young professionals will grow up with full acceptance of phone conferencing, e-mail goals, and spare-bedroom power offices. To them, it will seem natural that you only see your sales manager at quarterly meetings and that face-to-face sales meetings only happen during trade shows. Who's got time for office visits anyway? We have new markets to reach. Close the deal on the phone and fax the contract; e-mail the details to the home office.

A 1995 survey of 1,200 companies by the Outsourcing Institute found that 50 percent were outsourcing some of their information technology. Information outsourcing alone added up to $38 billion in 1995. Another survey in 1995 by Pitney Bowes found that 77 percent of U.S. corporations outsourced some of their business support services. Corporate America has been outsourcing for years; it's easy for them. There was significant money saved by cutting high-paying management positions. A chunk of inefficiency from outsourcing doesn't dent the savings they gain by using outsourcing because their in-house staff was never efficient. But for home-based companies, this is less of a problem since the home company works closely with its vendors and can spot inefficiencies even before they come up.

Outsourcing promises huge returns for the home business, even with the risk of inefficiency. Basically, outsourcing is the process of using independent professionals and vendors to do the work that was previously done by employees. This can apply to manufacturing, distribution, sales, accounting, and business support services. Everything but leadership can be outsourced. The advantages are twofold. One, you can use more sophisticated professionals if you are only buying services on a per-job basis. Two, you can farm out the tasks that do not draw on your strengths. Then you can spend more time, energy, and focus on the areas where you really shine. Outsourcing can turn a one-person show into a high-functioning business. And your customers accept it now.

Outsourcing Requires Its Own Management Techniques

The real challenge in outsourcing is management. Whether you're using independent professionals or vendors, you have to get good at managing outside help. The management requirements are different from those of employee management. You're not watching hours, breaks, or productivity. You're measuring results against a vendor's hourly rate or retainer. The challenge is to keep the right vendors in place and to make sure you can solve problems quickly from a distance. Flexibility is part of the management mix in outsourcing. One of the common denominators among companies that depend heavily on outsourcing is a continual change in the vendor base. This is such a big part of outsourcing that you can't even call it a problem; it's just part of the trade-off for the cost savings. If you prepare yourself for the continual vendor turnover when you begin outsourcing, it will be less of a shock. It will also help you avoid the danger of long-term contracts that tie your hands if you begin to notice that your vendor is not performing well and there is another company you would like to try.

You have less control over your services, since your people are not in your office. You can reduce this risk by using credible professionals and vendors, but you can't eliminate it completely. Employees are more expensive, but you have more control over quality and consistency. You may give up some stability when you outsource, but you can cut costs by 50 percent or more by going outside for services. With some experience, you can gain back the stability by choosing the right sources and then monitoring performance. If you're careful, you can outsource a higher quality level than you can employ. A growing number of companies believe the savings and the potential quality improvements are more than worth the headaches.

To overcome the shortfalls of outsourcing, you need to continually improve your management skills, from finding the best vendors to signing appropriate contracts. You also need good communication to keep your sources moving forward. Effective management will reduce your time shopping for new sources and will help you overcome the drought of good ideas that you experience when your time is scattered. Some companies bring their outside people together regularly to foster brainstorming and cohesion. These brainstorming sessions can be very creative and productive, sometimes more so than in-house staff meetings since outside vendors don't bring along the baggage of office politics.

Build Your Outsourcing Skills

Strong outsourcing skills are a big part of the future for most American business, big or small, but particularly for home-business companies, since outsourcing may be your only way to grow without moving out of your house. Outsourcing gives you the ability to compete beyond your in-house resources. It allows you to create a cutting edge without investing deeply in employee overhead. Low overhead can mean the difference between success and failure for the small professional businesses. For all its headaches and heart crunches, outsourcing can improve your competitive edge.

There are some basic skills you have to develop to make your outsourcing effective. They include selecting the right vendor, creating the right contract, and monitoring the service.

■ *Selecting vendors.* Just as an outside business owner needs to develop the skills to hire the right people, you will need to gain the skills to select the right vendors. This comes through checking references, asking the right questions, making sure the company is qualified, and trusting your gut instincts.

■ *Contract negotiating.* You need to be careful not to lock yourself into a contract with a vendor until you have tested the relationship and are convinced the services will be delivered on time and up to quality. Make sure you put a probation period up front so you can get out easily. Also, give yourself exit opportunities at periodic times, such as quarterly or twice a year, so you are not stuck with marginal service for two years if the vendor starts to slip. Make sure you have a clear statement about quality. If quality slips and the company doesn't improve, you should be able to get out of the contract immediately.

■ *Monitoring for quality.* You can't afford to let quality slip. Set up a monitoring system to make sure you're getting the quality you're paying for. If you sense a drop in quality of service, bring it to the company's attention and quietly identify a replacement company that can come in and take over if your vendor doesn't return to the appropriate quality level.

In selecting vendors for outsourcing, talk at length with their current clients. Ask those clients about the strengths and weaknesses of the vendors. Clients will usually be candid in these conversations. Unfortunately, most companies don't bother with these calls. Also, get clear agreements. Most disasters can be avoided if the agreement between the business and the vendor was well understood by both parties. A clear contract stating who does what and when can curtail tons of problems. Another safeguard is to give yourself alternatives. Keep a backup supplier in mind, and make sure you don't tie your hands with an exclusive contract. Go to your backup before you start missing goals. Finally, keep a good communication flow between you and your vendor. Keeping your vendor informed about how you view her services can help make sure the service level stays where it needs to be.

How Do You Find an Outsourced Vendor or Professional?

Networking is an excellent way to find vendors. Word of mouth is the most common way companies find services. Join your local chamber or a national trade association to meet other professionals with companies like yours. As long as you're not in direct competition, you will probably find your contemporaries candid about outsourced services.

The Outsourcing Institute can also help you in the process of finding vendors. This association of vendors and independent professionals offers a wealth of information on outsourcing. Check the Web site (www.outsourcing.com). It presents its members as outsourcing sources. Call 800/421-6767, or write to 45 Rockefeller Plaza, Suite 2000, New York, NY 10011. The yellow pages are also an excellent source for help. Either use industry directories or place a classified ad in a newspaper or trade journal. This works, but it takes more effort on your part to make sure you get the right match.

What Are Difficulties of Outsourcing?

Finding the right vendors is an ongoing process. Outsourced vendors are usually shorter-term relationships than employees. This means you're always on the lookout for new vendors. Turnover is usually high in marketing and manufacturing; accounting vendors tend to be longer-term relationships.

Another difficulty is that you're not necessarily the most important company to your vendor. A smart vendor will make it seem like you're his most important one, but sometimes your vendor just can't jump when you say jump because she has a parcel of other clients in addition to you.

Communication can also be a problem. Vendors are harder to control than employees. They are not in your office taking guidance on an hour-by-hour basis, changing the contours of the projects as you dictate. Missed communication can mean your vendor is days into a project before you notice it is going in the wrong direction.

What Are the Advantages of Outsourcing?

With outsourcing, you get top quality at affordable rates. You can improve the character of your business by improving the quality of your vendors. Systematic quality improvement is much harder to accomplish with in-house employees. With outsourcing, you are also free from the employee overhead burden. Plus, if the vendor doesn't work out, you don't have to jump through legal hoops to make a change; just go shopping for better services. In addition, you can buy as much or as little as you need. You can build this flexibility into most vendor relationships; no down time, and no production quotas. You buy what you need and no more.

Outsourcing—Points to Consider

1. Be aware that even outsourcing requires management skills. It takes some practice, but it's worth the effort since you can expand while keeping a low monthly cost.

2. Networking is the best way to find good vendors. Also, shun long-term agreements. Part of the power of outsourcing is that you can improve your business by improving the quality of your vendors.

3. Keep what you're good at and outsource your weaker areas. If you're good at sales, keep it; if you're lousy at accounting, outsource it.

Part V

Marketing—Your Driving Force

There's an old line, "If you can sell it, you'll succeed." Selling isn't the whole story of creating a successful business, but it is a big part of the job. Marketing is the most important skill for the business owner. All other skills can be learned on the job far more easily than marketing. This isn't because marketing is more difficult than other aspects of running a business; it's because the need for marketing begins on day one and continues to be crucial every single day you operate your enterprise. Even as you think about what kind of business you would like to own, you need to be thinking about how you will market your products or services.

Marketing involves a lot more than just selling. Some people don't even consider selling to be part of marketing, but for the home-business owner, selling and marketing work so closely together that you can't separate them. Marketing is the process of creating an environment that encourages sales. This includes getting your word out, but it also includes developing products and services that are marketable, since you have to continually adjust your products and services to fill the needs of your clients or customers.

Marketing includes publicity, public relations, product development, customer service, research, competitiveness, advertising, direct marketing, and selling. All of these efforts need to work in unison; all of them are crucial to your success. Because these efforts need to work closely together, it helps to have a marketing plan from the outset of your enterprise and to review your plan and make adjustments along the way. Some of your marketing efforts will work better than others, so you will need to continually fine-tune your plan.

If you do not have some professional marketing experience before you launch, you should learn as much as you can as quickly as possible. You should also consider hiring a marketing consultant with experience in your type of business and industry. Read marketing books and trade magazines in your industry or profession. Trade magazines usually have regular sections on how to market products or services. If you hire a marketing consultant, have him develop a marketing plan, rather than just hiring him to do your marketing.

Once you have a plan developed, you may wish to do some of the marketing yourself, while hiring the marketing company to do the marketing tasks that you are not as skilled to perform. This way, you get the benefit of the marketing company's experience without having to pay hefty fees for work you can do yourself. You may find that most of the work outlined in the marketing plan is work you can do, in which case go it alone. Use the marketing company's plan and revise it as you move forward. This may be the most efficient use of a marketing company if you are willing to learn and perform all of the tasks outlined in the plan.

Whether you learn how to do it yourself or hire someone else to do it, you need to provide professional marketing for your company. If you buy a franchise or business opportunity, you will receive expert instruction on marketing techniques that are tried-and-true. You will probably get the benefit of national marketing for the product or service the company provides. Even if you are receiving this support, it helps to learn the marketing strategies and techniques for your industry. The more you know about marketing, the better chance you will have of succeeding.

Sample Marketing Plan

Here is a sample marketing plan for a start-up company. It uses the Complete Home Business Web Site, the same company used in the sample business plan (see Chapter 10).

Complete Home-Business Web Site— First-Year Marketing Plan

Overview

During the first year, the company will test a wide range of marketing techniques that will include publicity, offline advertising, direct marketing, sales, Internet promotion, and networking. The goal is to determine the most efficient and effective ways to create traffic and turn at least 10 percent of our visitors into customers. Further, we will work to turn our customers into repeat buyers.

Given the wide range of marketing techniques we plan to test, we expect some of the efforts to be less productive than others. Next year's plan will be a trimmed-down version of this one. In the future, we will continue to experiment with new strategies, but not at the level of this first-year effort.

Our overall goal is to create 30,000 hits per month by the end of the first year. We anticipate 2,000 of these monthly visitors will purchase a product or service. We expect an average order of $65, which creates an average monthly revenue of $130,000. Given the low markup of 18 percent on our products, the net revenue will be $23,400.

There is quite a bit of competition over the Internet, but most home-business sites are doing very little marketing to promote their sites. By using the following marketing efforts, we can build a brand name that will keep our customers coming back. In order to hold our customers, we will need to continually add new information. We will also have to add new products and services regularly.

Publicity

There are innumerable publicity opportunities for the Web site. We will send out press releases announcing our launch and follow those with releases with announcements of new product lines and services. Since we will continually develop new partnerships with other sites and with franchise companies, we will always have fresh news to justify regular press releases. The following efforts do not include Internet publicity efforts since those are covered in the Internet section.

- *Press releases to local newspapers.* We will schedule releases to go out bimonthly. At that time, we will determine which recent events constitute the best news.
- *Trade magazines.* We will send press releases to selected trade magazines quarterly. These titles include the Internet industry and computer magazines.
- *Consumer business magazines.* We will send quarterly press releases to *Home Business Magazine, Small Business Opportunities, Working at Home,* and more. We will also send small articles to these magazine companies, since the articles come with blurbs.
- *Radio talk shows.* We will schedule at least one talk-show appearance per week. We will target the largest talk stations in the large and medium-size cities. Part of the publicity budget will be used to buy directories of radio talk shows.
- *Television.* We will try to get on both television talk shows and the local news. Whenever Shoe and Younger travel, they will try to get booked on local television talk shows.
- *Public speaking.* Shoe and Younger have experience in public speaking. Both of them will work to get speaking dates in front of groups of potential customers, such as entrepreneur groups and trade shows in the home-business, franchise, and Internet industries.

Advertising

This advertising section includes all offline advertising. The Internet advertising will be covered in the Internet section. A special-interest Web site needs direct advertising. Broadcast is too expensive and poorly targeted. The best bet for home-business entrepreneurs will be the home-business magazines. We will run ⅙-page ads that promote a free business plan template for those who visit the site. We will run an ad in three consecutive issues of each magazine. Since we will ask all visitors where they heard about the site, we can measure results against advertising costs. We will use the following magazines:

Home Business Magazine
Entrepreneur's Home Office
Working at Home
Business Start-Ups
Small Business Opportunities

Direct Marketing

The direct-marketing techniques that will be tested include direct mail, card decks, and ride-alongs. The direct-mail piece will offer something enticing, such as the business plan template.

■ *Direct mail to consumer business magazine subscribers.* We will use the same magazines that we choose for space advertising.

■ *Direct mail to business catalog buyers.* The catalogs can include those from NEBS, Staples, Office Max, PC Warehouse, Quill, and others.

■ *Card decks to entrepreneurs.* Card decks can include *Home Business Magazine, Entrepreneur, Success,* and *Self-Employed Professional.*

■ *Ride-alongs.* We will work with an alternative direct-marketing company to find ride-along opportunities. These can include computer box stuffers, credit-card bill stuffers for small-business credit-card holders, and more.

Sales

We will use direct sales to bring in franchise companies and business opportunities as partners in the site. We will offer our visitors the ability to search for listed companies. If one of our visitors chooses to participate with the franchise company or business opportunity, we will receive a commission on the fee.

- *Sales letters and proposals.* We will begin the sales process by sending a letter proposal to targeted franchises and business opportunities. The letter will outline our program.

- *Telephone sales.* Either Shoe or Younger will follow up the letter with a phone call.

- *Meeting with significant partners.* For companies that have great potential for consummating deals online, we will meet personally with the companies' leaders. Most of these meetings can take place at a conference or trade show.

Internet

We will test a wide range of Internet marketing strategies, including permission-based e-mail, newsgroup postings, board postings, links, and banner ads.

- *E-mail permission program.* We will encourage all visitors to register, which will give them a free subscription to our newsletter on home business. The registration will also alert them that they will receive periodic notices of new products and services they may be interested in hearing about. This registration allows us to target them based on a number of marketing criteria and also establishes that the e-mail they receive from us is not spam.

- *Newsgroups.* We will scour small-business newsgroups and offer answers and post notices. This public-relations effort will bring visitors to our site.

- *Boards.* We will also answer questions and post information on message boards to draw traffic to the site.

- *Links.* We will exchange links with a wide range of small-business sites.

- *Banner advertising.* We will experiment with banner advertising. Since banner ad click-throughs are down, banner advertising is becoming less expensive and is worth testing.

Networking

We will use networking as part of our sales strategy to line up franchise and business-opportunity partners.

- *Franchise and business-opportunity trade shows.* We will work trade shows to gather information valuable to our visitors; we will also market to franchise and business-opportunity companies to bring them into partnerships where we promote their companies for a commission.
- *Entrepreneur associations.* We will visit entrepreneur associations to promote the site as a place to get free information and discounted products and services.

Budget

Our total marketing budget for the first year is $100,000. It is allocated as follows:

Publicity: $5,000
Advertising: $25,000
Direct marketing: $22,000
Sales: $4,000
Internet: $40,000
Networking: $4,000

Chapter 20

Publicity—Your Birth Announcement and Ongoing Letter to the World

You don't need a public-relations firm to get publicity for your business, but you do need to develop a publicity plan and make sure the plan is implemented. There is no advertising that can equal the power of effective publicity. And there is no better time to get good publicity than the first year or two that you are in business. It takes creativity, persistence, and moxie to make it through the clutter on the desk of the editor or producer, but if you keep pushing, the rewards can be a strong boost for your business.

Public relations is your tool for managing your company's image to customers and potential customers. Most public relations is really media relations, which is your way of creating a positive image with the media, which then conveys that positive image to its audience. Most of this positive coverage comes in the form of publicity, which is your work to get the media to cover your company. Publicity takes a number of forms that include news coverage in newspapers and magazines, as well as broadcast coverage on radio and television. There are other forms of publicity as well, such as your presence at events and your presence on the Internet in subject areas that pertain to your company.

The great advantage of receiving regular publicity is that it creates an impression that you are a leader in your industry. It doesn't matter how big or little you are, if you are getting press, you get credibility and will be perceived as a business on the go. The fact that you're a home business will just add to your mystique if you're getting media coverage regularly. The home aspect can be a plus if you present yourself as the little company that could. If you're getting covered, most negatives can be presented as positives.

Many new business owners believe publicity comes to those who work with professionals and those with luck. Public relations and publicity professionals are effective, but it is because they know what the editors and producers want to cover and they present their clients in a manner that is attractive from the media's point of view. You can do the same thing if you learn the ropes of what gets covered (and why) and how to present your company in a professional manner. If you find a strong angle on why your company or its products and services are newsworthy and present the idea in a well-written press release sent to the appropriate person, you will get coverage.

The whole trick to successful media coverage is the matter of finding the newsy aspects of your business, learning how to create a professional press release, and doing the research to make sure you get the release to the right person. As you develop the skills to get covered and begin to understand how to be newsworthy, you will also start to see that there are some activities you can do as a business that attract attention, whether they involve initiating a charity drive or sponsoring a public event. So when you start to get coverage, begin to set up activities and events that will bring you additional positive coverage.

You can actually plan your media relations. From the first press release announcing the launch of your company to the time when most editors and producers in your town or industry know who you are, make publicity an ongoing part of how you do business. Draw up your battle strategy; make sure you get more than enough coverage.

Your Publicity Plan

A publicity plan is a section within your marketing plan that outlines your strategy to get positive coverage from the media. This plan will outline events, such as an award, the hiring of a new manager, an expansion, or a charity drive, that will bring media attention. Part of the plan will outline the kind of business news that gets covered. In some cities, the major newspaper's business section covers company anniversaries, while other papers only cover new hires and awards. As you learn the hot buttons that get you exposure, you can alter your plan accordingly.

Some companies set publicity goals, such as making sure they get some coverage each month or that they receive exposure in a set number of media outlets each time they do a particular charity drive or event. If you take your goals seriously, you will be more likely to make sure you get the desired coverage. Goals have a way of making you more effective than you would otherwise be, because they encourage you to put in the extra effort to make sure the goals are met. If you just list media coverage as a general company goal, you may never get around to sending out the kind of press releases that get stories. If you write down specific goals, such as getting on a particular newscast that features a different local business each week, you are more likely to make it happen.

Your goals should be very specific, such as the following:

- Get covered on the WXYZ nightly news business feature.
- Send an item to the *Business Times* at least once per month.
- Be a guest on a WABC or WDEF radio talk show once every three months.
- Try to get a guest-column item in the local business weekly.
- Create a charity event that will generate television, radio, and print coverage.
- Get a spot as a chat-room guest on the Internet every two months.
- Post and respond to newsgroup questions online twice weekly.

The list can go on and on. As you gain experience, your goals will become increasingly realistic and your ability to reach your goals will improve. The important part is to create a plan, monitor it to make sure you are doing all the necessary releases and research, and change the plan as you learn and develop effective media-relations skills. Once you become successful at this effort, you will begin to create an image of a company with credibility that is on the move. Usually the company in a particular niche that is getting the best press is considered the leader.

Print Media

Print media includes newspapers, magazines, and newsletters. You can approach print media as either a local story or a national story in your industry's trade magazine. The determining factor should be where you find your customers. If your customers are all local, don't bother with any national media. Likewise, if you sell business-to-business nationally, there is no reason to spend any of your time on local media. The whole goal of gaining publicity is to get your name before your potential customers in a way that fosters credibility.

There are also different types of publicity, including event notices and items about new hires, new projects, awards, and new products or services. These fall into the category of announcements; they can go in newspapers, magazines, and newsletters. They can often go in two sections of your newspaper, the business section and the section covering your subject. A publisher can send a notice about an expansion to the book editor and one to the business editor. Likewise, if you run a catering company, you can send your notice to the food editor as well as the business editor. Make sure each announcement is written individually and sent directly to each editor, in that editor's name; typing "Food Editor" on the envelope isn't enough.

With announcements, always include a photo. A photo helps for two reasons: It increases the chances that your notice will be included in the paper, and it makes it more likely that your notice will get read when it appears. If you send your announcement to a newspaper that runs only black-and-white photos, send a black-and-white photo of yourself. If the publication runs only color, or if the publication runs both black-and-white and color, send a color photo. The photo should be professionally taken and professionally developed. Many studio photographers can take a photo of you and produce copies both in black-and-white and in color. You should always have both on hand.

Print media is also a good place to push for getting an article written about your company. Attempting to get a publication to write an article about your company takes some research and creativity. First, make sure the publication you contact actually runs profiles on individual companies, then propose an article that fits your company into the publication's format. You can open your letter with a quick description of the angle that will work for the section of the publication, then say, "I believe my company would be a good fit for your 'On the Scene' feature."

Of course the letter should be addressed to the editor who is responsible for this particular feature. You can call the receptionist and ask who edits the feature. If the receptionist doesn't know, ask to talk with someone in the editorial department; whoever answers the phone will be able to give you the name of the appropriate editor. When you get the name, make sure you also get the correct spelling. If the first name is Jan, you will also need to find out if Jan is a man or woman.

Once you have identified who your idea should go to, make sure it's a great idea. It is not enough to say that your company is launching a Web site. Web sites were news in the mid 1990s, but everyone has a Web site now. Look for the angle that makes your story unique and timely. If you are about to launch a Web site that will offer the first home reading test that can determine whether your children's reading skills are above or below the national average, that's news.

Send the press release, giving the details of your break-through Web site, along with a cover letter by mail. After ten to fifteen days, call the editor to make sure she received your letter and release. Don't ask if she has read it or if she plans to run it; just ask if she received it. She will say either "Yes" or "No, can you fax it to me?" If she hadn't received it, fax it over and call her back in three days. When you know she has seen it, simply ask her, "Does this fit well with your 'On the Scene' section?" Don't tell her that it does, and again, don't ask if she's going to run it. If she says that it doesn't, ask where you missed, since you thought you had hit a bull's-eye. Whatever she tells you is gold for future reference or for rewriting your current release.

If she admits that your idea was right on target, let her tell you what her next move will be. Most likely, she will tell you what happens next. She might tell you that she'll get back to you for quotes in a week or so. She may tell you that she has a backlog of stories or that she has to take the idea to a managing editor for approval. Then, you ask if she needs anything more to strengthen the story. Don't tell her that it's a great story. Instead, tell her that it seems like a good fit with "On the Scene." Let her agree or disagree; if she disagrees, again, the words will be gold for your follow-up or next try.

The whole point of your approach is that you are knowledgeable and aware of this publication's feature requirements, and you know how your story fits into the feature. Beyond that, your job is to be helpful, not pushy. You are not trying to persuade her (your letter was your persuasion, not your phone call). In the follow-up phone call, ask if your judgment was correct; ask if she needs anything more. You are a professional checking in to make sure your correspondence was received.

If you use this professional approach, the editor will usually be open and responsive to your questions. By the end of this conversation, you will know what the next step is and have a contact person who may be helpful for years to come. The follow-up is very important. For one thing, if you don't follow up, your press release, and cover letter will likely find itself at the bottom of a stack of press releases that were "pretty good ideas." The follow-up gets your press release back on top and gives you a chance to redirect the release if it was a touch off mark.

Radio Talk Shows

Radio talk shows work whether you have a national market or a local market, since you don't have to be in town in order to do the interview. You can phone it in from your living room. Most cities have a number of radio stations that run shows featuring guests. Often the guests are authors, but most shows will also present nonauthor business owners if the subject is interesting. The reason for the proliferation of authors is that they are constantly working to get on these shows. Business owners can also get on most of these shows, but they usually don't try as hard to get the exposure. If you make it a point to get on as a radio guest and find a strong angle, you will likely be successful.

Radio shows come in different forms: Some are controversial political free-for-alls that thrive by being provocative; some are morning-drive entertainment formats with chummy male and female hosts talking about relationships; some are shock-jocks looking for ways to keep their listeners from pushing the button during the next commercial break. Sometimes you have a try a few shows before you get a feel for which format works best for you. Or you may decide it doesn't matter as long as you get exposure. Some business owners can do very well even with the controversial or shock-jock format by sparring with the host in a good-natured manner. If you can get some on-air chemistry going with the host, you will get invited back again and again.

Radio shows are very responsive to events. If your company is holding or participating in a charity event, it can be fairly easy to get radio guest spots. But even if you have an event, it still is important to create an angle. Raising money through an entertaining afternoon at the park is not enough; explaining that there will be a final trick at the event that involves you, a dog, and a goldfish will get their attention. Find an angle that will let the host have a good time with jokes and call-ins. It also helps if you prepare a list of entertaining or provocative questions the host can ask you.

To get on the show, find out who the producer is; it is usually the producer, not the host, who books the guests. The station receptionist will be able to give you the name of the producer. Develop your angle—the funny, offbeat, or provocative point you can make on the show. Using your angle, write down three or four fun questions the host can ask you. These questions will make the host appear informed about your subject, and it will give focus to the interview. Don't make the host do this work. Also explain your background or expertise in either your business or the particular charity (if you are promoting a charity event).

Then fax a press release that explains your angle and include three or four questions. Call the producer to follow up in two or three days. With radio, you don't have to wait as long to follow up as you would with a print editor. When you make your follow-up call, have your press release in front of you. Chances are the producer has looked it over and discarded it; you will have to remind him of your fax. You may get booked right then, after a couple of questions. Or the producer may ask you to fax the release again. If so, fax and follow up again. Don't get defensive about having to refax. The producer isn't being rude; he simply receives too many releases to remember them all.

If you get a no, ask why. If you have done your research and are familiar with the show, it is important to find out why you missed the target. Whatever you learn will help you in the future, so don't take a no without finding out what killed your shot. If you get a no, it's not because the producer is an idiot; it's because you somehow didn't get an accurate idea of the type of guests the show likes to book. A no means you need to do better research.

Don't worry about the charity taking up the focus of your visit instead of your business. You will be identified by your business even if you are being interviewed for the charity event. Besides, it only increases your credibility if you become the carpet-cleaning company that is the number one fund-raiser for the Red Cross. You don't have to mention carpet cleaning once as long as it's part of your identity. You can always slip it in if your host doesn't help on this point. When asked about how long you have been preparing for the event, just say, "Well, it's not just me. It's all of us at ABC Carpet Cleaning. Our whole office, small though it may be, really gets into this drive each year. Even some of our customers get involved." If you're discreet, the host won't mind, and the listeners will remember.

If the situation is right, you can also give away some of your products or services on the radio. Public-radio pledge drives are particularly effective for giveaways. If you offer free products or services as premiums for a fund drive, you can usually get a spot for an hour or two during the pledge effort. You will share airtime with a host and pitch the importance of listener contributions. Every few minutes, the host will tell the audience that you are here from ABC Carpet Cleaning helping out and that the next caller to pledge $75 will get a free living room carpet cleaned.

Even when you're off the air, your product or service will still be one of the premiums mentioned again and again for the week or two of the drive.

If you have a national product, radio works the same way, only you are on the telephone instead of in the studio. If you have a local tie-in, that's great, but it isn't absolutely necessary. I promoted a magazine through radio appearances throughout the country. I gave away subscriptions while I was a guest. This also worked for pledge drives at public stations. Although I couldn't appear in the studio, the giveaways were still effective for reaching listeners. When your product or service is used as a premium, the host will usually build it up to encourage pledges. You supply the two- or three-line promotion copy for the host.

Radio guest spots take a bit of research and follow-up, but like print coverage, radio can be great for building credibility. When people hear you on the radio, they automatically assume you're an expert. Your status comes simply from the fact that you are present on the radio; if you are articulate, so much the better. But you don't even have to be all that articulate as long as you come across as enthusiastic and genuine. Broadcasting experience isn't necessary either. The host will take care of that, and a good host will work to make you look good. You have already provided the questions for the host to ask, so there won't be too many surprises. Being a guest on the radio is easier than it sounds and goes a long way toward getting the word out about your product.

Television

Getting television coverage is more difficult than radio simply because there are fewer local shows that present guests and because there is fierce competition for the national shows. I usually recommend that entrepreneurs forget national shows entirely. I have seen too many businesspeople waste dozens of hours trying to get on Letterman's or Oprah's show without ever getting close. Often, in the effort to get on a national show, the local radio or television program that is possible gets neglected.

Whenever I or anyone I know has been able to get on a national show, it is because a local show was forwarded to a national producer or because a national producer saw a local segment that was picked up in a market near the producer. So, spend your time getting on local shows; you will be rewarded with success.

Though the opportunities for television are limited, there are a few worth pursuing. Many local stations do their own general-interest talk shows. These usually appear midday during the week or early in the morning on a Saturday or Sunday. They are often very open to guest suggestions. You can approach television in the same manner as radio, by faxing a producer, then following up with a phone call. Like you do for radio, wait only two or three days before your follow-up call. You may get booked right then, or you may have to answer a few questions and refax the release.

If you get a booking on the show, ask about appropriate dress. This doesn't mean formal or casual; your research will have already told you whether to dress up or down. You want to know about contrasts and colors. The producer may suggest high-contrast clothes or simple fabrics without intricate patterns. One of the big differences between the sharp appearance on national show and the relatively drab presentation on local television shows comes from clothing selection. Get whatever information you can from the producer before you take the chance of appearing washed out or gaudy.

Like the radio host, your television host should carry you through the appearance, using your set of interesting questions. This is even true on the major talk shows. Although the guests sometimes act surprised by one of Leno's questions, the surprises are rarely real. Most of the big stars would not appear on a show without first determining how the four or five minutes of exposure will be spent. It is the same with your visit. You certainly don't want to take the chance of having the host ask you a question you can't answer. Your host doesn't want that either, so she will be very willing to use your questions, especially if they have punch and are fun.

Soft news stories are another opportunity to get covered on television. Many stations regularly cover local businesses with positive stories. Charity events are also good for this type of coverage, although television usually likes to cover the event itself rather than alerting people to an upcoming event since television is a visual medium that likes to be on the spot with coverage. Study the local news broadcasts in the early evening and late at night to see if they cover local companies. You may have to watch twice a day for a whole week to learn the variety of soft stories they present.

Keep in mind that the early news usually runs different soft stores than the late news. The soft stories also run at different times on different stations. Sometimes they run just before the end of the program and sometimes they appear between sports and weather, but they are always in the second half of the newscast. If you don't see any type of coverage that could possibly fit your business or nonprofit activities, move on and study the next station. Don't waste your time trying to convince a station to cover you if it doesn't already have a format that is appropriate for your activities or business.

If you see a spot that would work for your business, fax a letter to the producer suggesting your company would be a perfect fit for the "Business Showcase" feature she runs on Tuesdays during the 6:00 p.m. broadcast. The more specific you are in placing your idea, the more credible your release. Also make sure you explain the visuals that relate to your story, such as the demonstration of your new chocolate-dipping machine. If you don't provide suggestions on what the visual will be for your story, she may pass. As with other broadcast releases, follow up in two or three days.

There are two strong advantages to getting covered in a newscast. For one, the audience is twenty to thirty times larger than that of a local television talk show. Secondly, the spot will be put together as a feature, which usually includes a visual shot of your chocolate-dipping machine in operation as the reporter explains your fascinating machine, interspersed with comments from you at your desk or at the machine, and ends with you and the reporter eating a finished chocolate-covered avocado. These spots usually run one to three minutes and are lighthearted in tone, so you can tape the feature and use it as a promotional item for your business.

If the feature is good, it gets sent out to the national network for potential use by stations across the country, which may bring any number of fun surprises. I know a Santa Fe cookie manufacturer whose business profile ran at 3:00 a.m. in New Jersey. An insomniac literary agent saw the feature, called the bakery in Santa Fe, and asked if the owner might be interested in writing a cookie cookbook. She said yes; six months later, she had a contract and an advance from Random House. Honestly.

Just as public radio runs pledge drives, you can get involved in your public television's fund-raising efforts. Much as you do in radio, you can offer giveaways of your products or services on the air. You may even be able to get a spot on camera giving a pitch about the benefits of public television with a station host. Whether you just give away products and services or also go on the air to pitch, you will give your company a goodwill shot in the arm that translates into business credibility. If you are on the air yourself, the effect is even stronger.

Unlike radio, television is a medium in which you can't get repeat coverage. If you do a fun job on the radio, you can return to the program at regular intervals. With television, no matter how successful your performance, you will not have the opportunity to return soon. Even so, it is worth the publicity efforts to get on television, because you can tape it and play it back at trade shows or in any other context that allows you to show a video to show a video to potential customers or investors.

The Internet

The Internet has exploded over the past few years. When I spoke to groups of entrepreneurs in the mid-1990s, I asked for a show of hands from those who were online. I used to see about 5 out of 100 hands go up. By 1999, most hands were in the air for that question. People are online learning about products and services. It used to be good public relations to make sure customers and potential customers could find you online; now it is a necessity. Even if your products and services are local, you may find that having a presence on the Internet is worthwhile and profitable.

You don't necessarily have to build a Web site to use the

Internet as a public-relations tool, but it helps. Your Web site is your online business card, the place where a customer can go to send you a note or reserve a time next Thursday for you to come by and pick up his collie for grooming. If you have a business that lends itself to visitors and newcomers, the Web can be particularly useful since more and more travelers and newcomers use the Internet to scope out the city they are about to hit. I know quite a few realtors who use the Internet to find customers who are about to arrive looking for a home.

There are a number of ways to get your name on the Internet. The techniques and strategies here are just the public-relations and publicity aspects. For the range of Internet techniques for direct selling, marketing, and advertising, see Chapter 24. Following are just a few of the publicity opportunities:

- Build your own Web site.
- Get listed on the Web sites of others, such as your chamber of commerce.
- Post questions and answers on newsgroups covering your subject.
- Network in chat rooms.
- Get booked as a chat-room guest speaker.
- Host a chat-room weekly.
- Post notices on message boards.
- Write articles for e-zines.

All of these activities can bring you in contact with potential customers. However, a word of warning: If you only have local products and services, stick to the techniques that directly work to reach your local customers. For some companies, such as commercial janitorial work, there are no Internet applications. Only use the Internet for public relations if you can determine that there is a stream of potential customers online who are seeking services such as yours. Close isn't good enough. If you know your potential customers are online but can't determine that they are online specifically to search for services or products like yours, the Internet isn't for you. It's the same with the individual Internet techniques listed above. If your potential customers are not specifically using one of these techniques to find companies like yours, then don't waste your time developing the technique.

But if you know that your customers are using the Internet to shop for your products and services, it can be a powerful public-relations tool. This isn't direct selling; public relations on the Internet serves a different function than sales. With public relations, your goal is to establish name recognition and gain credibility. If you sell sports cards, you can use the Internet to post the cards you have for sale and list the individual prices; that's sales. Public relations is a matter of establishing that you are an expert source for sports cards and that you can obtain cards that you do not hold in your immediate inventory. Moreover, you can coach customers in strategies for choosing the right cards to build a valuable collection and explain which cards hold their value and which ones appreciate. If you have the right business, public relations can bring you a lifetime client rather than just a one-time sale.

Web Sites

Everybody has a Web site. These are wonderful contact and sales tools, but don't expect anyone to come to your Web site just because it's there. Your Web site will only work if you send people to it. You may get picked up by a search engine, but the search engine will not necessarily send the right people. Unless you are well schooled in search-engine technology and politics, it may not be a very productive source for good traffic. Your best traffic will be the people you send to your site through offline marketing or through online exposure.

One of the best ways to get traffic to your site is to use your Web address in your online signature, so every time you correspond with someone online, you leave behind your Web address. It also helps if you print your Web site address on all of your offline marketing, from your business card to your yellow pages advertising. But don't just send people to your Web site for the fun of it; make sure your Web site is loaded with information regarding your specialty. For the sports-card dealer, the Web site can include in-depth articles on the appreciation of sports cards and how to select new sports cards for their potential growth in value. Give people a reason to go to your site, then deliver on that reason by offering useful information or resources.

You can also use your Web site to consummate a sale, whether it involves selling a sports card or making an appointment to price a landscaping project. But when you are promoting yourself through public relations, your Web site needs to be more than a store. Your potential customers are visiting your Web site because you are the expert in your field, so they rightfully expect to find information and resources that you have selected to help them learn. If you have your expert resources in place, visitors will be perfectly comfortable finding that the site is also set up for e-commerce. If they show up and your site is nothing but e-commerce, you will tarnish some of the goodwill you bought through your public relations. Most people will continue to buy from a sports-card dealer who is a constant source of education as well as a place to get a good deal on cards.

Newsgroups and Message Boards

Newsgroups are lists of questions and answers posted by people with a common interest, which can include everything from autism to Bob Dylan. They can be an excellent place to establish your professional credibility. The postings on a newsgroup are a combination of questions and news related items about the subject, which can include tips on good Web sites or breaking articles in e-zines and magazines. As an expert, you can go through the newsgroups and answer questions as well as post references to the latest articles on your Web site or in e-zines. The power of newsgroups is that the postings get read eagerly as long as they are information-based rather than promotion-based.

Make sure your postings reveal valuable information; also give your Web-site address so people can go there for more information. Be careful about making your communication too promotional. If it is perceived that you are only there to sell, the newsgroup audience will become skeptical about your notices. Avoid this by making sure all your postings and answers to questions deliver satisfying information, rather than being just a tease to lure people to your Web site. If people feel that you are consistently helpful and complete in your communications, they will be eager to go to your site to learn more about you and your services.

Message boards are similar to newsgroups except that instead of a stream of postings, they are organized by categories and topics. They are also set up to stay in place for extended periods of time. You may receive a response to a message-board posting a year after you posted your message. Like newsgroups, message boards can be used to post breaking news and answer questions. Because they are semipermanent, people will read through both the questions and answers, so your answer goes to a wider audience than just the person who posted the question. This is true of newsgroups, too, but the length of time your answer is easily accessible to newsgroup viewers is considerably shorter. With message boards, you can leave your Web address for further information, and you can make it easy for viewers by posting hypertext so they can click right on to your site.

Chat Rooms

Chat rooms can be a great place to network with other people who share your interests, and thus a potential source of clients and customers. I know a woman who actually sold a book to a major publisher in a chat room. The editor was visiting the room to learn more about a particular subject that she thought would make a good book. The writer was halfway through a book on the subject and had not yet found a publisher; she was there to do some research and find some contacts. They got to talking. These cybernetworking rooms are great for establishing your credibility and making contacts, even if you are just there as a visitor.

The best use of chat rooms is if you can be there as more than a visitor. Business chat rooms are often hosted by an expert. Your Internet server may provide weekly chat rooms on your subject. Find out if they need someone to spend an hour or so each week hosting a talk on the subject. You can also propose initiating a new chat room on your subject if your server does not already have one set up. The advantages of hosting a chat room are that you are always viewed as the expert on the subject, and when your server promotes your weekly chat, the server is also promoting your expertise.

A guest-speaker spot in a chat room is, as just stated, a way to establish yourself as an expert. Your server probably offers regular chats on individual business disciplines or subjects. Propose that you be a guest speaker at one of these chats. The server will e-mail all potential visitors a few days before your visit. At the time of the talk, a host will usually introduce you, and you will state some interesting or provocative thoughts about your subject. From then on, it is a free-for-all of questions. If you are not a good typist, it can be quite a ride, but it's fun. You will invariably meet people who will contact you later at your Web site or by e-mail.

Another plus to chats is that most servers make their past chats available to anyone who is interested in the subject. I once did a chat on how to launch a magazine from scratch. There were about thirty attendees in the chat room, but over the course of the next year and a half, I received about fifty e-mails from people who read the chat and had further questions, which made me wonder how many people read the chat and never contacted me with a follow-up question. You can meet so many people who are interested in your subject while you're in a chat room that it is impossible to predict what may happen from the networking: maybe nothing, maybe a customer, maybe some credibility, maybe a book contract.

E-Zines and Archives

The Internet is also a good place to post articles about your subject. E-zines are electronic periodicals that come out on a regular basis. Some come out daily, but most are published weekly, monthly, or bimonthly. E-zines contain news and articles by experts; there are e-zines on every subject imaginable. One of the advantages of e-zines is that you don't have to be a professional writer to get your article placed. Your information has to be professionally presented and must contain useful information, but articles don't face the same rejection odds of magazines, so it is fairly easy to get an article placed in an online publication.

After the periodical circulates to its online subscribers, the article is often put into the e-zine publisher's archives. Your article can stay there for years. If the Web site indexes it well by subject, you can get responses to your article for years to come. As with newsgroup and chat rooms, you need to make sure your information is helpful; at the end of your article, include the hypertext so readers can click right to your Web site for more information.

Internet marketing is still developing, but online publicity is already mature. This is because the Internet was conceived and developed primarily as a research tool. So it was natural for experts to use this vast form of communication to promote their expertise. Even though e-commerce is growing quickly, the online world will always be a strong place for people to seek information and learn. If it helps your business to present yourself as an expert before groups of people interested in your subject, the Internet provides you with inexhaustible opportunities.

Sponsorships

You can promote your business through sponsorships, which can include public events, charity drives, fund-raisers, trade shows, and numerous other activities that gain public attention. Sponsoring an event can give your business strong name recognition without the high cost of advertising, but it only works for certain types of businesses or certain types of events. A public event that draws hundreds of consumers may work for cleaning services, such as Merry Maids, but it would be a poor choice for a CPA. Yet a CPA may find it worthwhile to sponsor a reception that includes a half-day workshop on how to launch a business. The determining factor is whether potential customers are likely to see the sponsorship promotion.

Keep in mind, sponsorships are an indirect method of both advertising and public relations. You get to put your name out, but you don't get to send your message. Sponsorships work best if you are already reaching your market through more direct forms of advertising and are using the sponsorship to underscore your name and distinguish your company from the competition. You also get the benefit of the affiliation with the organization or charity that is producing the event. This can bring some goodwill to your company, but the goodwill is only meaningful if the attendee of the event already knows what your company produces.

If your CPA business is already listed in the yellow pages and reaches potential customers through cross-referrals from attorneys, the sponsorship of a business launch seminar to reach new prospects makes sense. Just remember, no matter how attractive the numbers may appear in a sponsorship program, you will only get your name out, not your message. The public event only makes sense if you are already successfully promoting your name.

Public Speaking

Speaking about the subject of your business can be a very successful way to build credibility for your company, if you have the kind of business that requires professional expertise. If you run a janitorial service, public speaking may not do much to help you gain clients, but if your business is management consulting, marketing, Web site design, accounting, or almost any other professional practice, speaking in public can bring you credibility and exposure. Some professionals use public speaking as their primary way to gain customers as well as establish a reputation and name recognition.

Public speaking brings more than just the chance to present yourself to an audience. When you speak at a function, your talk is often promoted to the group's membership and even to the public. The exposure you receive through the press that goes along with your talk can be as valuable as the talk itself. The promotion for the talk usually includes background information on you that helps to build your credibility. The talk itself will create additional goodwill for you and your company.

There are a variety of public speaking opportunities available in any community, profession, or industry. If your business is landscaping, you can speak to gardening groups about the particular advantages and disadvantages of your local climate. An attorney can speak to entrepreneurs about the different forms of business organization. A clown can talk to children's groups at the school library. Most businesses have related opportunities for the owner to get out in public and talk about her expertise. But note that public speaking is not an opportunity to talk about your products or services; It is a chance to share your expertise. This alone will elevate your company in the eyes of the audience, and even in the eyes of those who read about your talk in the newspaper but didn't attend.

Getting Media Coverage—Points to Consider

1. Draw up a publicity plan that consists of monthly goals for getting press releases out to print media, getting bookings on radio shows, and getting exposure on the Internet.

2. It is easier to get newspaper, magazine, and radio coverage than it is to get television exposure, so put the greatest amount of effort into print and radio where your chances for results are best.

3. As more people spend time online, the Internet is becoming a better and better place to gain exposure for your business. Visit chat rooms and answer questions on newsgroups; these activities will draw traffic to your Web site to further your business.

Chapter 21

Advertising—Get Their Attention and Keep 'Em Coming Back

Advertising expenses can eat through start-up funds faster than you can say, "I need a new round of financing." The trick is to make sure that each advertisement you buy is both efficient and effective. Your advertising should be more than gambling. A seasoned marketing consultant or small advertising agency can save significant dollars by making sure that each advertisement you buy is appropriate for your product or service. A good advertising professional will also make sure you can track the results of your advertising.

Advertising is more important when you first launch than at any other time, since you have to reach out to new customers and clients and there is no awareness of your company in the market. This varies a bit if you have just purchased a franchise that is strong with national advertising, such as Subway or Jiffy Lube, but even then, you have to tell your potential customers about your location. Advertising requires a very delicate balance: You will fail if you apply too little of it, and you will fail if you spend too much on it. If you use exactly the right amount, it can spell success in big letters.

If you have some experience with advertising, including the strategies for placing it and the means for measuring its effectiveness, you can save yourself considerable expense. If you are just learning the techniques of effective advertising as you launch your company, you will be best off hiring some experienced help, then paying close attention to everything your expert does to make your advertising dollars effective. During this time, do considerable reading to educate yourself about good advertising principles. In time, you will probably learn enough to begin placing your own advertising, which will save you considerable expense.

Advertising agencies charge you in two ways. One, they bill you for all the work they do on your behalf, which can include planning, market research, creating print and broadcast advertising, and tracking the results of the advertising. They will usually either bill you for these efforts on a monthly basis or charge you a monthly retainer based on an estimated workload. In addition, they will buy your ads at 15 percent less than the going rate and charge you the full rate, thus pocketing 15 percent of every advertising dollar you spend, in addition to their monthly billing. Your costs for using an advertising agency can add up very quickly, so most new businesses look for an alternative to hiring an ad agency.

If you do not have the expertise to go it alone with your advertising, one of the alternatives is to use a marketing consultant. The consultant can be hired to develop your plan. You can implement the plan yourself, using the consultant for particular functions, such as putting you in touch with a designer, giving you feedback on the ads the designer proposes, and placing the ads (buying the media). Have the bill go to you, not to the consultant, so you take the 15 percent deduction. This can be a very efficient and effective way of purchasing expertise without tying yourself to an expensive advertising agency.

However you choose to develop and place your advertising, make sure you get some expert input until you have a very strong idea of what works and what doesn't work. If you have just launched a business that comes from your professional experience, your instincts about what will be effective may be a better barometer than anything an advertising agency or marketing consultant can offer. Ultimately, as you spend day in and day out with your business and its customers, you will develop strong instincts for the ways to find, attract, and keep customers.

Approach All Advertising With Caution

All advertising is expensive; misplaced advertising is especially dear. Many savvy marketing people approach all advertising with deep skepticism. As they review the various advertising possibilities, they keep one question at the forefront: "Can I do without this advertising buy?" If they can't find a good reason to shoot down the idea, they try it for as short a time as it takes to get realistic results. In time, the advertising mix becomes a blend of formulas that have been successful in the past, with a few experiments here and there. With a good marketing program, some experimentation is always part of the mix.

Unless you launch a franchise or business opportunity, all your advertising buys will be new at first. In order to carve out a reasonable marketing program, you have to find out how similar businesses go about attracting customers and clients. You can learn a great deal by simply asking other businesspeople with similar companies what they find works. If you run a comic-book business, your competitors in town are not likely to help you figure out what works to find sellers and buyers, but a few calls to other towns can be very illuminating. Not all business owners are willing to tell you what works in their advertising mix, but some will talk endlessly about all the advertising they tried over the past five years if you are not a direct competitor. If you call five dealers in other towns, you will likely get two who will tell you what works. Explain that you just set up shop and are curious about what advertising has been effective. People love to talk about what they do. Offer to send a gift certificate for lunch. The information you get is invaluable.

Pay special attention to what your competitors, particularly your successful competitors, are doing to get customers. Notice where they are advertising, and study the message of their advertising closely. Note the attention-getter and the offer in the ad. Is the come-on low price or high quality? You should do this work before you launch your business. Do it as part of your research to determine what business to launch or buy. Certainly you should do this before you begin to meet with potential marketing professionals.

The research you gain from talking with noncompetitors and examining your competitors may be better information than any advice you receive from a marketing or advertising professional. Bring this knowledge to your meetings with your consultant. A good marketing ace will have already done this research. If you find that you know more about how to market your product or service than the professional, look for another marketing consultant or go it alone.

The one thing you don't want to do as you launch your business is experiment with all aspects of advertising. You need a foundation of tried-and-true vehicles that work again and again with your product or service. If you are a plumber, make sure you are prominently displayed in the yellow pages, up toward the front, with a large ad and a message about being quick and affordable. Don't worry that all of your competition in town is also in the phone book. Most people call a plumber when they have an emergency; they check the yellow pages. Get in there too, and get your share. Then look around for advertising experiments that might increase your business.

Create an Advertising Budget and Plan

The worst way to buy advertising is one chunk at a time, as you can afford it, trying a different ad and different media as you go. Advertising should be a continual discipline, with an ongoing budget and a strategy for placing the biggest ad push to coincide with your strongest seasons. Whatever you do in advertising, it should have a budget and a plan. Most businesses create monthly budgets, with the lion's share of the budget going to the meat-and-potatoes advertising efforts that bring in a predictable amount of business.

The plan should outline your goals, which can include the following:

- The number of potential customers you plan to reach
- The number of customers you plan to attract
- The dollar value of your customers
- The percentage of ongoing or repeat customers

After the goals, your advertising plan should show the different forms of advertising you plan to use to meet these goals on a month-by-month basis. This should be reflected in your month-by-month budget. The plan should also state which forms of advertising constitute the basic ad placements for your type of business and should also explain which advertising is more experimental. Likewise, some of the ad budget should be fixed for the year (as with yellow pages advertising), and some should be discretionary (a budgeted amount available for experiments or opportunities).

At first, your advertising plan may be a completely fictional work with considerable guessing of both the appropriate budget levels and the appropriate advertising buys. By studying your competitors and others in your industry, and working with a marketing professional, your first plan will probably have some useful content mixed in with the guessing. Review the plan monthly and revise it quarterly. After about a year, you will begin to have a very good idea of what works and what is ineffective. Your second-year plan will be based mostly on your experience, so it will be a much more effective plan.

Don't Let the Sales Rep Drive Your Advertising

I have been an advertising sales representative for a number of ad products, including the advertising space in my own magazine. From that experience, I can testify that most business owners and marketing directors do not follow a plan like the one I outlined above. A surprising amount of advertising is sold by advertising representatives based on persuasion rather than investigation. This is a poor way to put your advertising program together. When you work outside of a plan, it is hard to focus your advertising as an effective tool to create business.

As I sold advertising, I noticed that most of the strong business owners held to their plan and only considered my pitch as an experiment that would be funded out of the discretionary portion of their budget. If it was successful, they added it to next year's plan and continued to fund it from the discretionary dollars until the new plan came into effect. This is the disciplined approach that keeps the advertising effort under control while still allowing for opportunities that may emerge during a plan's cycle.

Be careful not to bounce from one form of advertising to another simply because the sales rep has a very persuasive argument. I used to work with a very strict advertising plan for a book publishing company. I still listened to pitches from ad reps, but most of them did not have a clear idea of how books are promoted and sold; nonetheless, their pitches were very intense. These were well-trained professionals who knew how to listen and persuade, but they didn't know how to sell books. I experimented with some of their programs and always found them lacking. When I explained that the program didn't work, I was usually told that I needed to commit to a longer-range program and buy more exposure in order to make the ad medium really effective.

Occasionally I would meet with an advertising representative who was particularly well informed about my product and the effective ways to promote it. These people were usually very helpful and informative; they were also rare. Most advertising sales reps know a lot more about their advertising programs than they know about how to sell your products and services. No matter how skilled they are at sales, if they don't know what it takes to get people to buy your products and services, they can lead you down an expensive blind path. Stick with your plan. Let the sales reps move on and sell to your competition.

Choose Your Advertising Options Carefully

Telephone Directories

For many companies, the yellow pages are the best source of new business. This can be true for a wide range of professionals and people with skilled trades, including attorneys, accountants, plumbers, electricians, florists, even comic-book dealers. Just by looking through the advertisements in your section, you can get a good idea of which words work to make advertising effective. It may be speed and cost, as with plumbers, or it could be reputation and effectiveness, as with attorneys. The size of the ad is important; so is the order in which it appears.

Alphabetical order can be important, but sometimes this edge is obscured if the section is preceded by ten or fifteen full-page ads that are slotted on a first-come, first-served basis. You will find this to be the case with plumbing. By the time you get to the alphabetical listings, you have thumbed through a thick handful of full-page ads. If your section isn't crowded, then you will appear earlier if your name begins with the letter A. That's why so many companies go by the name AAA or A-1.

In most communities, you now have a choice of directories in which to advertise. This usually creates a very competitive environment, with ad reps deriding their competitors' product. The best way to determine which directory to use is not by price or by what the sales reps say, but by experience—preferably not your experience, since learning by experience can be expensive. Find a noncompeting company that appears in both directories; call the owner and find out which one pulls best and by how much. It may take two or three calls before you get some good information, but it's worth the time because it saves you the considerable time and money of running your own experiments.

You may find that you need to be in both directories, but it would make sense to place your largest ads in the stronger directory. You can bet the directories do not set their prices by results. If one directory works only half as well as the other, its pricing will probably only be 10 percent or 20 percent less, if at all. If you can only afford to go into one of the directories, don't necessarily choose the least expensive one; choose the one that gets the best results, even if it means you have to choose a smaller ad. It is better to have a smaller ad in the leading directory than to have a bigger ad in one that isn't as well read.

After you decide the content of your ad, study the advertisements of the leaders in your niche. If they have been around for a few years and have been successful at attracting customers, pay close attention to the layout. Is it clean, using mostly type and logo rather than pictures? What is the headline? Is there color in the ad? Don't try to do a prettier ad if all the other ads look plain and simple; they are probably plain and simple because plain and simple works. People don't browse the yellow pages like a magazine. They go to the category they need and look for price, speed, quality, geography, ease of payment—all the basics. Make sure your advantages are prominent.

Print Advertising—Newspapers and Magazines

Use print advertising, newspapers and magazines, if it is known to be effective for your type of business. This is a very expensive form of advertising. Only use it if you know that you have to place print ads in order to get the traffic you need. If this isn't clear to you, don't even experiment with print. But if your competitors are running advertising regularly in the newspaper, you need to at least investigate it as a source. Keep in mind that most print advertising is not very strong on direct response. This is particularly true of magazines. When you advertise in print, you may never know how effective the ad is unless it is the only advertising you are doing.

When was the last time you ran to a newspaper or magazine to find a source for something you needed to buy? What was the product or service? A movie? A tire sale? A couch? A used car? Most print advertising is not direct. A good deal of it is image advertising, designed to reinforce and work with other forms of marketing. If you have products or services that belong to a category that people go to a newspaper to find, then newspaper advertising may work, but don't hold your breath. Print advertising is not effective as a single source of marketing unless you run a restaurant or movie theater.

A significant exception to this rule is special-interest magazines and trade publications. A magazine for fly fishermen can be a very strong and direct advertising source for those who produce flies or other related fishing equipment. Many enthusiasts comb their magazines for products. The same is true for many trade magazines. Businesses will often respond directly to the advertisements in their trade magazines, and they will often keep the annual trade sourcebooks all year long and refer to them just as a consumer refers to the yellow pages. The real advantage to using a print medium that produces direct response is that you can track the results to find out if the business you received from the ad warrants the cost.

Radio

Like print, radio only works for certain types of products or services. Radio is very good for events, national products, insurance, real estate, fast food, cars, and large consumer goods. One of the advantages is that you can do some demographic targeting, based on the station's format. For example, it can help you point your advertising to men who are ages twenty-five to thirty-five and at a particular income level. This kind of demographic focus is usually only meaningful if you sell consumer products to a large audience—good for Wal-Mart, but not so good for a clowning business or a management consultant. If you produce events, radio can be very effective.

If you do try radio, don't worry too much about the production of your advertisement. Most stations will produce an ad for you, using the voice of one of their on-air personalities. The on-air voices work very well to give credibility to your ad. The station will also help you write the ad to make it appropriate for a listening audience, which means heavy repetition of dates, times, and phone numbers. You can spend hundreds of dollars for an agency or production company to write and produce an ad that will pull no better than the simple read of a trusted on-air voice.

Television

Even with the inexpensive alternative of cable, television is by far the most expensive form of advertising; it is also the least effective for targeting your customers. There are few home businesses that produce products that can benefit from the high exposure and high expense of television. Buying the time is only part of your expense. Production costs for television are extremely high. With television, there is no inexpensive route like radio's on-air voice; every ad on television costs a fortune to produce. And for all this expense, television is still an indirect and untargeted medium. If television is applicable for your business, you will need to get professionals involved in the production and placement to make sure your money is not wasted.

Outdoor Advertising

Outdoor advertising can include billboards, bus panels, public benches, or any other surface that inventive advertising professionals dream up. The Dallas-Fort Worth Airport sells the vertical panels on its escalators. Like radio and television broadcasts, outdoor advertising reaches a wide range of viewers and does not work well for targeting potential customers. The only targeting you can do is by neighborhood. Plus, it cannot be easily measured for results. Outdoor ads work best for retail and events or in conjunction with other forms of advertising, such as a roofer who also advertises heavily in the yellow pages. There are few home businesses that can utilize outdoor advertising efficiently.

If you decide to test outdoor advertising, do it out of your discretionary budget and not as a main source for reaching customers. You can pick out a billboard that seems appropriate and call the owner; the owner's name will usually be posted at the bottom of the board. You can work directly with the board owner to develop your message, get it produced, and put it up. Take the owner's direction on your message. Outdoor ads are very limited, since most people view them as they are driving by and cannot focus carefully. A good outdoor message is quick to read, uncluttered, and easy to grasp.

Specialty Advertising

Sometimes I think the specialty advertising industry exists only because of the persistence of its brilliant networking sales force. All over the country, business owners give in to the pitch from their next-door neighbor who sells trinkets from a colorful catalog, thinking, "Oh, why not. I have to buy pens anyway, so why shouldn't I buy some with our name on them." Specialty advertising is the vanity side of the advertising industry. It is such a soft ad buy that its salespeople never enter into a discussion of advertising reach, return, or tracking. My guess is that most specialty ad buys come out of the office supplies budget rather than marketing.

In short, specialty advertising is a range of products, including pens, baseball caps, T-shirts, coffee mugs, even peanuts, that have your company logo and phone number printed on the side. If you choose to go this route, don't list it in your advertising budget. Specialty advertising is not a vehicle for reaching customers and selling them on the quality of your products or services. If you buy specialty advertising items, take the expense from the same budget you use for your business cards or stationery—and don't expect it to bring you any additional customers. At best, specialty advertising will contribute very softly to name recognition and remind some of your current or past customers that you exist.

Choosing Your Advertising—Points to Consider

1. Develop an advertising budget, then stay within that budget. If you want to experiment, leave room in your budget for testing, but don't exceed your ad budget unless you decide the budget is too small. If so, create a new budget and stay within its limits.

2. Before you spend much on advertising experiments, find out how your successful competitors are advertising and work with their models. Don't begin experimenting until you have the basic tools that work in place.

3. Track all of your business to find out what source of advertising produces sales. You won't be effective with your ad dollars unless you know where every customer heard about you.

Chapter 22

Direct Marketing—An Expensive but Effective Targeted Pitch

Direct marketing includes direct mail, the Internet, and scores of other alternate marketing methods that are characterized by the ability to reach customers directly and to track the exact results of the marketing effort. Direct marketing is expensive in most cases, but it gives accurate feedback. You don't have to spend any time wondering what's working and what's not. Not all products and services lend themselves to this direct approach, but if your business can use direct marketing, you can learn a great deal about who your customers are, which offers work best, what prices are most effective, and which of your products are strongest. You can even test a new product's acceptance before you create it.

The most common form of direct marketing is direct mail. Some call it junk mail, but direct-mail advocates say it's only junk if it goes to the wrong person. Other forms of direct marketing include ride-alongs (the ads you get in your credit-card bills), coupon books (filling your mailbox), door hangers (the pizza offer on your doorknob), and even telemarketing (the long-distance phone industry). All these forms of advertising share the ability to select recipients by gender, age, income level, neighborhood, profession, personal interests, willingness to buy through the mail, and dozens of other qualifiers.

You can go to a list broker and ask for a group of women

doctors between the ages of thirty-five and forty-five who have purchased from a catalog in the past six months, own a cellular phone, subscribe to at least five consumer magazines, own a home computer, have an annual income of over $100,000, and live within fifty miles of Seattle. You can ask for either home or office address, and you can request their phone numbers for a follow-up call after you send along a mail package. The power of direct marketing is your ability to target, to pinpoint, your customers.

The cost per prospect is vastly greater than print, radio, or even television, but with those forms of advertising, up to 95 percent of the people you reach are not likely to be interested in your product. With direct marketing, you can come close to making sure that 95 percent are very interested in your product. When you calculate the cost of actually reaching someone who is interested in your product, direct marketing may be less expensive than the broader forms of advertising. Plus, with direct marketing you can test different mail packages to find the right combination of offer and price that turns prospects into customers.

Direct marketing works well for many home enterprises. It can be effective for cleaning services, yard work, consultants, network marketers, commercial janitorial services, clowns— virtually any service for homes or businesses. Different forms of direct marketing will work for different services. For yard work, door hangers may be more effective than direct mail. For commercial ground maintenance, direct mail with telephone follow-up is effective. These differences can be determined through experimenting, since direct marketing lends itself to testing.

Many direct-marketing practitioners believe that testing should never end because the market is always changing and there is always a fair chance that, by testing, you will come across new direct efforts that beat your best previous efforts. Once you get an understanding of how your competitors have successfully used direct marketing and begin to make it work for yourself, you can do it without the help of a professional. Very few companies that successfully use direct marketing also use an agency. You may use both a list broker to help search for appropriate prospect lists and a consultant to design a test package, but once you get your program in place, you can run it yourself. But first, you have to learn the direct-marketing basics.

Facts About the Direct-Mail Business

Before you set out on your direct-marketing journey, learn some of the basics. Your community may have classes in direct marketing. These are more likely to be taught through a community college or continuing education program, than your university's business school. Practical marketing is not often presented on the university level, but that is just as well, since it's best to learn from a practitioner rather than an academician. The best direct-marketing teachers are those who are in the trenches all day long. Many of these teachers are also available for consulting if you need some help in putting together your initial programs.

You can also learn a great deal about direct marketing through books. This form has become so widespread that you can now find books on direct marketing at most well-stocked bookstores, such as Border Books or Barnes and Noble. You can also learn about direct marketing through Internet sites, but the information on the Web is fragmented. A thorough book is the best place to start unless your area has a good class. Unlike most forms of advertising, direct marketing really can be taught in a book, since examples of direct-mail packages can be illustrated and explained.

The Direct Marketing Association (DMA) also presents conferences that offer expert advice on the latest developments in direct marketing by leading practitioners. The DMA also offers seminars year-round in the New York City area. Even if you are not able to attend DMA programs, the association offers a range of learning aids to help you develop skills in direct marketing. In addition to all these sources of information, there are two or three direct-marketing trade magazines that are free to those who qualify. You can meet their qualifications if you are actively using direct marketing as a significant portion of your marketing.

By using these resources to learn about direct marketing, you can quickly gain enough information to begin testing ways to reach customers and bring them to your business. As you continue to study the field and apply the techniques you learn, you will become a direct-marketing expert on your own business. The beauty of direct marketing is that you only have to learn about the efforts that are successful for your business. In general advertising, you have to be well-rounded to effectively grasp how advertising functions. With direct marketing, all you have to learn is what works for your company.

Types of Direct Marketing

Direct marketing comes in a number of forms. Direct mail is the version that is most prevalently used, but the other forms of direct marketing share direct mail's qualities of targeting and measurability. Here is a quick description of some common types of direct marketing.

Direct Mail

We are all familiar with direct mail since we receive so much of it. The hallmark of direct mail is that you create an opportunity for your customers to consummate a sale without their visiting a store or contacting you by phone or mail. Many companies do all their business using this method. The customer receives an offer and the customer buys. Catalogs work this way, as do magazines, book publishers, correspondence schools, and a slew of other products and services.

Some direct-mail programs require a second step, for example, the yard-maintenance company that sends an offer for a discounted first visit. The direct-mail package sells the visit, but the customer must call to make the yard-care appointment. Most home businesses that use direct mail require a call to complete the transaction. Seminar presenters, accountants, house- or carpet-cleaning services, lube services, and a wide range of other products and services are sold by enticing customers or clients to a call.

A direct-mail program can be as simple as a letter or as complicated as a Publishers Clearing House package. The package has a clear goal: Get a customer to buy the product and/or service or to make the phone call. Usually the copy is loaded with words, such as *free, now, special offer, don't miss,* and *winner,* that are designed to get the recipient to act. Some companies create their direct-mail packages by finding a mailing they like and copying its salient elements. This can be a way of saving on the expense of using a consultant as long as you make enough changes in the package so it is not a recognizable use of the original. If you take this inexpensive and effective route, make sure you choose a package that is selling a product or service similar to yours and is successful.

Ride-Alongs

When a noncompetitor of yours is mailing to the same people you need to reach, you have the opportunity to test a ride-along program. Ride-alongs include such things as the credit-card offer you receive in your record-club monthly mailing. They offer a huge savings, since they only cost a fraction of the expense of sending the same offer to the same consumer as a stand-alone. If you know of a noncompeting mailer that is already sending packages to the same prospects you need to reach, call and find out if they are willing to include your brochure or flyer. You can also find comailers through professional brokers. You will find these brokers advertising in *Direct* or *DM News.* These brokers are also listed in the materials you will receive with a membership in the DMA.

Ride-alongs work both ways. If your stand-alone package is large enough, you may be able to include other noncompeting mailers in your envelope. I used to do regular mailings with four ride-alongs. The total revenue from the ride-alongs paid for all my costs on the package, making my effort free. All I did was make a few phone calls to noncompetitors who needed to reach the same people my mailing was going to. The comailers who received a good response stayed with me for future mailings; those who didn't dropped off. Direct mailers are usually ready to test any reasonably good idea.

The disadvantage of ride-alongs is that the response is considerably lower than with stand-alone mailings. But the beauty of direct marketing is measurement: You take your reduced costs and compare them with your reduced response and calculate your cost per sale over your profit per sale to determine whether the ride-along is a good source of customers. If it is, you repeat and keep calculating your response versus cost. If it's not productive, you're down the road to the next test.

Coupon Books

We all receive local-retailer coupon books in the mail. You can hire franchises that put these books together. If you have the right kind of business, then you may participate in these books. They are fairly inexpensive, but they only work for certain types of retailers. Take a close look at a number of previous books before you test this source. If you don't see a business similar to yours included, approach this source with caution. The types of retailers that succeed with coupon books include pizza restaurants, food stores, video-rental shops, dry cleaners, carpet and home cleaners, and pet groomers. Usually the offer is a generous discount. For most retailers, the coupon book is used to take business from a competitor, so the discount needs to be very attractive.

Door Hangers

If you want to get your printed material to a home without going through the postal service, you are not allowed to use the mailbox. Door hangers are an alternative to the U.S. Postal Service. You can either prepare a door-hanging offer and send out a crew yourself or use one of the services in your community that places bags of offers on residences. Like ride-alongs, going into a bag with other retailers will hurt your response, but it will also cost you much less. It may be worth testing both methods to see which one is most cost-effective. Marketing through door hangings work best with types of services homeowners need, such as house painting, yard maintenance, handyman or fix-it, pet grooming, and house sitting.

Telemarketing

We all hate to get telemarketing calls, but they continue for one reason—they work. There are two different kinds of telephone sales: One is telemarketing, which is direct marketing over the phone; the other is conventional selling, with the phone as your tool of contact. Conventional selling over the telephone is covered in the next chapter. Telemarketing is a whole different matter. Telemarketing, like all direct marketing, is a tool for targeting customers and consummating a sale during that contact. It is usually done on a mass scale, using phone scripts designed to overcome objections and move to the close. The service is usually provided by telemarketing companies that charge by the call.

Similar to direct mail, with telemarketing you buy lists of phone numbers based on consumer demographics and buying habits. Telemarketing is one of the most expensive forms of direct marketing, and it only works for a small range of products, including magazine renewals, book clubs, long-distance telephone services, fund-raising, and financial services. Most of these do not apply to a home business. The telemarketing companies usually contract only large jobs, and effective telemarketing is not feasible as an in-house operation.

However, there is an abbreviated version of telemarketing that is frequently utilized by home-business service companies— appointment setting. If you offer services as a management consultant, tax accountant, insurance agent, financial consultant, or real estate agent, you can hire someone to make calls to consumers or business owners. The caller qualifies the prospect over the phone and sets up an appointment for you to visit and explain your services. You can have a caller do this from her home, using a short and simple script. You pay your caller by the hour with a small bonus for every appointment that she sets up, and an additional small bonus for each sale you make.

Lists and More Lists

They say the three most important elements for retail success are location, location, and location. The three most important elements of direct-marketing success are lists, lists, and lists. In the good old days before I entered the direct-mail business, an average response to a direct-mail effort was 5 percent. By the time I started using this form of marketing in the mid-1980s,

2.5 percent was great. By the early 1990s, I struggled to reach 2 percent; in the late 1990s, 1.5 percent is respectable. This continual deterioration of response makes list selection ever more important. You can no longer put together a dynamite package and watch it work over a wide selection of lists. Now, you need a great package and a great list.

Buying lists is like buying airline tickets; you use a list broker the same way you use a travel agent. The broker gets paid a commission on the list orders you place. You don't have to pay the broker for his services. The list broker is more than just someone to negotiate the purchase of a mailing or phone list; he is a marketing consultant who can help you determine which lists to test and who suggests effective ways to test those lists. All this consulting comes at no direct expense to you.

When you work with a list broker, he will give you information on a variety of lists on the market that are likely to work for your product or service. The information he provides will include the size of the list, the cost per 1,000 names, the source of the list (magazine subscribers, catalog buyers), demographic information, and some buying habits. As with a travel agent, any list that is on the market is available to your list broker, so don't bother going through list catalogs. You can find list brokers by combing the ads in *Direct* or *DM News,* or by going through the resources that come with a DMA membership. It is best to shop for a list broker nationally rather than going through your local yellow pages.

Database Marketing

Another form of direct marketing is the use of your own collection of names as a source of future sales. When you gain a name through direct marketing, you usually save it on your computer. The name may come from someone who requested information but didn't buy, or it could be a customer who has repeatedly bought from you. This collection of names is called a database; you probably have this database segmented by category of prospects (those who inquired but didn't buy), new customers, and repeat customers. You may also have these names gathered by the type of product or service they bought.

You probably have this list on your computer in an inexpensive file-management program, such as File Maker Pro, which offers a wide range of selection options. If you have all this, you have a customer database. If you don't already have this database, think seriously about creating one. There is very likely gold in those names, and it is just waiting to be mined. The way to use your database is to remind your existing customers to continue to use your products or services and to announce both new versions of old products and altogether new products. If you are an accountant, you may use your database of current customers, past customers, and "almost" customers to test their interest in the services of estate planning for tax avoidance. If your file is segmented by age, this test could be particularly effective.

This type of product and service testing, using your customer names, can be done by most home enterprises. A dog groomer could test a program of pickup and delivery for a 20 percent premium, or free if the customer agrees to a regular schedule of grooming. A lawn-care company could test the viability of a tree-pruning and -planting service. House-cleaning services can test upholstery and blind cleaning. A janitorial service can test the addition of an office plant-and aquarium-maintenance program. Your database can be a source of testing additional products or services. If the test is successful, you can take your database profile and market your new service to non-customers. You can then take the new customers you gain for your new service and cross-sell them your traditional services.

All this takes is the ability to imagine related services that extend from your core business. Janitorial services know their customers would probably prefer that their plants and aquariums be maintained by a crew they already trust and who would take care of the servicing in the evening when it would not be disruptive to business. The same goes for window cleaning. Using your database to promote this related service is a way of testing the new service on a larger scale than just your present customers, without the expense of an outside marketing effort. If the database test proves successful, you know that it is worth the risk to invest in aggressive marketing. If the database test is not successful, you have tested a product or service extension at little cost.

The Internet

Until very recently, the Internet would not have been considered a direct-marketing source. Spam e-mail certainly doesn't rise to the level of effective direct marketing, but changes in Web-site marketing techniques that appeared in the late 1990s constitute wise and effective direct marketing. They go beyond well-targeted e-mail into the segmenting strategies of database marketing blended with affinity sales. ("Would you like fries with that order?") The visitors to your Web site can create a quick pool of names that work like a database to test new products and services.

Beginning in 1999, a number of software companies introduced programs to help Web stores track buyer patterns and test affinity products. These software programs help the Web owners develop programs for their Web visitors and customers. The Web site offers to provide regular updates on the subject matter to the visitors in the form of regular e-mail correspondence on a daily, weekly, or monthly basis. These e-mails contain subject content and product offers. A fly-fishing Web site can entice its visitors to receive fly-fishing tips twice each week. Along with the tips, the customers receive promotions on new lures, reels, and rods.

Using this push technology that blends direct e-mail with database marketing and affinity marketing, the Web site can continually test new offers and products with a base of interested consumers at very little cost. You can even test product interest before you create and deliver the products. If there is market acceptance for the product, you will obtain orders and begin purchasing the products for resale. If there is no interest, you pass the orders to a manufacturer for fulfillment and cease promoting the product. This virtual testing lets you test any product your customers could possibly want at very little expense.

Direct marketing is expensive, but it is also measurable. As long as you can measure the dollars spent against the dollars received, you can decide which direct-marketing efforts are worth keeping and which ones need to be dropped.

Choosing Direct Marketing—Points to Consider

1. If you do not already have direct-marketing experience, learn as much as you can through books and magazines before using this form of advertising. A poor direct-marketing letter can destroy the response of an otherwise good package or list.

2. As with general advertising, study your competitors. If they repeatedly use the same packages, it is probably because they are effective. Be careful with your experiments; tailor them to your business. For lawn-care services, door hangers work while direct mail is more expensive and less effective.

3. Remember, in direct marketing you are always selling benefits and asking for the order. Over and over, tell them what they'll get and ask them to buy.

Chapter 23

Sales—The Personal Persuasion

For some businesses, persuasive selling is the most effective way to gain customers. This is true of network marketing and most professional services, such as investment counseling, advertising sales, and management consulting. Often this type of selling can be enhanced by seminars and presentations. Much like direct marketing, sales bring you continual feedback. If your product or service mix isn't right for your prospect, you find out immediately. There is a variety of ways to sell. The same techniques that work to sell an advertising program will not necessarily work to sell janitorial services to an office complex property manager. You will become efficient and effective in your selling when you learn the techniques that work best with your potential customers.

You don't have to try every selling technique to learn what's best for you. One of the first things you can do to set up your sales effort is watch what your successful competition is doing to bring in customers. If they are successful, chances are their sales techniques work. Try those strategies first; work on improving those strategies once you have a flow of business coming your way. I did some marketing consulting with a home remodeler. The owner had started his own company after working as sales manager for the city's leading remodeler. Once he was out on his own, he didn't use any of the leader's sales techniques, believing he was more likely to succeed by using different strategies. His business floundered.

When I came on the scene, I examined his ineffective sales strategies and asked what the common techniques were for remodelers. He explained what the leader was doing and said, "But we need to be different."

"Why?" I asked.

"Because they are already doing it."

"Who cares!" I exclaimed. "Let's try it."

Needless to say, the techniques that were being used by the leader were successful for my client. His business picked itself up off the ground. When I'm working with any company on its marketing, the first question I always ask is, "What strategies are the winners using?" That's the place to start. Once you have implemented a successful program, then get innovative. If you start right out with experiments, you may not gain a solid foundation of business before your start-up dollars run out. Until you are on your feet, steal from the winners.

One-On-One Sales Calls

Eyeball-to-eyeball sales meetings are not as common now. People are busier than they used to be. They are also more accustomed to technology, so the sales visit is usually used only when your client is very interested. In the mid-1980s, you couldn't sell a magazine advertisement without paying a personal visit. You didn't even try to sell by mail or on the phone. You only used the phone to set up the appointment. Now you can't get the appointment, so you have to sell by phone and mail or you're stuck. Not all industries have changed so dramatically, but most have moved away from sales calls as the primary way to sell products and services.

Just as time is valuable for your prospects, it is also dear to you. So you shouldn't even try to get an appointment unless your prospect is well qualified and there is a reasonably good chance of getting a sale. As you make your calls, always measure your rate of converting visits into sales to make sure face-to-face selling is worth the time. The average sales call takes two hours and fifteen minutes from the time you leave your office until you return. For some businesses, you can keep that time down, but even if you are nearby, a sales call consumes a great deal of time. With some products and services, it simply cannot be avoided, but save the visits for the likely sales and not for prospecting. Use the phone for prospecting and qualifying before you make sales calls.

Also, make the most of your sales calls by always moving toward the close. You don't have to rush by asking for the sale before it's clear that your prospect is ready, but you need to be aware of moving things forward at all points in the conversation, even if you are talking lightly. At all times, keep in mind that you are there to help your prospect; your product or service will help fill a need. You should spend most of your time asking about your client's need rather than talking about your products or services.

If you provide grounds maintenance, spend the meeting discussing the prospect's grounds rather than discussing your background. Once you have a thorough understanding of your client's needs, it will be easy to explain how you can solve these needs with your high-quality services at a fair price. There is no reason to begin talking about your services until you have a complete understanding of your client's needs. All through the meeting, you should remember you are not there to sell your grounds maintenance; you are there to offer solutions to the property manager's need for quality services. You have already determined that your services are a good match for this prospect's needs or you would not have asked for an appointment.

Telephone Selling

Telephone selling has become a very acceptable way to develop a customer, since meetings are no longer the predominant way to sell. This is especially true now that more companies sell throughout the country. Phone selling can be used to build a relationship and develop consultative sales. Your clients actually prefer it since it saves time and can complete a great deal of the sales process.

There are tricks to making phone sales work from home. For one thing, if you are alone on the phone, it is difficult to ask someone to call you back since most likely he will not find the line clear. You need to ask your prospect's receptionist when an appropriate time to call will be. Then you can leave a message saying you will call at a certain time. This is assuming you have already established a rapport. If you are making an introductory call, you should try again later rather than leaving a message.

Forget call waiting. Even if you choose to ignore an incoming call, your customer will be very distracted by the clicking. If you put your customer on hold to get the incoming call, you can expect your customer's mood will have changed during the break. At this point, you are no longer carrying the call. No amount of apologies will earn you back the lead in the conversation. Choose voice messaging instead. People are far less put off by voice messaging; most people have fully accepted it.

Since you are not meeting your customer in person, you have to put more effort into learning her needs and personality. Some people never warm up on the phone, while others drift into time-consuming chitchat. During a personal meeting, you can fill in blanks by observing body language and office furnishings. Over the phone, you can easily misread your prospect's intentions and hot buttons. The best solution is to learn as much as possible about your customer's company and its purchasing habits beforehand. Without being able to observe the surroundings, you will have to ask more questions.

Always state the reason for the call in your first sentence. Even if your call is exploratory in nature, make a positive statement, such as, "We have a program coming up that is designed to take care of your needs in this area, but I want to clarify your exact needs so I can send along a detailed proposal that really makes sense." At this point you have stated your purpose, and you can begin gathering valuable information without coming across as vague and prying.

Do not fear voice messaging; it's your friend. Some people leave voice messaging on to avoid interruptions. Make sure every voice message takes you a step further. Introduce yourself and state your purpose. Then say something to the effect of, "I just need to ask you two quick questions to find out if this is an appropriate time in your budget process to consider new equipment. I'll try again tomorrow around 10 a.m. If that time doesn't work for you, please let me know a better time." Chances are the person will get back to you or will be available at 10 a.m. Now you are obligated to keep your end of the bargain and make your questions quick.

Sales Letters

Strong sales letters have not gone out of style. In some sales situations, there is nothing that can beat a well-written letter. When you want to explain how your products or services will fill a prospect's needs and to present the argument in a logical and compelling manner without leaving any aspect of the case to a give-and-take phone call or sales visit, a letter can be the perfect tool. With a letter, you can explain exactly how your service will work to fill a prospect's needs and give all of the supporting information, piece by convincing piece.

Always focus on your customer, not your product. Don't rave about your company's service, talk about your customer's needs. Make yourself an understanding listener. If you communicate real understanding of his problems, your credibility grows. It is simple: If you truly understand the problem or challenge, then your proposed solution has merit. If you cannot convince him that you understand his problem, how can you convince him that you are offering the best solution?

Use your letter to outline his challenge. After this is done in detail, begin to explain how your product meets his challenge. Don't worry about going on too long. He won't tire of reading about his problem and a solution to that problem. But if you spend any time talking about your product without relating it directly to his challenge, you will lose him.

Show your prospect the promised land, and do it in quick bullets. The process of explaining the problem is called "poking the bruise." Next, you need to offer comfort and resolution. Tell your prospect that it doesn't have to be this way; you have a solution. Outline that solution in quick readable bullets. Don't tell her about your product's features; talk about how it solves her problem. Offer a quick sketch of the solution at work, then give her the image of a well-solved problem.

The letter needs to be clearly personalized, without repeating the customer's name every two sentences like a computer letter. One of the best gauges of natural, personal language is reading the letter aloud. If your voice stumbles on a sentence, that sentence probably needs to be rewritten until it's smooth. If there is anything in the letter that is uncomfortable to read aloud, change it until you can read it in a very natural, relaxed voice. The best way to personalize a letter is simply to refer directly to the customer's predicament. Don't talk generically about your product or service. If you address the prospect's business needs in specifics, the letter will come across as personal.

Nobody wants another expense. But we all realize we need to invest in order to move forward. Make sure your letter makes this case. If the purchase is not an investment to move the business forward or solve an uncomfortable problem, then the purchase doesn't need to be made. Focus on the results of this purchase, positioning the purchase as an investment that will bring greater returns than the outlay. If you offer a payment plan that allows the customer to realize return even before the purchase price is fully paid, emphasize this leverage.

Close your letter with a very specific explanation of your next contact. Do not leave this ball in your customer's court. One good way is to mention that further information is on the way and that you will call at a certain time to answer any questions. This imposes an obligation to read your material, or at least to prepare for a decision. By sending another package of supporting material two days later, you remind your prospect that you intend to follow up. At the very least, this process will clear out a good number of the maybes.

Proposals

For some businesses, including consultants or anyone contracting for long-term projects (such as grounds maintenance, advertising agencies, and book publishing), the proposal is one of the major selling tools. Add to this list anyone who contracts with the government, be it federal, state, or city. If your selling process necessitates a detailed description of the services you will deliver and when they will be delivered, and if you also have to document why your company is best suited to deliver these services, then you will need to get very good at writing proposals.

Proposal writing is a skill; great proposal writing is a talent. One of the most important skills involved in writing effective proposals is the ability to write persuasively. You need to develop a command for the language that explains how well you know the project and how well your company can complete the services. If your writing is not strong, the reader will have doubts about how strong your services will be. A command of persuasive language can create the impression that you will also have a command of the project at hand.

This is not a false impression. Most professionals are competent writers. Most professionals who deliver excellence are more than competent writers. It isn't that writing comes naturally to those who are good consultants or excellent accountants, but people who strive to excel come to the realization that in order to present themselves as someone who can deliver high-quality work, they have to be able to communicate very well orally and with the written word, so they take the trouble to learn a command of both oral and written presentations. The trouble someone goes through to groom her communication skills comes through, and it fosters confidence. If you want to present yourself well in the context of proposals, get some training in writing. You can do this through seminars and continuing education classes.

The look of your proposal will vary from industry to industry. When you submit a proposal to a government office, it needs to be presented in a very plain manner. Plan proposals with compelling writing are acceptable in most professional situations, with a few exceptions. If you are proposing work as an ad agency or marketing consultant, some colorful examples of your past brochures and ad campaigns can be just as important as the writing in the proposal. But even in this case, the proposal has to be strong, and it has to hit all the hot buttons for the company that receives it.

The goal of a good proposal isn't to simply rave about the quality of your company's services; the goal is to make it appear that your company is logically and irrefutably the appropriate company to get this project. You make it look as if your company was born to get this bid, not because you're so great but because your company is just the right fit. You accomplish this by explaining all the aspects of the job at hand and showing, point by point, bullet by bullet, that your company can perform these tasks as well as or better than anyone else. You don't have to be the best around on every point; you only have to be the best around on the two or three points that make a difference on this particular job.

Every job has these two or three points of real contention. Find out what they are before you write your proposal. For grounds maintenance, the company you are proposing to may have had problems in the past with a contractor that was irregular in its visits, sent over uncouth workers, and left hedges untrimmed, even though its price was good and it did a great job with the lawn. Price will always have a strong bearing, but in this case, reliability, a professional team, and thoroughness will be strong points. Make sure you know what the spots of contention are before you write your proposal. Every job has these in one way or another.

Presentations

If you are bidding on a big project that requires a significant investment on the part of the organization you are pitching to, you may have to do a presentation. A presentation is a talk to a number of people involved in the purchase. You spend ten to thirty minutes explaining your view of the project, then answer questions for another ten to thirty minutes. If you are selling your marketing services to the Manufactured Housing Association for its annual exposition, which comes with a $125,000 advertising budget, you will probably have to make a presentation to the board after they have reviewed your proposal. Your portion of the $125,000 may only be $10,000 or $15,000, but through your recommendations, you will determine how the full budget will be spent.

Before the board members turn their purse over to you, they want to see you sing and dance. The presentation is a credibility test. Each individual board member wants to see for himself or herself that your proposal wasn't smoke and mirrors, that you really do have the knowledge and competence to spend the association's hard-gathered dollars. This isn't just formality, this is human nature. They are not going to turn over their money unless they individually get a gut feeling that you will do a commendable job for their association and that you won't make them look like fools.

By the time you get to the presentation, you have a good understanding of the project, you know who the leaders of the group are, and you know which members are the key members to convince. Be aware that in most groups there is always a buffoon, and the buffoon may be the one who seems most supportive. If you sell to this person, you'll lose the group. Find out who the credible leader is and sell to that person. It may be someone who hangs back quietly, but when this person asks a question, the whole room hangs on it. During the presentation, make eye contact with each member, but especially this opinion leader. If you win this person, you usually win the group.

You can often find out who this leader is before you get to the presentation by talking with the executive director or other members of the board you happen to know. You can't identify this person by title. It may be the president, but it could just as easily be the past president or treasurer. When you get enough experience in selling to groups, you will learn to identify this person while you are at the presentation and meeting everyone in the group for the first time. Usually this key leader will not be the one doing all the talking. But as you make your points—particularly when you get to a sensitive point—all eyes will turn quickly to the opinion leader. This is quick, then the eyes go right back to you; but now you know whom you are selling to.

As far as presentation effects, use what is customary for this group plus a touch extra. Don't go overboard with bells and whistles or risk a backfire. If they are used to overheads, don't bring a video, bring slides, a step up but still in the park. Keep the selling focused on the organization's needs as much as possible, explaining your strategy to ensure you'll surpass their goals. But don't overpromise. If you overpromise, you could fall below your promise while still exceeding their goals. Instead of being a hero, you look like a bum.

Also, don't be afraid to answer, "I really don't know. I'll have to get back to you about that." You can't have all the answers. You may get an unreasonable question that is thrown in just to test you. The danger here isn't that you will be stumped; the danger is that you will act as if you're not stumped even when you are. It's okay to be stumped (we all get stumped), but it's not okay to fake it when you're stumped. By the way, it is usually the opinion maker who throws out the stumper.

Using Sales Techniques—Points to Consider

1. One-on-one sales calls are very time-consuming. Use one-on-one sales if it is clearly the only effective way to consummate a sale in your profession or industry. If it can be done by phone, use the phone.

2. Telephone selling has become very effective. You have to be careful not to sound like a telemarketer. Use the phone to prospect, to initiate, and to further relationship selling.

3. In our busy world, sometimes the best way to get a prospect's attention is through a personal business letter with a follow-up call. Personal letters are so infrequent that they are becoming an attention-getting novelty, especially if they are truly personal and do not sound canned.

4. An effective way of selling is to research your customer's needs, send a personal business letter explaining how your product or service fills the needs, follow with a fact-finding phone call, and send out a proposal. This is effective if you are trying to establish an ongoing relationship.

Chapter 24

The Internet—Personal Contact With Millions

The fantastical growth of the Internet provides unbridled opportunity for entrepreneurs, especially since it has just barely started to grow as a place to do business. For the first few years after the Internet became popular, there were questions about whether consumers would ever overcome their reluctance to spend for goods and services online. During the Christmas season of 1998, consumer spending online had a surprising breakthrough. Before 1998, consumer spending online was below $2 billion, a speck on the nation's $5,130 billion in retail sales. But retail spending hit $4.8 billion for 1998 with the Christmas breakthrough. The average online company's increase was 270 percent for the year (these numbers come from Forrester Research in Cambridge, Massachusetts).

The growth is expected to continue. Retail sales are predicted to hit $17.2 billion by 2002—still just a speck, but a growing speck. But retail sales are just a portion of the story. In 1998, business-to-business sales were $8 billion, almost twice the amount of consumer business. And what's in store for business-to-business in 2002? Forrester Research predicts business sales will hit $327 billion in 2002. That's nothing; International Data Corp. projects $500 billion in business-to-business receipts for 2002. No, that's not a typo. The real story in online sales is those who are selling to business, not CD sales.

GE alone plans to spend $5 billion online in 2000 and 2001. Why? Because there is a big savings to be had by being online where purchase managers can get discounts from companies that don't have to maintain an outside sales crew for their online catalog. The sales crew comes with a heavy commissions price tag. Take the commissions away, and you can give some pretty hefty discounts. GE expects to save $500 million by making purchases over the Internet.

So where does that put your tiny home business on this exploding Internet map? It's an open game, but the wonder of the Internet is that the itsy-bitsy business tucked away in a spare bedroom in Vermont can look just as impressive on the Internet as any Fortune 500 monster. The online market is very democratic; you don't have to be an economic giant to wield the power of the technology that helps drive online sales. As long as you have the right products and services and are clever enough to reach customers, you can get your own thin slice of this magnificent pie.

E-Business Funding

In 1999, venture capitalists began pouring $300 million per month into Internet start-up companies. That constitutes over 30 percent of venture funds in online enterprises. And what are these venture capitalists looking for in a new company? Fancy offices? Principals in expensive, well-tailored suits? Seasoned businesspeople with two or three decades of experience in high-technology firms? Ph.D.s with degrees in computer technology? How about college dropouts in their early twenties working from home, maybe even mom and dad's home? These are people who may not be savvy enough to keep their clothes from clashing, but they have their fingers on the pulse of the Internet heartbeat.

Why on earth are the venture capitalists wooing such an untested crowd? Well, how about Amazon.com with a 1999 stock value of $21.4 billion—who had ever heard of this company in 1995? Try the auction company eBay with a stock value of $19 billion—who had heard of this company in 1997? Yahoo! with $35 billion! The list goes on all day. Even if the bubble pops and this group collapses by 50 percent, its gain is staggering. If you're a venture capitalist, how many of these long shots do you need to justify the investment? One out of 20? One out of 50? You can imagine the participants of venture capitalist funds asking their managers, "How come we're not in on this Internet thing?"

The investment dollars are not necessarily going to the team with the snazziest technology. Web technology is very contagious; as soon as it is introduced, technology speeds through the online world. It's like a bad cold traveling through an airline cabin. Everyone gets it. So there is no big interest in chasing the next technology. Consumers and businesses don't buy from the sites with the strongest technology. They buy from the sites that have the strongest online brand. That's online brand, not offline brand. Just ask Barnes and Noble as it desperately chases Amazon.com.

If you decide to stake your claim to some of this pile of venture dollars, keep in mind that they want to see a brand, not just a good idea. Don't try to dazzle them with all the bells and whistles that will drive your Web site. Everyone has the bells and whistles. You need to have a brand that will catch on with your customers. Your brand needs to be sharp, snazzy, irreverent, sassy, colorful, fun, and thorough. Want to know what's cool about Amazon.com? The fact that it's complete? No. Being complete is simply necessary. Amazon.com is cool because any idiot can search it effectively, and it lets you write a review and post it. It lets authors write comments about their own books and post them. It tells you what additional books were purchased by others who purchased this book. It suggests other books you might like if you like this one. Amazon.com is a fun place to visit.

Venture capitalists want to see these elements in the proposals they review for Internet launches. They also expect you to know a great deal more about the Internet and online culture than they do. If they begin to get the idea that you are less aware of what is happening online than they are, their eyes will begin to glaze over. They are willing to put up with inexperienced businesspeople with great online ideas for one reason only: The venture capitalists believe these new, young Internet entrepreneurs are more in touch with the market than anyone else. If that's you, and if you have a cool idea for a brand, then you may have a chance to get funded.

E-Mail Marketing

It didn't take long for e-mail marketing to get a bad reputation. It will take years before e-mail recipients will trust e-mail marketing again. If the reader doesn't recognize the sender, zap. Direct postal mail still works because, contrary to popular belief, most people actually look at their junk mail. Not true for e-mail. But who cares if you can send out a gazillion e-mail messages for little more than a computer click? This indiscriminate and crass use of e-mail has poisoned the waters for legitimate direct marketers who would really like to send a message to people who are interested in their products and services.

So forget blind e-mail. There is an alternative that is becoming effective. It's called push marketing, based on push technology. The concept centers on waiting for the consumer to make the first move. Web-site owners invite their visitors and customers to receive information on new developments in the subject of the site. Music Blvd., one of the largest sites selling music CDs, did this by creating My Music Blvd. in late 1998. The Web site invited its customers and visitors to sign up to receive notices of new releases, reviews, online interviews, and online concerts by their favorite artists.

Music Blvd. originally designed this program for customer retention. It wanted to make sure its customers wouldn't drift away. But as it turned out, visitors signed up as well, and a good portion of these visitors became customers. When visitors to the Web site sign up for My Music Blvd., they can choose to receive notices daily, weekly, or monthly. They can choose artists and categories of music. The updates come to the participants as e-mail messages with hypertext click-throughs that take the recipient to an online concert, interview, or to Music Blvd. itself if the recipient wants more information on a new CD release.

The wonder of this push marketing is that the recipient welcomes the e-mail since she recognizes its source and remembers requesting the information. When Music Blvd. sends along discount offers, the recipient doesn't automatically delete the message; after all, the communication was invited. To provide the considerable content for the program, Music Blvd. teamed up with some music-content providers. When customers click on the note about the tour dates for the latest Rolling Stones tour, they go right to a content provider who offers this content regularly. The content provider is happy to receive this flow of qualified visitors, and Music Blvd. doesn't have to go into the content-providing business. It's a clever concept that benefits all participants: the music lover, Music Blvd., and the music-content providers.

Music Blvd. was one of the first companies to provide this service for its customers. Within two months, this marketing concept was widely available across the Internet. It has been a successful way of using e-mail as a marketing tool. Originally designed to keep customers, it also works to capture new customers. This is quickly becoming the new model for successful Web sites. Internet technology allows you to use direct-marketing techniques of targeting and apply them to a mass audience. A program like My Music Blvd. lets you send individual messages to millions of recipients simultaneously.

Web Sites

While Web-site owners twiddled their thumbs waiting for consumers to get up the nerve to type their credit-card numbers into their computers, they developed some effective ways of communicating with their customers to encourage commerce. Some of the experiments tried by various Web sites have been gathered together by software companies to sell as packages to Web stores. As of 1999, these packages have not been available at a reasonable price for the small entrepreneur, but like all other software products, it's just a matter of time before the merchandising tricks contained in these software packages become widespread and inexpensive.

Blue Martini Software in San Mateo, California, was one of a number of software producers to develop Web-based products to help Web stores make the most of their customers and visitors. At the beginning of the Internet explosion, the focus was on getting people to come to your site, but after a few years of watching 30,000 people breeze in and out of Web sites with a "just looking" online attitude, the focus turned to converting a portion of these visitors to customers. Blue Martini Software's e-merchandising software is designed to analyze customer preferences and product affinities for Fortune 1000 Web sites.

What does this mean? This is the "Do you want fries with your order?" equivalent for Web stores. The software manages the Web store and its merchandising processes to identify what customers really want and to cross-sell them additional merchandise. Using this software, the Web site can electronically ask the suit buyer whether she needs any accessories. It is called micromarketing, but it is actually just a program that greets the customer and makes sure he doesn't forget to buy new socks and underwear as long as he is here buying pants.

The beauty of these programs is that they remember their customers' preferences for a long, long time. When was the last time your shoe retailer called you up on the phone and said, "Well, it's been seven months since you bought those running shoes. In the past, you have run through your shoes in about eight months, so we thought you might be ready to consider a new pair. By the way, we know you like the light air-filled crosstrainers, and we just received a newly designed version that gives you increased durability without increased weight. Just thought you'd like to know." That's the magic of the Internet: an electronic robot retailer that knows your preferences better than your mom does.

A Wide Eye to the Future

The next wave of innovations that will expand Internet commerce is probably already cooking on some small sites few of us know about. Once the word gets out about these new commerce tricks, within a few very quick weeks, every Web site will be utilizing their devices, their software, their attitudinal effects. This is why you can't interest investors with e-commerce tricks. But you can look for ways to deliver your brand in an effective manner. The Internet isn't a medium for creating new products or services; it's a medium for communicating about existing products and services.

The future of Internet commerce will continue to be tied to

existing merchandise. Take a look at the major successful Web sites such as Amazon.com, eBay, and 1/800-FLOWERS. Take a look at the successful categories such as travel agencies, office supplies, and catalogs. They all share one thing in common: They offer traditional merchandise and services in a more convenient and less expensive manner. So, for all the innovation on the Internet, all that is really going on in commerce is the same old products and services sold faster and cheaper. The Internet offers a great step forward with its research capabilities and the convenience of e-mail, but research and e-mail are virtually free.

There will come a time when the Internet begins to offer new products and services that are endemic to the Internet. This will probably not begin until the Internet comes through a bandwidth that allows for images and sound that equal or surpass our current CD players and televisions. Then, there may be a chance that the Internet will offer young entrepreneurs a playground to develop new forms of entertainment and education. For now, the Internet brings us new ways to shop for and purchase items that are already available through traditional channels. The winners in the short run will be those who continue to use the Internet to improve on the shopping and ordering of traditional consumer and business goods and services.

Doing Business on the Internet—Points to Consider

1. If you are launching an online company, you will find investors are much more interested than they used to be. They are also likely to be comfortable with the fact that your business is run from a home.

2. Pay attention to the development of *permission marketing* online. With this marketing, you invite Web site visitors to receive information, including product and service information, from you.

3. It is worth the time and attention to subscribe to one of the Internet marketing publications listed in the resource section at the end of the book. Follow the online marketing trends for ideas on how to grow your company.

Chapter 25

Networking—Meeting Your Customers Socially

Networking has become a well-accepted and effective way of marketing a variety of business services and consumer products. The kinds of business positions that can be marketed effectively through networking include those that depend most heavily on establishing an ongoing business relationship. These include real estate agents, marketing or management consultants, travel agents, financial-service brokers, accountants, attorneys, and any other professional who needs to communicate credibility through interaction and participation in groups and associations.

You do not necessarily have to network in a professional group, as long as you can gain personal trust through the networking opportunity. If you and an accountant are both members of a board of directors for a nonprofit group, you may decide to use the accountant to do your business taxes without any direct experience with the accountant's work. You know and trust the accountant by virtue of your common interest and commitment to the group you serve. This is the magic of networking. It allows you to develop business relationships based on personal trust rather than professional inquiry.

Networking opportunities are around us all the time. I know a real estate broker who rides with cops. He is part of my city's volunteer police officers' group. Mike started riding along with cops before he entered the real estate business. He is known and respected among police officers, and when one of them needs a real estate agent, they call on Mike because they know him and because he knows and understands their needs. He never intended to use his association with the police as a networking opportunity for his real estate business, but it has become a significant source of new clients, not because they can tell he's a great agent when he's riding with them but because they know they can trust him to be a truthful representative for them in a business where trustworthiness is crucial.

Marketing through networking is not an opportunity to show off your abilities in your profession. Networking gives you the chance to develop personal relationships and establish personal credibility. People will choose to do business with you because they know you and feel that you will "steer them straight." Networking works both ways: As well as meeting potential clients, you will also meet potential vendors, suppliers, and partners. The same volunteer cop hired a builder to construct his 4,000-square-foot custom home. And where did he meet this builder? They served together on the board of a local church.

What constitutes a networking opportunity? The answer is any association that fosters trust and gives you the opportunity to meet people who are potential clients. If you offer a service that is common to most people, such as real estate or insurance, even your neighbors provide networking opportunities. If your services are more specific, such as subcontracting granite stonework for kitchens and bathrooms, your networking may be limited to your state general contractor's association, in which case it behooves you to get very involved in the association, and take a leadership role if possible. If a leadership role is not likely, then get very involved in high-exposure volunteer activities, such as the member-development committee.

With a little practice and the right attitude, networking is not work at all. It's fun and it can quickly become part of your recreation and social time. The trick is to choose networking opportunities that appeal to you personally. If you are limited in your choices for networking, then try to find activities within the groups that appeal to you. The granite subcontractor mentioned above may choose to form a golfing event with the contractors as a charity project. If you can have fun in the context of your networking, it will seem natural and you will be more effective than if you view it as a necessary part of work.

For some professions, networking is the primary form of marketing. Some insurance agents and real estate professionals join a range of associations and groups to meet people and gain trust. One of these professionals may be part of six to ten organizations. My brother is a mortgage banker. He is a member of the chamber of commerce, the Rotary, the Elks, a church, a marketing group, the school board, and various other groups that come and go. He also plays on a softball team and is on a bowling team. Most of his lunches are taken up with club obligations. He enjoys it greatly. He also knows it is a big reason that his business is successful.

Association and Group Involvement

It isn't enough to join an organization and sit at a back table during dinner meetings. Networking is most effective if you participate in the group. The real relationships are formed and grow when you work with people on committees and on boards. And don't worry about it being difficult to get involved. Every organization on earth is struggling to get more volunteers. The membership committee always needs more members. It is also an excellent place for networking since you get to meet new people, and the people you meet will not view you as a newcomer to the association. To the new member, you are the association.

I know professionals who evaluate their networking results when it's time to renew a membership in an organization. Unless your group attendance mirrors a personal interest, such as a church or a specific activity (such as the riding-with-cops real estate agent), you may have to judge your participation based on the results. Give the organization a real chance first. I remember a time I headed my state's chapter of the American Marketing Association. Many of the new members were there to look for business or to network for a job. I watched these people lose interest in the group when their business or job needs were not filled quickly. I also watched other members roll up their sleeves and get involved, abundantly giving their time, energy, and talents. These people often succeeded at getting business or finding employment through their participation in the association, but you would never be able to tell by their involvement that the networking was anything more than a secondary concern. These were givers. They weren't standing around waiting for the association to give to them. The people who had business to give and jobs to fill were much more likely to turn to those who were eagerly participating in making the association a success, rather than turning to those who were just there for the networking.

Trade Dinners and Meetings

Networking isn't effective unless you show up. Having your name listed in the club-membership directory isn't enough. Attend meetings and get to know people. Sit next to someone new at each meeting. Force yourself away from talking only with people you know, even though it's natural to spend your time visiting with friends. The discipline of meeting and greeting new people is good both for the group and for networking. Your club leadership will appreciate your efforts to make new people feel welcome. And of course, the new people you greet will also appreciate it.

Don't worry about making mistakes in the process. You will make mistakes—so what? I remember greeting a new face at a group I had attended for about six months. I introduced myself to a woman, saying, "Hi, I haven't seen you here before. Welcome to our dinner."

She smiled curtly and said, "I'm one of the founding members." Of course I felt ridiculous, but how was I to know? She hadn't attended a meeting in six months. You can't avoid mistakes like that, and you shouldn't let the urge to avoid the faux pas stop you from reaching out to people. I've made every mistake: I've introduced myself three different times to someone I've already met; I've spilled a glass of wine on the dinner table; I've given a dinner talk with my fly down. But I have never regretted reaching out to people and introducing myself. On the other hand, I have regretted the times I've stood to the side, feeling

too uncomfortable to walk right up to a stranger and say, "Hi,
I'm Robert Spiegel. What brings you to this meeting?

When you participate and get involved with a group, these
lunch and dinner meetings are a chance to get introduced. If you
are active on a committee, you may be asked to stand up and
give a quick rundown on the committee's work. Jump at these
chances. Everyone notices who you are if you stand up in front.
The next time you stand around and visit with people before
dinner, someone will pipe up and say, "You're part of the legisla-
tive committee, aren't you?" Boom, a contact, a reference point.
This may seem small, but these little reference points move you
right into the person's next question, "What's your business?
What brings you to this group?"

Trade Shows and Conferences

Many associations and groups hold annual trade shows and conferences. These can be excellent opportunities for networking,
especially if you are involved in putting the show or conference
together. Look for tasks that will put you in touch with a variety
of people, such as lining up sponsors or selling booths. With an
event, even a small one, you get to network with people outside
your group or association. The affiliation with the group will
lend you some credibility if the group is related to your profession. If you are a marketing consultant and are lining up speakers
for the local marketing association's conference, you may be calling on people who also use marketing services such as yours.

When the conference is over, you can call them and they
will know who you are and will be much more likely to meet
with you and hear about your services with an open mind. During the show, you can even mention that you provide marketing
research and that you would like to come by sometime for a
quick visit. Then, when you call to follow up, your prospect will
be open to setting up an appointment. When you mention this
at the event, be quick and don't go into detail. You are there to
meet people; you're not there to sell. If your prospect begins to
ask questions, don't go into detail, no matter how tempting it

may be. Gently suggest that you would love to get together after the conference and that you'll call.

Conferences and trade shows offer a good first step to public speaking. Volunteer to be a moderator of a panel or to introduce sessions leaders. This is a very undemanding way to put your toe in the water, since the attendees are in the room to hear someone else and it isn't up to you to deliver the content. When you step up and speak, everyone gets to know who you are. The role of host for the speaking event helps to build your credibility. People will remember your name and they will remember your face. When you sell to them later, you won't be a stranger at the other end of the phone, you will be a fellow professional with a profile position in a group that presents the leaders of your profession.

Public Speaking

Speaking in public is one of the strongest ways to establish your credibility and meet people who are interested in your services, especially if you talk on a subject related to your business services. Some consultants use public speaking as the primary way to establish expert status and to meet clients. I know an accountant who derives most of his clients from giving seminars on how to start a business. He presents the seminar at a very low price to draw a good audience. He knows that the people who show up are likely to be in the market for an accountant if they go ahead and launch the business. He establishes himself as an expert by the content of his talk.

When he presents the seminar, he is careful not to promote his own services. The audience will judge his professionalism on the quality of the seminar. If he delivers solid information that is helpful and not self-serving, he will come away with respect and trust. If he uses this platform to promote his services, it will have the opposite effect of diminishing his credibility. This is one of the cardinal rules of using public speaking as a way to gain credibility and meet potential clients: Deliver strong and useful information and you will win their trust; pitch your services and they will distrust you. When you introduce yourself, you can explain your background and expertise on the subject matter and quickly describe your company; after all, it is part of your credibility. You can also make your cards and brochures available at breaks and at the end of the seminar. This exposure is sufficient; the rest comes from the quality of your presentation.

Other professionals I know who rely heavily on public speaking to promote their businesses include consultants, attorneys, stock brokers, psychologists, landscape architects, remodelers, and martial-arts instructors. The list can go on and on. Whatever the subject of your business, there are seminars you can put on to establish yourself as an expert in your field. Usually it is writing and public speaking that establish the experts in their field. So as soon as you stand up in public to give a talk, seminar, or workshop on your subject, you will be perceived as an expert.

Another benefit of public speaking is the exposure you will receive in conjunction with your talk. If you speak at a group's lunch or dinner, you will be promoted through the newsletter, and the write-up will explain your background and expertise. If the group promotes its programs to the general public, which is common with many groups, you could get covered by your local newspaper, again with your background and expertise listed with the details of the event. If the group is not consistent in getting out publicity, you can volunteer to do it yourself. Most groups will be thankful for the help, and the publicity benefits you as well as the group. Cut out these items and build a clipping file. These items can be mounted and copies can be included in your promotional materials.

The more public speaking you do, the better you will get at it. As you improve, you will get more requests to talk. In time, as you develop your skills at presenting an entertaining and informative program, public speaking can become a source of income. You can develop your public-speaking skills through Toastmasters. This organization has small groups that meet all over the country in almost all communities. The groups require minimal dues and meet once per week, at either breakfast, lunch, or dinner, so that people don't have to take time off from work or family responsibilities in order to participate.

I attended Toastmasters for two years to develop public-speaking skills. The program is very practical and relies on peer training. At each meeting, everyone gets at least a few minutes of speaking time, some prepared and some impromptu. You receive a small fine every time you say "um" or "ah." The participants are taught to be positive in their feedback, and all members get their turns at both speaking to and critiquing their peers. The support is warm and encouraging. Most people who spend a few months or more in Toastmasters come out of the program with a clear improvement in their speaking as well as a stronger confidence in getting up before an audience and talking like a professional.

Public speaking is a great way to distinguish yourself from your competition. Most people are terrified of speaking in front of a group. In surveys, most people list speaking in public as one of their greatest fears. Statistically, it ranks above death on the "most scared of" list. If you embrace public speaking, you can gain more attention, exposure, and credibility than the competing professionals who are not out in public talking to groups. People will always have more confidence in the person who is out on the circuit talking about the subject.

I remember a business magazine editor who said, "You know, the guys who are out there giving seminars on business are the ones who really know what's going on." Of course they do. They are the ones who are meeting the audience, hearing the questions, and taking the heat. It is a widely held belief: If you want to meet the real expert, talk to the person who is out there giving the speeches about the subject. If you want to put yourself at the top of your field in your community, get up and start talking about your subject.

Leadership Roles

The strongest way to bring credibility to your company is to take a leadership role in your industry or profession. Leaders have credibility simply because they are leaders. It brings you attention and fortifies your role with your clients and customers. If you're a landscape architect, you can bet your clients are going to feel they made a wise choice when they see you getting interviewed on television about how to get through the current drought. And when prospective clients see your marketing materials that mention you are the head of the state professional association in your industry, they will see this as an endorsement by your peers. That inspires trust.

Leadership positions also give you a high profile that can be its own marketing effort. I know a real estate agent who ran as the Democratic candidate for Congress against a popular Republican incumbent. When he launched his campaign, he was worried about how it would affect his business. For one, he would be distracted from marketing and building his client base. For another, he worried that he would never get another Republican client. As the primaries came and went, he was tagged by his party, and he started getting calls. All summer long, his phone rang off the hook. Everyone knew he would lose to the prominent incumbent, but his exposure as a candidate plastered his name and reputation all over the district. By the time the campaign ended (and he lost), he was turning away customers. The exposure took his business to a new level, where it remained.

Why was his candidacy so successful at bringing in customers? People liked him. The press discussed his profession, so everyone knew he was a real estate agent. People were impressed that he had a credible run against the incumbent, and they didn't hold it against him when he lost. Your customers will be impressed by any exposure you receive as a leader in your community. When you walk into a restaurant and see a plaque thanking the owner for running the most successful Red Cross fund drive in your state's history, it will fortify your decision to eat at that restaurant.

Taking leadership positions comes from getting involved in clubs, groups, and associations. As a business owner, you already have credibility as a leader. Many organizations look to their business-owner members to take leadership roles. All organizations are on the lookout for people who can take leadership spots. They look to those people who are involved in the committees and those who volunteer to help organize events. Some members are tapped for board positions because they did a particularly good job in running an event. So if you want to take a leadership role in a group, get involved. If you do a good job with your involvement, you will get asked to take leadership roles. It will probably start with committee leadership, which is fine since committee heads are usually on the board.

The skills you learn by taking a leadership role with a volunteer organization can help you with your own business. I learned a lot about budgeting after a few years on the board of my church. I also received some good experience in public speaking since I spent a couple of years as board president, and one of my tasks was reading the announcements and introducing guest speakers on Sundays. As leader of my state's American Marketing Association, I spent a good deal of time with professional marketers of considerable experience. Working with that group taught me a great deal about solving problems, promoting membership, and getting the word out about events, all of which helped me in my company.

Every business has its networking opportunities. Search these out for your business. When you run a company, you are part of a community, and the enterprises that are most successful are those with owners who are involved in their company's community. As a home-business owner, involvement in your business community can be particularly satisfying since you probably spend a good deal of your business day alone. We all need social stimulation. For home-business owners, networking can be a form of business interaction that is a pleasant treat after a hard day in the back bedroom.

Networking—Points to Consider

1. Join associations and groups in which you are likely to meet potential customers. This is much more effective than spending time in the company of your competitors.

2. Get involved in groups. Working to run and grow a group gives you much more credibility than you receive by simply attending functions. Getting involved also gives your potential customers a chance to get to know you.

3. Attending trade shows is another effective way to meet potential customers. Getting involved in the show by giving a seminar or participating on a panel gives you even more exposure and credibility.

4. Public speaking is the best networking of all. It gives you credibility in your industry or profession; it also gives you exposure. Public speaking positions you as an expert and leader.

Part VI

Watch Your Step—One False Move and You're Revising Your Resume

One of the most useful aspects of a detailed business plan is that you know you're in trouble before it's too late. This part shows how to save a business that is heading down the wrong road, as long as you know it in time. This section also covers ways to avoid business calamities and to transform your business into a stable enterprise that you can rely on to produce income over many years. Getting a new business on stable ground is no small task; anyone who is able to successfully launch a business should be commended. It usually takes far more grit than it appears from the outside. If you're like me, business ownership will teach you new respect for all your past bosses who were business owners, just as becoming a parent teaches you new respect for your parents.

Early on in my first business, I read an article in *Inc* magazine about a business owner who claimed that you don't really learn how to run a business until your money runs out, at which

Growth

time you learn quickly or fail. I thought that was tantamount to saying you don't learn about how to make a marriage work until your spouse threatens a divorce. I read this grim assessment just as I was running out of money. It certainly was true for me. As long as I was well funded, my spending was unfocused and my marketing efforts were fuzzy. As I ran out of funds, I suddenly became the most penny-pinching owner you've ever seen, and I made sure every marketing move was productive. If a method was less than profitable, it was scrapped instantly.

There is a quality of sharpness that comes with being on the line for your income. There are a hundred tools and techniques you can use to learn about business, but you don't really know what works until you're in the thick of it. I used to give seminars on launching magazines. My attendees would come with all their plans and their research and ask what I thought. These were professionals who had prepared themselves well for the road ahead, but they hadn't yet started their journey. There was a ''greenness'' to these people, no matter what their age or how well they had prepared themselves.

When these people asked about their chances for success, they invariably started talking about the quality of their idea and explained how the research they had done indicated they had a superlative concept. They would ask, ''So don't you think this should succeed?''

My answer to this question was always the same: ''It depends on how much you like the rigor of running a business and how quick you are to learn. I can guarantee you one thing—you will get into trouble. If you can get out of that trouble, you may succeed.''

This little speech was usually greeted with a blank stare. These people really wanted to talk about their idea, which they thought was so good it would bring them business success. There is no such thing as an idea so good it paves the way for the business. One of my attendees called me weeks after a seminar saying she was about to launch. She explained her idea and said she had done her research but that before she launched, she just wanted to know if there were any holes in her idea she couldn't see. I told her that until she called advertisers and asked them to commit to advertising, there was no way to tell if she had found a market. I also told her that until she got into trouble and got back out of it, she would have no idea if she had the stomach for business.

She was not disappointed by my answer, which was a good sign. I told her it was a good sign that she had called me, and I encouraged her to keep calling people for advice. I told her not to get so attached to her idea that she couldn't change it to make it more marketable. I asked her to do the needs test— "Who needs my product or service?" I also asked her to send me her first issue. After five years, I'm still on her mailing list. The magazine gets better-looking every year. Next time I'm in a bind, I may call her for advice. God knows I still need advice.

Following are some chapters covering troubles and corrective maneuvers, mentors and sage wisdom, and methods for bringing credibility and stability to your enterprise. This stage comes when all of the planning is over, you've quit your day job, and your money (and other people's money) is on the line. This is where the rubber meets the road, where you get to test your mettle, where your ideas take their hits. If you are in the planning stages of your business, you may just skim these chapters, you'll find them much more interesting when your business is eight months old and you are trying to figure out how to pull yourself out of a ditch.

Chapter 26
Trouble Signs and Corrective Maneuvers

Sometimes you can fall so in love with your product or business that you ignore the danger signs that develop around your young company. This blind faith can pay off in some circumstances: It can keep you going when all evidence says stop, and then the business turns around from all your effort and commitment. Often, though, unheeded danger signs can result in a failed business. Even if you cannot save your company, recognizing the inevitable can help you retain some of your assets. This chapter covers the process of recognizing trouble and creating solutions.

Difficulties can hit a business at different times, but they usually come during the first eighteen months; eighteen months tends to be a turning point. By the time a year and a half has passed, your start-up funds are gone, and either you are creating cash flow or you're out of business. By the time eighteen months have passed, you will have run into problems and hopefully solved enough of them to keep going. The following suggestions will help you get over the business hump that hits when your start-up funds are dwindling and you are still not all the way profitable.

There are other difficulties that can hit later in the company's life. I had two different friends who owned small video-rental stores when supermarkets entered the video-rental business and large chains, such as Blockbuster and Hollywood Videos, began claiming the portions of the market that supermarkets didn't get. One friend quickly launched a tape-duplication business and survived. The other friend sold the inventory at a small fraction of the original investment and started a catalog business. Market changes such as these can hit a stable company and throw it into chaos. Seasoned businesspeople often survive like my friends did, by simply moving their skills into a new enterprise. This takes the ability to see the trouble before all resources are gone. In the case of both of these video enterprises, the owners shifted gears while they still had enough resources to launch a new product or service and started an entirely new business.

Part of the trick is to recognize the trouble soon enough to act. This is where the new businessperson sometimes gets stuck. In business, you often have to change direction to get back on a positive road. If you can't see the trouble coming, you may not have time. If you are not creative in your business thinking, you may not be able to see what road would provide a more positive direction. This is where it helps to get expert assistance. A business mentor can often suggest a new direction simply by asking the right questions. Your tools to stay on the right road and get back on a good path when the going gets rough are planning, additional financing, and expert advice. If these tools prove fruitless, then you need to land as softly as possible to avoid adding a personal financial disaster to your business calamity.

Financial Planning—Measure Your Cash-Flow Needs

How long will it take before you begin to be in the black and turn a profit? Three months? Three years? No idea? This is where your pro forma comes in handy. The pro forma is a projection of the expenses you will incur each month and the revenue you can expect to receive. For most companies, when you do your planning, there will be expenses you didn't anticipate and the revenue will come both in smaller amounts and more slowly than anticipated; this is normal. Some business advisors say that you should calculate your expenses, then double the projected dollars to find out how much you will really need.

Well, the good news for the home business is that you stand a better chance of getting your projections right since you will start with a small overhead. Even so, there will be surprises. Take your pro forma and revise it as you go along during the first few months of operating your business. As you revise it, you will get a much better indicator of how long your start-up funds will last. Your original plan may have indicated your funds would last twelve months, but once you get going, you may find that you really only have enough to keep you going for six months, which means you need to quickly determine if your revenue stream can get up to an appropriate level before you are out of money.

Revise your pro forma, using your income statement, every month during your first year so that at any given point you know how many months you have left before you crash. You may find that after seeing the cushion of time shrink from twelve to six months, your sales pick up and you begin to gain months, and suddenly it will be seven months till you go broke instead of six. These are the types of measurements that are crucial to your success. Taking these measurements will not be the least bit boring. Most successful business owners are nearly obsessive about taking their company's pulse, just as they also get good at hanging onto their dollars and pushing up their revenues. The alternative is gloomy: If you don't track your business very carefully, you may find you're about to run out of money next week.

Second- and Third-Round Financing

You have all your start-up funds in place and plan to turn a profit in about six months. But after eight months, you're still in the red. Is your business still alive? If it looks likely that you can turn the corner in just another few months, will you have the resources to stretch that long? Many companies take a number of rounds of financing before they push into the black. This isn't surprising; it is hard to get a good bead on the relationship between your expenses and revenue until you're up and going. But it is important to see what additional funds you might need while you still have time to round them up.

A good pro forma will give you the measurement to tell how much longer you have to last before you're out of money and how much longer you need to keep going in order to reach profitability. A well-tracked pro forma will show you how many additional months of support you need to get on your feet. It will also show you how much you will need each month. Once you have this information, you will be able to calculate how much more funding you require. Since business progress is usually incremental, you could come up with a configuration that says you need an additional $3,000 per month for the next three months, $2,000 per month for the following three months, and $1,000 per month for four months after that, which means your new round of financing will need to be $19,000.

To be conservative, you borrow $20,000 with the ability to go back for an additional $5,000 if necessary. If you are watching your numbers carefully, you may be able to predict all the needed funding a good five months before you actually need it. You will also be able to predict how soon you can get the funding paid back, using the same calculations. This isn't a very difficult process, but it does require that you look very closely at what is happening in your business. It takes the ability to measure what is really going on rather than projecting hopeful scenarios. All businesspeople hope they will land that great contract in the next couple of months. Great if you do, but don't build that into your projections until it happens.

The Turning Point—Should You Throw Good Money After Bad?

The start-up money ran out; you went into your stash to get you through another four months. That money ran out, so you took out a second mortgage, then a third. Now you're about to call Uncle Carl because your credit cards are maxed out. You just can't seem to let it die. "It's going to turn around or else," you keep telling yourself, but the bills just keep mounting up. There comes a time when you just have to let it go and focus on a better future direction for your life.

How do you know when to quit throwing good money after bad in your business? This is a tough question when you are wrapped up in your business. Some owners answer this question by continuing until all options are spent. Then the business just folds and the question answers itself. This is not the best way to fail if you're going to fail, but sometimes it really seems it will all turn around in just a couple more months. This decision is worlds easier if you are working with a spouse who can offer a different point of view or if you are consulting a good business advisor or mentor.

I once launched a second business in a neighboring state because I saw a good opportunity that would help my core business. I kept two offices, one in each state, and spent a week in each office. The second company didn't take off like I expected, so I tried harder. My core business started having trouble since I was only able to work it half-time. I was at my wit's end. I felt absolutely committed to the new business because I had brought along a minority partner. I went out to coffee with my wife one morning to brainstorm ways I could turn it around. I filled my wife in on the problems, and the first thing she said was, "Why don't you just close the new office?"

It was so simple I didn't even get it. "I can't."

"Why can't you shut it down?" she asked.

"Well, because Jim's involved. He invested in it."

"He's not going to get his money out of it if you keep going. If he still likes the idea, let him go run it."

She was right. I told Jim he could have the new business if he wanted, but I wasn't able to continue with it. I told him I would give him back his investment if my core business didn't fail. I shut down the new business and my core business flourished. I even paid back Jim's investment dollars. If my wife hadn't said "Shut it down," I very likely would have stayed with it until both companies failed. Sometimes an outside voice is absolutely crucial. Entrepreneurs can easily fall into the problem behavior of the gambler who loses $200 and is so upset he loses another $2,000 trying to get it back.

An Option—Bringing in Experts to Correct a Downward Spiral

How dizzy do you have to get in your downward spin before you get some help? Don't go the route of the alcoholic who has to hit bottom before he asks for help. Ask for some help with your failing business before it's too late. A seasoned businessperson can help you see through the numbers to tell if your business stands a chance of success. You can often get a volunteer who will be able to take a look at your situation and help you determine whether it is worth continuing with the company.

If you don't already know someone who can help review your finances and explore your options, you can call the SCORE office of your local Small Business Administration. SCORE is a service that provides retired business executives who are willing to informally consult with entrepreneurs at no charge. These executives are often well schooled in business and can help you figure out whether your business is likely to turn around in a reasonable time. They will help you explore other options you may have in marketing to grow your business more quickly. They may also have some suggestions for shutting your company down if your prospects do not look hopeful.

Sometimes a passionless, clear eye from someone who has experience with small business can give you a completely different view of your enterprise and can make suggestions that can change your pressing circumstances. As business owners, we can get caught up in the struggle and fail to see a door open across the room that would bring a brighter alternative. It can be difficult for many entrepreneurs to admit that they need help, but business is not easy. It is rare that a business owner can get a company up and going without some assistance along the way, even if it is just a short visit with an experienced hand who says, "Hmm, have you tried this?"

The End—Choosing a Crash or Soft Landing

Okay, you tried your darndest. You can see the writing on the nasty wall. Much as you tried to avoid it, you just can't pull the nose of your business up. So how do you land? Go down head-first and let the business crush your family's financial life? Or is there a way to get this business down softly on some patch of grass? Look for ways of closing your business while keeping your personal finances afloat. For many entrepreneurs, a soft landing isn't possible because they try so hard to make the business successful that the attempt soaks up all available resources.

But if you can see that your business doesn't stand a chance in time, you usually have some positive options. For one, you can go to a competitor and sell your equipment, supplies, and marketing lists. This may actually bring you some needed cash. You can also go to a credit-counseling service to work out settlements on the outstanding loans you may have. These are nonprofit services that help you negotiate settlements with finance companies and credit cards. Many of your creditors would rather take a small portion of what you owe them if the alternative is bankruptcy.

Handling Business Difficulties—Points to Consider

1. Be prepared for the necessity of a second round of financing sometime between six and eighteen months after your launch; this is a very common need. Make sure you know where you will get that capital when the time comes.

2. If you continue to need new capital beyond a second-round infusion, give it a hard think. Many entrepreneurs will prop up a bad business idea until all of their resources are depleted.

3. If nothing seems to work, try to close down the business while you still have some remaining resources. Die-hard entrepreneurs can gear up to try again.

Chapter 27

Finding Mentors and Sage Wisdom

Locating Mentors

A study in the 1980s looked for the common traits of successful people. The study found that people of high achievement came from all backgrounds and circumstances. But the results showed one outstanding common characteristic: Successful people almost always had a mentor during their career. Often rising entrepreneurs have a number of mentors along the way as they grow their business from one stage to another. One of the wisest moves you can make to ensure your success is to identify a mentor and ask that person to periodically offer advice. A mentor can make a significant difference to a business, and it is surprising how willing people are to help a new entrepreneur.

A mentor can help in a number of different ways. For one, your mentor provides a model of successful behavior. How does your mentor live? What are her principles? Does she take breaks, vacations, time away from the business? Does your mentor keep outside interests alive, and does she volunteer in community projects? Not all of the value of your mentor comes in the form of business consulting; some of it comes from watching how your mentor lives and seeing what her values are. These qualities can be just as important as the professional activities of business negotiation, marketing techniques, or team building.

Your mentor can also be a source of inspiration, a boost to keep you going when the future begins to look gloomy. Most businesspeople experience tough times. The successful entrepreneur is usually someone who is good at getting up and trying again after a bad go-around. Your mentor may be someone who has hit bottom harder than you ever will and was still able to get up, learn from the experience, get back in the game, and achieve beyond the limits of the first failed attempt. When I struggled with my first business, I would look to my mentor not for business advice or direction, but simply so I could know and understand that it's not the falling down that matters; it's the willingness to keep getting back up.

Attending Business-School Programs for Small Business

Some academic programs are worthwhile for small companies, and others are a complete waste of time. If you want to learn how to run a business, get into a class taught by a successful business practitioner. All of the theory and principles can't help you figure out how to grab the two ends of your business and force them to meet. That isn't to say you shouldn't learn some of the rules of market research or methods for assessing new product acceptance, but remember, university programs are designed to prepare students for future corporate employment. Most of the models they use or theories they profess are designed for large corporations.

Most business schools now have small-business centers or entrepreneurial study programs. But these classes are still taught by academicians. You are not likely to find a successful entrepreneur or small-business owner teaching one of these classes. For one thing, most academicians don't believe any local entrepreneurs are managing their businesses properly. Professors are likely to view most entrepreneurs as hustlers or riverboat gamblers who take advantage of market forces without any idea of what really drives commerce. They certainly don't want any of these people stepping into the classroom and muddying their students' waters with uneducated ideas of what makes a business successful.

You may find some practitioners teaching in continuing-education programs. Many of these classes are practical and useful. If the teacher is a former or current business owner, you may be able to learn a great deal about how to operate a small business. You may also meet someone who can act as a mentor or informal consultant to help you along the way. Most teachers naturally welcome questions from eager students who are struggling with the same problems they have overcome. You may find your instructors guidance is so useful you will bring him in as a paid advisor when your business is doing well enough to justify the expense.

Getting Expert Advice for the Price of Lunch

A New York magazine entrepreneur once told me that most people will try to give you a hand if you just ask. We were in an elevator in New York. "You know," he said, "if Mayor Giuliani walked into this elevator right now and I told him I was an entrepreneur trying to make my business work and had a favor to ask, he'd probably say, 'Tell me what you need.' That's just the way people are." Well, you can call my friend an optimist, but time after time he used that line when calling people for favors. More often than not, people responded, "I don't know if I can help you, but tell me what you need."

When I launched a magazine company, I found a couple of magazine professionals who were willing to let me pick their brains for the cost of lunch. These professionals worked for magazines that were not direct competitors with mine, so they were surprisingly free with their information. I was very direct in my approach: I simply called one of them at work, explained who I was, and said, "I know you have done a good job building circulation at your publication, could I buy you lunch and pick your brain about getting subscribers?" Every single time I asked a question like this, I received a yes. People like to talk about their jobs, and there is always the networking possibility that I could help them in their career down the road. Or maybe it's just simple goodwill.

Most people are flattered when they are asked to give their

thoughts about what works and what doesn't in their job. For example, someone may report the good news of her recent accomplishments to her boss without going into the details of what made the success. At home, she may find the details of her job to be beyond easy explanation. But then you call and want all the details: What worked? What failed? How did she get through it? Has she tried this or that? On top of that, lunch is free. Most people see this situation in a very positive light. You may wonder why someone would give you free advice. But they will, and sometimes you can learn more from these lunches than you can from a three-day conference.

Using Consultants

Asking friends, acquaintances, or strangers for help is one thing, asking a consultant for help is another. As soon as you ask a consultant for help, he'll look at his watch and say, "Okay, start now. I'll keep track of the time." Sometimes the information you need is so specific and so necessary it's worth hiring a consultant. If you do, have clear ground rules before you get going: Outline the exact problems you want to address; set a specific number of hours to explore the problem; and request that the results be presented in written form in addition to the verbal instructions you will receive. Most consultants are accustomed to these parameters.

There are some good reasons to bring in a professional consultant. You may want someone in your industry who spends his time examining companies like yours to come in and make suggestions on how you can cut expenses and increase revenue. Or you may be seeking suggestions on finding additional products and services you can add to your mix, but first you want to hear from someone who has helped other companies like yours add similar extensions. You may also want an evaluation of your long-term prospects. Whatever the reason, you can count on receiving better direct information about your company and high-quality suggestions for improvement from a consultant than you will get from informal lunches and advisor meetings.

Buiding a Board of Advisors

You can take all your informal professional helpers and create a regular meeting time to exchange ideas by building a board of advisors. Unlike a board of directors, the advisors bear no responsibility for the business. All that is required of your board of advisors is that they are willing to attend meetings and share their brilliant thoughts. You don't have to pay these people; you can find many persons you know who will attend simply because they are asked. Most of your vendors will be happy to participate. Your vendors will probably include an attorney, an accountant, and business owners of services you regularly purchase. These boards work best when they meet regularly, and when the agenda and length of the meeting are set beforehand.

I was on one of these boards that met on a specific day every two months. The meeting was a strict two hours long, and the business owner provided coffee and pastries. She sent out the notice two weeks ahead of time and sent a reminder fax two days ahead of time. The notice was a one-page agenda that listed the topics. The note came with the list of participants along with their phone numbers, which was a handy networking tool. I have always been surprised by the quality of advice that came from these meetings. I never failed to learn from these gatherings, even though I was just a participant. And all this expertise comes free for the asking.

Joining Entrepreneur Clubs

Many cities have a club or association of entrepreneurs that gets together once per month for lunch or dinner and presents speakers who talk on topics such as how to find and sell to venture capitalists. These clubs or associations have a mix of professionals as members. Some are people who would like to start a business and are in the process of getting educated. Others are active entrepreneurs who are seeking new and helpful information as well as spending time socially with people of like mind. Another group is people who make their living selling services to entrepreneurs. This group includes accountants, bankers, attorneys, even copier salespeople.

If you get involved with an entrepreneur club, you will get more out of the experience than if you just attend meetings. The greatest value of these associations is creating friendships and networking with other entrepreneurs who may someday be of great help when you need advice or a partner in a new enterprise. You don't get this benefit from sitting at a dinner table listening to a thirty-minute talk. Roll up your sleeves and work with these people to run the club. Friendships will build naturally. Then when you need a boost, some encouraging words, or an introduction to a venture capitalist who is working with your fellow board member, these connections can be invaluable.

In order to make these clubs or associations work, you have to be just as willing to give as you are to receive. As you move forward in your enterprise, you are developing new skills and gaining new insights into what it takes to get a business up and going. When you first join one of these clubs, you will probably feel like the greenhorn who can barely understand the terms these people use. Within a few months, you will start to notice there are some members who have even less experience than you do. Make your resources available to these newcomers just as the old timers coached you. If you want to have a mentor, be willing to be a mentor.

Learning From Various Resources—Points to Consider

1. Look to workshops and conferences rather than business schools. Usually the workshops and conferences are taught by practitioners who deliver current, from-the-trenches information.

2. Another way to learn is to take experienced people out to lunch and pick their brains. If you are not in direct competition with them, many businesspeople are happy to answer questions over a free lunch.

3. You can formalize expert input by creating a small board of advisors. Your vendors will be particularly willing to participate.

Chapter 28

Building Credibility and Stability

Don't be surprised if your first year of business is a complete roller coaster. It usually takes awhile to find your "sea legs" as an entrepreneur; instability is the nature of the first year of business. This rough time needs to be as short as you can make it. The goals are credibility and stability. The two work together. They should be part of your overall direction, just like profitability. Income rests on credibility and stability. Without that foundation, it is hard to stay profitable. There are a number of tools you can use to get your business on an even keel. A high level of professionalism goes a long way toward creating credibility and demonstrating stability. Even if you're scrambling to make ends meet, you have to deliver excellence in your products and services in order to gain and hold customers.

Keeping Your Quality High As You Get on Your Feet

There is a large portion of consumers who look for quality and not just price when they make their selections of products and services. Although you can never ignore the importance of good pricing, you should also work hard to make sure your business produces quality that is easy for your customers to perceive. If you offer yard maintenance, you should work to make your business the expert in the field of yard maintenance. A big part of your competitive edge will be your quality and expertise. You want your customers to say to their neighbors, "This company really knows what it's doing. Every time June's over here with her crew, I learn more about my yard. I pay a little more for her, but not that much more, and she makes sure the yard looks great."

Create, foster, and communicate that expertise. Expertise and quality are your best tools for keeping your customers and clients coming back. Most of your customers won't go shopping for new services if they are satisfied with your work, even if they can get a better price across town. Usually people will not start comparison shopping on price alone; they go out looking for a new company when the old company falters a bit.

If your customers see any negative change in your products or services, they will quietly start looking elsewhere, and they usually won't come clean if you ask them directly why they left. They won't tell you, "You seem to be having business problems and your service just hasn't been what it used to be, so I found a company that's more stable." Instead, they will usually tell you they just wanted to see what else was out there. But you can bet that if your customers get the feeling things are not right with your business, they will begin to drift away.

Planning Cash Flow to Stay Out of Trouble

Okay, you finally got the ends to meet and the business is actually giving you a regular paycheck, a bigger salary than you ever received as an employee. Now it's time to open a new location. For a lot of entrepreneurs, the first sign of black ink means it's time to take more chances. Before you take your business winnings and put the whole lump on the next roulette number, plan your cash flow so that your business extensions don't threaten your company. If you have an insatiable desire to extend and grow your business, do it in a way the strengthens your business rather than putting it at risk.

You can do this by balancing your cash flow so you always have a cushion of resources to fall back on if your second location or new line of products fails. I have seen some very talented entrepreneurs stake all of their resources on a new company, location, or brand extension only to have the failure of the new venture take the original business down as well. Consolidate your winner. Take the proceeds from your winning business and invest them in your new company, but don't mortgage your successful company and gamble it on risk. Once you go into business, it pays to cultivate a conservative side to your nature.

Setting Up Milestones and Warning Signs

Most good business owners naturally create milestones. They may not even use the term, but they know that if they fall below a particular monthly revenue level, they need to make some changes. They also have a good feel for how many months they can operate below that level before they're looking through the want ads. To help stabilize your business, you need to take a calculator and put these milestones or water-level marks on paper. Then you will know that after, say, four months of falling behind a set level, it's time to take some action to turn your operation around before it's too late. It is okay to wait some slumps out; some downturns are periodic or seasonal. But you should always be aware of how much time you can spend holding the same course before it takes you underwater. A set of clear milestones can provide the guidance you need.

Building a Cushion That Accommodates Change

You burned through your start-up funding, went through your nest egg, and borrowed against your house. But hooray, it was worth it. Your business succeeded. Now you need to pay yourself back because in business you never know what's going to happen next, and you need to create a new cushion if you used up your former cushion to launch your business. I once had a business that failed. It was my third business and the previous two had been successful, so I was a bit overconfident. As the third business failed, I hadn't fully replenished my cushion and found myself with less resources than necessary to save the failing company, so I had to let the company go. If I had replenished my resources before launching the third company, the outcome may have been different.

Most business owners go through a period of deferred gratification. You stop spending on yourself and your lifestyle in deference to the greater good of creating wealth through a business. After a few years of holding back your spending, it's hard to take the early proceeds from your newly successful business and sock it away to replenish depleted savings accounts and sky-high credit-card balances. It is very tempting to take your new proceeds and finally replace the beat-up car, the dryer that knocks, and your out-of-style clothing. You have to put some toward a better lifestyle or you'll go crazy, but it is also important to begin replenishing your resources. The business may yet go through some rough months, and you may need to retap your savings or credit.

Creating Credibility and Stability—Points to Consider

1. Produce high-quality products and services again and again. Quality always wins the day. It will hold your current customers as you gain new ones.

2. As you establish your business, build a cushion of capital to sustain your business if the market or the economy turns down.

3. As you stabilize your business, continue to refine your planning and cash-flow goals. As the months and years go by, this will become very predictable.

Part VII

Mature and Comfy or Up and Out of the Nest?

What are your long-term goals for your home business? Is your house the launchpad for a business that will eventually move to an office and build a staff? Have you chosen to launch your business from home because you truly want to work in your spare bedroom? There are no right answers to these questions; it depends on what you want. Some people find that after a couple of years in the home they're happy to drive to an office. Others grow their company so large it can't stay in the home, but they regret the move to an outside location. The more you know about what you really want, the better you can plan for it.

Growth

Each direction comes with its own major challenge. If you decide to move out of your home as the business grows, you will have the challenge of taking on the additional overhead of an outside work space. As mentioned in earlier chapters, this additional overhead can be formidable. For many businesses, working from home constitutes almost zero overhead. Whatever reasons you have for leaving home, whether it is business growth or difficulties in running a company in the family environment, jumping out of the cheap nest will have a profound effect on your cash flow. Prepare for it well because it can be a shock.

For those who decide to stay at home and enjoy its inexpensive comforts and flexibility, the challenge is how to grow a business under the limitations of your home space. You have to figure out how to grow without employees, grow without becoming a burden to your neighbors, and grow without having your work space progressively encroach on your family territory. We discussed using the tools of outsourcing to accommodate growth in Chapter 19. There is also the option of avoiding growth by choosing clients and jobs that offer better pay. This is a way of improving cash flow without enlarging your business.

Whatever you choose, few home companies can avoid working through these challenges. Like the start-up challenges, they require some soul searching and good communication with your family. It could be that you never intended to use the home for more than a launchpad, but once you started working in your home, you fell in love with its advantages. You may have to initiate a sit-down with your family to explain that the recent inconveniences are about to become permanent. Or you may find that you simply can't afford to move out, so you will continue in your home for financial reasons. Whatever happens, keep your family informed and continue to educate yourself on all the options and strategies that are available.

Chapter 30 in this section discusses an emerging strategy for growing a home business: running more than one company. This is the new home version of the rural Southern tradition of keeping two companies under one roof. Even today, drive through Southern Louisiana and you'll see signs such as Mel's Bar and Towing or Jenny's Hair Salon and Palm Reading. My favorite is Henry's Pet Grooming and Taxidermy; one wrong move of the clippers and you simply shift your client from one business to the other. These are the twins and triplets of home enterprise. If your company only produces the income you need and growth efforts are not productive, perhaps your answer is to start a complementary business alongside your existing company. This strategy comes with its own challenges, but if you proceed carefully, it can be the move that brings you success.

Chapter 29

Is Your Home a Launchpad or a Permanent Place to Stay?

If you know your home office is temporary, you can plan for the eventual move. The move will be more difficult if it's not expected. The answer to the question of whether your home business is temporary or permanent will direct all your decisions concerning growth. If you are only at home for the incubation, then it is simply a matter of timing your move with your space and financial needs. If you intend to stay at home, growth is a continual process of outsourcing. These decisions can easily change along the way, since it is hard to tell how well you will take to working at home until you begin doing business in your den, and it will be hard to get a feel for your cash flow until you're lining up clients and selling your services. So be prepared to change your plans if necessary.

The Launch—Set Your Long Term Goals

As you put your business together for a launch, set some long-term goals as well as the necessary short-term milestone. Imagine yourself and your business five years, ten years, twenty years down the road. Few of us look at our lives in this manner. Even when we get married or have children, we don't often draw the picture of how we would like things to be in ten years. When you start your business, it helps to do this work. Just write out your long-term goals. Do you want to retire and be independently wealthy in fifteen years? Do you want to create a business that you can run well past conventional retirement age? Many people start a home business for this very reason.

Whatever your long-term goals may be, they can affect the decisions you make during the very first year of business, and the first year of business can also affect your long-term goals. As you push your business forward, reviewing and revising your plans along the way, take a look at your long-term goals. You may find they need adjustment and revision as you learn about your business and about yourself. There are some aspects of running a business that you cannot anticipate until your company is up and going. You may like it more than you thought, or you may like it less than you thought. These revelations will have a bearing on your long-term goals.

The Home Office—Is This the Preferred Space?

Even if you plan to eventually set up your business in an outside office, your home can be a great launchpad. The low overhead during the first year or two can make the difference between success and failure down the road. You can easily save $1,000 to $3,000 per month by staying at home. If you remain in your home incubator for two years, the total savings can range from $24,000 to $72,000. That chunk of capital can be all the difference for a small business. It can even be attractive enough to sway your decision to move out, or at least to delay your exit. You may decide to stay in your home because it's comfortable for your company's bottom line, not because it is the ideal place for your work style or your family's lifestyle.

Under these circumstances, housing the company in your home is one of the inconveniences that comes with the start-up years of the business. All things have to be weighed. It very well could be that by keeping the company at home, the financial pressure can be lifted, so even though it's uncomfortable having work-related equipment, furnishings, and products all over the house, it's nice having all the bills paid. Many families will take an extended period of home discomfort over extended financial discomfort. For an emerging business that launches from home, this is not an uncommon choice.

The Next Step—Plan Your Flight From Home

If you know your home is just an incubator for a business that will outgrow your home, plan the transition ahead of time so your company gets the best launch and so your family has a clear idea of the game plan. When you launch a company from home that will eventually be too big for your spare bedroom, you will probably outgrow your home before you actually depart. It is not uncommon to hire part-time people who work in your living room while you find your outside space and prepare it for your business. Your family will be more tolerant of the inconveniences and stress of the business if they know the game plan. A family can take six months of inconvenience knowing when the end will come more easily than they can take two months of it if it seems without end.

Since you will also face a sharp increase in overhead when you move out of your home, it's wise to set aside some resources to make sure the change doesn't set your company back financially. Think of your move as a semi-launch that will require a stash of "just in case" capital. If you do not have this stash, you may want to delay your move until you can set a cushion aside. The last thing you need after sweating and scrimping to get a company on its feet is to go back to the long days of work and the long nights of sweating over bills.

The Prodigal Business—Be Prepared to Move Back Home

Here's a common story: You start a business in your home. It grows wonderfully and within six months you're in the black, writing yourself paychecks and making payments on your loan. The growth seems steady and strong, so you move out to an office and hire two employees to help you with the work. Suddenly your office overhead has grown from a few hundred each month to a few thousand. In a few months, your growth settles down to steady but small increases. You're no longer in the black, and you have to borrow to make payroll. You haven't paid yourself in months. Is this the time to scramble for new loans? Or is it time to let your employees go and move back home?

The home offers powerful overhead savings. The largest killer of small companies is the weight of overhead, so don't be surprised if moving out of your home brought back the devil of red ink. Like the prodigal son, perhaps it's time to reconsider whether your young business was really ready to go it alone. You may be able to keep your employees by sending them to their own homes to work. As long as you haven't committed to a long lease, moving home may be the way to save your company. Even if you did sign a lease, there's always the chance of subletting.

I know a number of small-company owners who solve some of the home-business space difficulties by building additional rooms onto their home. If you know that the construction will be for the purpose of housing your company, you can build a private entrance and extra off-street parking for employees. This will keep your business space out of the living room while you grow, plus you get the benefit of adding value to your home while the business foots the bills and deducts it as a business expense. And don't worry about the difficulty of selling a home with a built-in home office. More and more homes are getting advertised as being a home/office.

Moving Your Business Out or Staying at Home—Points to Consider

1. If your long-term goal is to up and leave the home when your business is big enough to support its own overhead, plan the transition carefully. It is often more expensive than anticipated.

2. Over the long run, it may actually be less expensive to add an addition to your home than to move to a rented office.

3. When you move out, you may lose much of the flexibility of your home enterprise. It won't be as easy to wander over to the computer after dinner. That productivity can be a real loss.

4. Be prepared for a potential move back home. Some home-business owners find the outside world is much more expensive and a lot less comfortable than the back bedroom at home.

Chapter 30

Twins and Triplets—A Nest of Young Companies

If you drive through the small towns of the Deep South, you'll see dozens of enterprises that offer odd business combinations: Myrtle's Hair Salon and Dog Grooming, Miller's Feed and Propane, Wayne's Mortuary and Palm Reading. These special concoctions actually work. In a small community, each individual business may be marginal. Bring two together and you have a thriving enterprise. Many home-business owners are also combining enterprises. Some of this simply derives from opportunity: Many computer-system consultants find themselves calling on clients who also need a Web site; many multilevel marketers know their vitamin customers are open to cosmetic purchases.

With a home business, you can gain the same advantages, but your strategy for creating a combination is completely different. In small communities, the combo-enterprise is selling completely different products to the same customers. The reason for the combo is location. Nobody wants to drive to the next town to get the dog groomed. With a home business, location is usually not the major factor, it's a common market. You need to create a combo that sells a number of products or services to the same customer.

The easiest way to build a combo-business is to ask yourself, What else does my customer need? If you're in the house-cleaning business, your customers may need carpet and upholstery cleaning. If you sell natural vitamins, perhaps your customers will also want natural facial and hair-care products. For computer consultants, how about a small software catalog designed specifically for the needs of your client base?

Most businesses can find a tie-in for a second or third business. Building a combo-business can make the difference between success and failure, or it can offer a low-investment way to increase profits. Sometimes, you may find the second launch is more profitable than the first. In most cases, the start-up costs are significantly lower, and there is much less risk since you already have customers.

Five Combo-Business Rules

There are five basic rules of the multiple-business road. Follow these rules to keep your risk to a minimum and your potential profits at a maximum. One warning: Don't try to launch two businesses at once unless your rich uncle left you a couple of small fortunes. Adding a second or third business to a successful enterprise can be a wise idea, but launching twins is dangerous.

1. Market to the Same Customers

It's hard enough to reach one market; it takes learning, experimenting, testing, and lots of money. The charm and profit of a second or third business is that you don't have to go out and get new customers. If you break this rule, you may as well be launching a business from scratch. In the best of all worlds, you sell your new products to your existing customers to get a toehold with the new launch. Then, once you are stable, you take the new product out to new customers and then sell your original product to these new customers. Each business profits from its sibling. Using the house-cleaning example, the new carpet and upholstery business eventually attracts new leads for house cleaning.

2. Choose Easy-to-Manage Suppliers

Be careful with your new addition. You don't need a problem child. Don't bring new difficulties to a smooth-running business.

If your new addition hurts the performance and quality of your original business, you may be adding real trouble. If you sell mail-order items and the new business hampers your ability to ship full orders in a timely manner because suppliers for the new business are slow, you may be hurting yourself more than helping yourself.

Likewise, make sure your new addition lets you provide strong customer service. One of the potential downsides of an additional business is customer-service problems. Plan your customer-service strategy from the outset, just as you plan your marketing.

3. Create a Single Simple Image

Don't let your new business confuse your customers. Choose an add-on that supports and strengthens the image you want to project. I remember the owner of a carpet-cleaning company who gave me a pitch on buying gold coins. His carpet-cleaning background didn't add any credibility to the coin pitch, but the coin sell undermined his credibility as a reliable carpet cleaner. If he had pitched me on yard cleanup, handyman maintenance, or duct cleaning instead, he would have improved his image positively. You look like a huckster if you are pitching completely different items.

4. Cross-Sell at All Times

Assuming you are convinced that launching a new business complements your core business, you need to discipline yourself to cross-sell at all times. Make sure all your customers know everything you have to offer. If you are in mail order, send out the new product catalog with all your orders. Offer samples from your new business as premiums or gifts to your core customers. Don't make your customers try to figure out what you have to offer.

Present your addition as a strategy to meet all your customers' needs in a particular area. When I leased a copier and the salesperson proposed a fax machine as part of the package, it was appealing. There was service convenience and one monthly note for both machines. I began to see my copier company as a source for office machines, not just copiers. My computer-network consultant offered solutions for an additional workstation. She provided the computer and printer and wrapped the price into the monthly payments I was making on the network. She was selling computer solutions, not just network installation.

5. Don't Stop Testing

All business is a test. You never have a final product, a final formula, or a set marketing and product strategy that ensures continued success. Just ask IBM, GM, or Kmart. If you can remember that you are always testing your concept and your product or service line, you keep from getting stale. Think of yourself as a problem solver for your customer. This view works with any business. Position yourself as the expert for your product or service. As an expert, you draw on a number of solutions for your customer, all related to your core business. If you keep this view, you can add and subtract products and services accordingly.

Twins and triplets are simply a matter of offering your customers choices and solutions. When adding a second or third business, ask yourself, Does this solve an additional problem for my customers? Also ask yourself, Does this new business give me access to a new market that will bring new customers to my first business? If you can answer these two questions with a yes, and if you follow the five rules above, your additional business may take you to a whole new level of profits.

Running a Combo-Business—Points to Consider

1. If you add a second line of products or services, make sure they complement each other. It makes sense when your carpet-cleaning company offers blind-cleaning services, but you'll feel queasy when your carpet cleaner starts to tell you about vitamin supplements.

2. Cross-sell at all times. Not only will the second business give you additional products for your existing business, but your new line will bring in customers who can be sold on your original line.

3. If it doesn't work to add a blind-cleaning business to your carpet-cleaning business, try upholstery-cleaning or duct- and chimney-cleaning services. Always test and keep testing.

Part VIII

Planning Your Exit—Nothing Is Forever

All things—good and bad—have an ending. Your new business start-up will someday be gone. You may sell it when it grows to a value that creates wealth, or you may pass it on to your children. You may even leave the business with hired managers who will run it for your family. The more you know about your intended ending, the better you can plan for it. Your company's ending should have its place in your business plan just as its inception did, even if the proposed ending changes many times through the years.

Sudden, unplanned changes also need to be taken into consideration. Although we work hard to keep our lives and businesses in some semblance of control, life is unpredictable. The one thing you can do in the face of an unknowable future is to develop contingency plans so that if something sudden happens, whether it is temporary or permanent, there is a clear path for your company. Your business, after all, may be your family's greatest asset, so it must be protected if something happens to you. Fortunately, there are strategies you can put in place to save your family from the chaos and economic damage of an unfortunate turn of events.

Exit Strategies

Chapter 31

Planning Your Sale at the Outset

It is best to have an idea of the ending of a business right from the beginning. If your dream is to build a business up to sell it in ten years, this decision will affect most decisions you make during those ten years. If you want to sell your company to investors (who may include family members) in five years, your decisions will be different. The sooner you know the expected outcome, the better prepared you will be when that time comes. You may not have a clear idea of what you will want to eventually do with your business, but even if you don't name an exit strategy at the outset, the decisions you make when you choose a business will have a strong bearing on your options when you are ready to let go of your company.

The last thing on your mind when you visit a franchise and business-opportunity show is the end of your business. You are probably completely involved in evaluating a business's start-up costs, income potential, likelihood for success, and required owner experience. But the decision you make can have significant consequences in future years. You may find there is a similar company that can be purchased as either a franchise or a business opportunity. The business opportunity is vastly less expensive and the potential income seems even, so why on earth would someone spend the extra dollars on the franchise?

Well, imagine this scenario taking place in the mid-1960s with a potential business owner weighing the difference between purchasing a McDonald's outlet and a Happy Jack's Burgers restaurant. If Happy Jack was just a business opportunity, it very well may have cost far less than the McDonald's, but twenty or thirty years down the road, the McDonald's location might sell for $1.5 million while the Happy Jack's Burgers, if it is still in business, might bring only $75,000. Back on the day of purchase, it could be that the McDonald's was only selling for $15,000 above the asking price for Happy Jack's Burgers.

If you knew from the beginning that equity growth was important, McDonald's would have been an obvious better choice, since it was a franchise and would offer its owners much more in support and national promotion. If equity wasn't on your mind, if you weren't thinking about the eventual end of the company, the clear advantage of buying the McDonald's may not have seemed the least bit important. If you know that in the end you want to sell your business for a good return, the types of companies you examine for potential purchase will be completely different from those you would consider if you weren't concerned about selling the company at a later date.

Is a Sale in Your Long-Term Interest?

If you expect to sell your business one day, this goal will affect a wide range of decisions all through your business life, from the selection of the business you launch to the market you choose to chase. As you test new products, enter new markets, establish a public-relations program to give your company expert status— all of these efforts and activities contribute to the value of your company. If you are running a professional practice, none of these matter in the long run because your business will only last as long as you are practicing. But if you are creating an enterprise that can be sold to a new owner who can pick up where you leave off and continue building income and value, all of these efforts have two aspects: their contribution to income and their contribution to your company's sale price.

I know a doctor who left his lucrative private practice in conjunction with a hospital and took a pay cut to open a clinic with two partners. He worked longer hours for less pay, but he did it because he knew he would not be able to sell his private practice when he retired. He wanted to create a business entity in addition to creating income, so he was willing to take a smaller income to build a business. At first, the clinic did not produce a profit, but it was able to give him a modest salary. Five years later, his salary had grown beyond that of his private practice, plus he was receiving one-third of the clinic's profits. In another five years, he will have the choice of retiring and taking the one-third profits indefinitely or selling his ownership position and walking away. The value of the partnership was estimated to be in excess of $2 million.

Another way to look at it is that owning a business with the potential to grow in equity is like investing in yourself. Owning your own business is just like owning any other stock: The value may go up, or the value may go down; the big difference is that you have most of the control over whether the value of the business goes up or down. Every decision you make about introducing a new product or service can have a direct bearing on the value of your business. You can even evaluate product or service introductions based on whether they are likely to add to the value of your company.

Who Should Sell Your Business, a Local Broker or an Industry Broker?

When I sold a magazine I had launched and built over a ten-year period, I met with a local business broker and I met with a magazine industry broker. The local broker evaluated my finances and determined that the appropriate asking price was $500,000 and that I should be prepared to accept $350,000 to $400,000. When the industry broker looked at the same finances, he said we should ask for $2 million and be willing to accept $1.5 million. I went back to the local broker, who was very puzzled by the industry broker's assessment. He sat right down and showed me why my company couldn't possibly bring more than $400,000. I hired the industry broker and sold the business within five months, getting a figure that was within the range the industry broker quoted. Was the local broker an idiot? No, not at all. He just sold companies to a different market, and that market evaluated finances in an entirely different manner from the national industry market.

Business valuation isn't like horse trading, different business markets evaluate companies with entirely different precepts. As you shop for a business, look at these factors. Some companies do not have an industry context for valuation. A house-cleaning business will usually be sold by a local broker, or in conjunction with the franchise company if it's a franchise. But a Web site, like many media companies, may have a strategic value for a potential buyer who needs to get a toehold in the market where you have established credibility.

Other companies that may offer strategic value within their industry include publishers, Internet companies, specialty food producers, and catalogs. Any company that allows you to market products and services nationally may have the ability to command a higher selling price than a company that can look only to its local market for a buyer. This is one more consideration to think about as you evaluate businesses that you can buy or start.

How Do You Set the Sale Price of Your Company?

The price you set for your company will depend on the options you have for selling it. And certainly the decisions you make about your business along the way will affect the selling price of your company. If you have a company that holds strategic value within your industry, your options will be much different than if your company is likely to be purchased by a small-business person in your town who intends to make her living running the business while paying you over time out of the proceeds from the business. If you sell it locally under those circumstances, your asking price will probably be your proceeds beyond a modest owner's salary, times five. How does that work?

Okay, say your company produces $500,000 per year in sales, and say your profit (or income) on that revenue is $125,000. Let's further say that it would take $50,000 per year to hire a manager to do your job. That means your company is really earning $75,000 per year, even if you pay yourself the full $125,000 since we can call $50,000 a necessary expense to run the business. Your buyer will need to pay herself the $50,000, and the $75,000 will be available to pay off whatever financing she needed to buy from you. There is a five-year payback rule of thumb for business purchases on the local level. That $75,000 will also have to cover the interest on her financing.

Given those figures, you are justified in asking about $300,000 for your company. If you are willing to finance the purchase yourself, you could ask $375,000. Now you may argue that your company's income has been growing by 10 percent each year, and that that growth needs to be part of the asking price. The answer to that claim is no. All growth (sometimes called blue sky) belongs to the new owner since it will be up to her to sustain it. She may be counting on that growth to increase her income over the years that most of the company's income is used to pay back the purchase price.

A strategic buy is vastly different. For one thing, you don't have to be profitable in order to attract interest from buyers. They may be a bigger company that can take a look at your business and see that they can bring efficiencies to your operation that are not available to you. Although you're not profitable, they may be able to make your business instantly profitable. Or it could be that owning your Web site gives them a vehicle to expand their present business, thus strengthening their company while adding profits. Given the numbers in the above scenario, you might get $650,000 for your company instead of the $300,000 that would be reasonable with a local purchase.

How Do You Make Sure the Business Stays Sold?

I know several people who have sold their companies more than once. A restaurant owner I know sold one small crepe restaurant five times. This may seem strange until you have been through a business sale. When you get to see the whole picture, it can begin to seem more surprising when a business does stay sold. You can end up getting your business back in your lap if you finance the purchase, which happens in most local-business purchases. If you sell to inexperienced businesspeople, they may not be able to run that company at the same income level you were able to produce. Since the asking price of the company means that all profits above salary go to the purchase agreement, if the new owners can't match your performance, they won't be able to meet their payments.

Your purchase agreement will spell out the details of what constitutes default and what options the new owners have of getting caught up. If these measures fail, the business returns to you. You get to keep the down payment and all other payments they have made on the business, but the company you get back may not resemble the company you sold two years earlier. You now have a company that is not making its past income, which means many of your old customers are gone. When I have seen this happen, most business owners have been able to pick the business up and dust it off. Usually within a few months, the owner has the company back to its previous glory. But that's not so great; after all, he was trying to sell the darn thing.

I know one case where the owners were not able to repair a company that landed back in their laps. A couple ran a mom-and-pop video-rental store. They sold it during the boom of mom-and-pop shops and came away with a good return. Two years later, the market fell out of the corner video-rental stores. The new owners failed, and the former owners could not reestablish their shop in the decimated video-rental market. They sold off the used videos and closed the store.

There are a couple of ways to avoid these calamities. One, you can reduce your asking price for a complete cash-out, which motivates the buyer to borrow money in order to pay you. Then, if the new owner fails, you're in the clear. Another way to protect yourself is to screen your purchasers carefully and refuse to sell to inexperienced businesspeople. This may not be practical, since businesspeople with a strong background in running companies would probably rather launch a company to compete with you than buy your business. Yet another way to secure your sale is to ask for personal collateral. These safeguards can help somewhat, but in most business sales the owner sells to inexperienced owners and crosses his fingers that all will go well.

How Do You Reverse an Unsuccessful Course?

Whatever course you choose for selling your company, test the waters while there is time to reverse an unsuccessful direction. Say your business is carrying $50,000 in debt from an equipment purchase. Also assume that you plan to sell the business and use some of the proceeds for your retirement. Are the closing proceeds on a potential sale likely to let you cover the business loan so that your ability to make good on the loan is not tied to the ability of the new owner to make payments? Can the loan transfer from you to the new owners?

You could easily find yourself having to settle the loan at the same time you are cashing out your broker. That means you could sell the business and still have to reach into your own pocket for, say, $20,000 and yet be up against a tax hit for the full amount you received to cover the loan. Boom—you sold your business, you had to come up with $20,000, and now you owe an additional $15,000 in taxes. You may be due a good return over the next six years, but the first payment may be eighteen months away. God forbid, but it may be cheaper to shut the business down and sell the equipment.

Selling Your Business—Points to Consider

1. Determine whether your company will be sold by a local business broker or an industry broker. The difference can greatly affect your sales price. Check to see how companies like yours are sold.

2. As you get within a few years of selling your company, begin meeting with potential brokers, both local and industry brokers if possible. As they look at your business, you will gain an understanding of how it should look when it's sold. Then you can spend the next few years getting the company into appropriate shape.

3. When it's time to sell your business, pick the right buyer and make the right deal to make sure it stays sold. Be patient. If you sell to the wrong buyer, you could get the business back a year later in hopeless condition.

Chapter 32

Leaving It to the Young

Just like the planning involved in preparing a business for sale through a broker, you have to plan ahead if you intend to leave your business to your children. This long-term goal will affect a whole range of business decisions you make from start-up through to the end. The particulars can get complicated with families. Not all children are equal in their interest in the enterprise. Should those who take an active interest receive more? Even if they were fairly compensated for their participation? These questions can take on biblical proportions unless you prepare the atmosphere before the carving and dividing begin. A game plan that's in place from the beginning and that changes along the way can solve these problems in advance.

It can be very satisfactory for a business founder to pass the enterprise on down to her children. This has been the story of human enterprise from our earliest days. The eldest son is the apprentice in dad's carpentry business. When dad tires out, the son takes over and all the other kids fend for themselves. Times have changed, of course. Statistically, the daughter is more likely to take over pop's business now. Give us one more generation and we will see sons taking over their moms' companies. The big problem now is that the other siblings are no longer content to just go out and fend for themselves. If sis is the only child who wants the business, she still has to settle up with her brothers and sisters. If the business is not producing enough to compensate them, she may not be able to take over. Probate is likely to say sell the darn thing and divide the proceeds. Sure, and under a court order, you'll get one heck of a good return on the sale of the business.

Your guard against a war among your heirs is to set the plan before the business leaves your control. If you have a clear and detailed will, probate will not step in and cut the baby in half. If your will is clear, in the above situation you would leave the business in the capable hands of sis with instructions for her to buy out her siblings over the course of a number of years that account for business downturns and a period of time for sis to get on her feet. Then, the business stays in the family and the other siblings get their share, but not at the expense of sis and the business.

Set Your Transition Plan From the Beginning

Even though you know things will change along the way, you need to set some guidelines in case the unexpected occurs. As the business grows and as your family matures, you will have to adjust your transition plan. If one of your children is particularly well suited to take the reins, put it in writing for that child to take over the business in the event of your passing. If it happens while you're alive, so much the better. But be firm with this child's siblings. Make it clear that they will get their fair share as the business grows and thrives. If they want their fair share right now, it often means tearing the company apart. The only thing that can stop this is your hand, either at the moment of transition or in an explicit will.

If things change, you can change your plan. Sis may get tired of waiting for dad to let go, and in her understandable impatience, she may go ahead and launch her own business, in which case he needs to identify another interested child or stipulate that the business will be managed by someone of his attorney's choosing until a suitable buyer can be found. There are a hundred ways to configure your transition, but make sure you, rather than the courts, are the one calling the shots on what happens to the business. Under a court order to sell and distribute the proceeds of the business, your heirs will not receive a fair return on all the years of your efforts.

Check In on the Next Generation

Does anyone in your family want your business when you're ready to walk away? When it is left to the next generation, will your children just maintain it or put it on the auction block? These questions will have different answers at different stages in the life of your family. You may find that it is time for retirement and all of your children live in different states, deeply involved in their own lives. If you know none of your children are interested in assuming control of the business at the time you're ready to retire, you can oversee the sale of the business, and the proceeds become part of your retirement nest egg. This can be the easiest transition since the proceeds will flow evenly to your children when you pass, and there will be no conflict over control of a major asset.

Train Your Kids

If you know one or more of your children want to keep the enterprise going, get them trained in the basics. Some business owners bring one or more of their kids into the business well in advance of the transition so the reins can pass without a business hiccup. If one of your children is interested in carrying on and your other kids have their own interests, this is an easy decision. The only difficulty will be fairly compensating your other kids without putting too great a strain on the company.

One of the most difficult scenarios is when two of your children are interested in the company and both have worked in the business through the years. This can be a thorny problem after you pass. While you're there, you're in control, so there is no dispute over who directs the company. When you are out of the picture, what do you intend to leave behind? Do you want your kids stuck with a partnership, that two-headed beast that pulls in two directions at once, or do you want to assign control of the business to your most capable child? It's wise to be tough here and put one of the two in charge. Better that than to let them fight it out after you pass. If you don't have the stomach to designate one of your kids as leader, just sell the business and divide the proceeds.

Hands Off, Mom and Dad

A common and difficult problem that can arise during a business transition is the reluctance of the founding generation to let go of the business. Here's how it goes: Dad brings in his daughter to take over the business, but he stays on for a transition period that isn't specified. Daughter is okay with the indeterminate nature of the transition out of deference to her father, who launched the enterprise. As the arrangement starts, he explains that he will turn over the checkbook to her shortly and will stay on as a consultant for a brief period. A couple of months go by and he still has the checkbook, and daughter is more or less nothing but an employee.

After six months, she asks what his plans are. He explains that he just wanted to get through this recent tough patch. Another six months go by, and daughter decides to take a job with another company. Dads says he's disappointed, but he is secretly relieved. He stays on with the business until his death, at which time the business is hastily sold. Another common version of this is that the daughter stays on for years waiting for dad to turn over control and he never does. Finally death puts her at the reins only to find that her siblings have suddenly taken a keen interest in the enterprise.

Passing Your Business to Your Children— Points to Consider

1. Make sure your children are just as interested in running the business as you have been. You don't want your kids to take the business out of a sense of obligation.

2. Train your kids to manage it effectively. Impart as much knowledge as you can, turning the business over to them while you are still there as a consultant.

3. Then, finally let go. One of the most difficult parts of a business transition happens when the owner brings in the kids but retains all decision-making control. This can kill your children's interest in the company.

Chapter 33

Planning for the Unexpected

Planning for the unexpected takes real discipline. Who wants to prepare for death or disability? When you are running a business, there are more urgent tasks, and certainly more pleasant tasks. When the business day is over, the last thing you want to do is go over scenarios of what to do if something awful happens. But thinking about what happens when a family isn't prepared to deal with mom's business can give you serious pause. Who's going to run the company when it's in probate because there were no legal preparations? You owe it to your family and you owe it to your company's possibilities to develop a plan of action if you are suddenly yanked off the scene.

Designate Temporary Reins

No matter how young you may be when you launch your business, you should designate someone, if something happens to you, to run it until it can be sold or passed on to the next generation. Even if you know that your number three daughter will take control, it can help for a transitional figure, such as your attorney, to maintain oversight until your daughter comes to an equitable agreement with her siblings and remaining parent, or until the prearranged agreement has taken effect. It can be very difficult to negotiate the emergency transition if one of the kids has her hands on the wheel of a major family asset.

You should have that emergency transition plan in place in case anything happens, from an accidental death to a serious illness. The plan should have a couple of elements: a plan to keep the business going until you're back up and going, and one to cover a situation in which you will not return to the company. You don't have to go into great detail as long as you explain what you believe would be the best course of action for all involved. Write it out in a couple of pages. You want it to be flexible enough for your family to apply it in a practical manner, but the guidelines should spell out who you think would be the best steward of the company.

Give Your Plans Legal Status

To further make your emergency transition plan effective, you should give it legal status by turning it over to your attorney and explaining to those concerned that you have made provisions for unexpected events. Since this is an emergency or contingency plan, it will operate differently from a will. If you expect to be back at the wheel in time, the plan is simply instructions on who can keep the business afloat until you return. If you are not going to be able to return, the document gives instructions on how to guide the business until your will takes effect. It is the will itself that will provide the detailed instructions of how ownership is passed on, but since this process may take days or weeks, the transition guidelines give your family instructions on how to care for the company until it passes to your heirs.

You don't want your family members to ask each other, "Well, what do you think dad would want us to do?" Spell it out in a couple of pages and give those to your attorney. That will end the hand-writing that can come at a difficult time. Your attorney can simply talk to your family members and explain how you wanted business matters handled until either you get back on your feet or until the will passes ownership to your designated heirs. These guidelines will bring relief. Even if your instructions are not followed exactly because of mitigating circumstances, at least your family will have your guidance.

Communicate to All Involved While You Can

You don't have to go into elaborate detail about your transition plan with those concerned, but you should at least alert them to the fact that you have some emergency plans developed. Go over them quickly with someone close, like your spouse or a grown child, who might be named as a person to help out with the company or actually take control. Ask for some input. You will probably get a response such as "Whatever you want to do is fine with me," because nobody likes going over what-if scenarios. It's hard to conceive of an abrupt event that would change your situation dramatically. But if something happens, the person you confided in will be greatly relieved that you have made contingency plans.

Have Disability and Life Insurance

In Chapter 13, we covered some of the reasons to add disability and life insurance to your business overhead. Here is the situation where insurance considerations pay for themselves. The disability insurance will provide income while your company grapples with the unexpected circumstances. You certainly don't want a financial crisis to be part of your period of disability. If your family is not able to keep your company going at the level you ran it, at least there is a flow of income until you're back at the helm. If you die suddenly, the life insurance can be a major relief from financial calamity. Most business owners make sure their life insurance is adequate both to cover outstanding liabilities and to provide some additional cash to help the family stay solvent.

You can designate how you want your beneficiary to disburse the insurance proceeds that keep the business from losing value during this transition. Spell out how much of the proceeds are needed to settle old obligations, how much should go into the business to keep its bills paid until ownership passes or a buyer is found, and how much should pass to your heirs. Even if new circumstances dictate some variations on your plan, the guides you provide can offer a foundation to keep your business from losing value and keep your family out of a financial crisis.

Sometimes you are not able to plan the business transition. Life has the potential to throw you a curve. Your business may be your family's greatest asset, and it may be the most vulnerable asset if you do not have emergency plans in place.

Making Plans for the Unexpected—Points to Consider

1. Designate a person to run the company in the event you can't. In a few pages, explain who should take over the company if you are temporarily unable to function and what should be done if the change is permanent. Give the details to your spouse and attorney.

2. Also, since the business is a family asset, put the details of the transition in your will. If you choose to have the business sold upon your death, jot down a plan so it won't be done hastily, since a quick panic sale will not bring the potential full price.

3. Disability and life insurance can greatly help your family through an abrupt change in circumstances. Your family may need to use life insurance proceeds to hire a business manager to run the company while it's up for sale.

Part IX

The Loneliness of the Long-Distance Runner

Marathon runners are probably the best suited for small-business success. They are accustomed to forging ahead while in pain. They are able to train day in and day out to ultimately run an unreasonable distance. In their toughest moments, they are alone, knowing that the positive outcome they desire is on the other side of a hard and painful wall. They are not completely sure of the outcome, but they are sure of their commitment. Are you suited for this pursuit? I can tell you one thing: You cannot get a real feel for what you're up against until you're well into the race. Here's where business ownership differs from running: The runner can train with long runs; the business owner doesn't really get to know what the race is like until she enters it.

You can take fellow business owners out to lunch every day of the week and still not get a clear idea of what it's like to run a business. It's overwhelming, stressful, frustrating, exhilarating, frightening, and hard. During the first year, you will have many nights when you wonder whether you've made a terrible blunder, but in the morning you'll go back to it. You may find that after a few weeks your spouse is the worst person to talk to about your difficulties because it's so upsetting. Your spouse may come to dislike the business and your obsession with succeeding. But it won't seem like an obsession to you. It will just seem like the logical way to respond to a very difficult job. Launching a business is a personal challenge like no other. Within a few weeks, you have dropped the thought, 'I hope I succeed,' and you will replace it with, 'I must succeed.' And it will seem natural, not extreme or excessive.

You will lose interest in many of your past concerns and pastimes. You will probably even lose interest in your appearance, except inasmuch as it helps your business succeed. You won't notice the weather; you won't notice if your children are starting to draw on the white wall behind your desk. But you will note every tiny inch closer you get to closing a sale with a major client. You will be intensely aware of the tiny percentage increase you have gained this month over last month's receipts. You will also notice how your voice changes as you talk to your printer and say, "I know you quoted $1,350 for the brochures, but is there any way you can do it for $1,200? Can't you at least give me a 20 percent overrun?" You never thought of yourself as a demanding customer before, but you've come to see that the demands get met, and that you owe it to your company to get the most from every dollar spent.

You may find yourself getting up in the middle of the night with a knot in your stomach. At that moment, you will probably have some doubts about whether you are cut out to run a business. You'll wonder if it takes someone who is cut from a tougher piece of cloth. These doubts are natural. Every business owner I know has experienced these dark nights. To succeed in business, most people have to reach inside and transform part of themselves. It changes you, just as parenthood changes you. The transition is not smooth, and it is not all pleasant, but coming out on the other side is exhilarating. By the time you move through the tough, dark tunnel, you come out enlightened.

There are ways to cope with some of the pressures. Regular exercise, stress-relieving activities, a healthy amount of sleep—they all help. But the real solution is a combination of getting the business into profitability and accepting that there will always be stress-producing events in business, whether it's a customer who is unreasonable or a key vendor who turns around and goes into business as a competitor. One high-level GM executive once described the business world to me: "It's like a lake. On the surface it appears serene, smooth, and beautiful, but underneath that gentle surface, all of the creatures are desperately trying to eat each other." That's a mighty grim image, but I get his point.

I think it's more like the sky. It can appear blue and clear, but once you get up there, you find out there are some rough and exciting winds. They can come from any angle and they can suddenly vanish. You can find yourself dropping, just to discover that with a few corrective moves you're back on an upward curve that takes you higher than you've ever been. It's scary up there, but the view is tremendous. The air makes you feel alive all over. The longer you stay in the wind, the stronger you get. And in time, you begin to see that no matter how fast you drop and how hard you hit the ground, you can get back up and lift yourself into the wind again.

Chapter 34

Judging Your Own Suitability

A strong, persistent desire to own and run a business is necessary for starting a company. It will not work if you are halfhearted. You also need the ability to endure frustration, to learn from your mistakes, and to keep a sharp focus on what's important. It helps if you have considerable background in the business, particularly sales and marketing experience. It also helps if you have done all your background research and have chosen a business that will work particularly well for you. Beyond that, business ownership will require you to keep your wits about you, use your imagination and creativity, and stay persistent.

Because you are launching from your home, the odds are in your favor to succeed. There has never been a better time to launch a business, and home is the very best place to do it. Launching from home gives you a better than fair chance for success, which is the best odds for starting a business since these statistics started being compiled. This is a far cry from the early 1970s when business experts predicted the demise of the small business. It was believed that business success necessitated a source of significant capital. Back then, the experts were too shortsighted to see that the currency of the future was not capital but information. Now, to start a business you need desire, intelligence, imagination, gall, determination, and persistence, but you don't need much capital.

How Do You Weather the Surprises of Business Ownership?

No matter how successful you may be in your business venture, there will be surprises along the way. A surprise can take the form of a key vendor who goes into competition against you or a sudden change in your market. Just before I launched my first business, my former boss, whose business I had helped build, said that I would probably not enjoy being a business owner.

"Why?" I asked.

She looked me dead in the eye and said, "There are things that happen in business that you will find are very unpleasant."

Once I was up and going for a few months, I began to get a good understanding of what she meant. Not everything goes right, no matter how hard you try and no matter how hard your vendors try. She was right. I did find some things that were very unpleasant, but I came to view those as just part of the price you pay to be independent. I find that isn't too high a price to pay for the freedom that comes with business ownership. It just becomes part of the background. Disturbing at times, sure, but generally if you stabilize your company and keep it up-to-date, there is far more pleasure than there is distress.

As with any aspect of life, surprises can always come, but most seasoned business owners come to the realization that surprises and sudden changes can be addressed, and there is a solution to every problem that appears. As long as you stay confident that you will pull through, the ups and downs are just part of being the owner—they come with the territory and it's okay. As Norman Vincent Peale said, "I haven't had any problems lately. Lord, don't you trust me anymore?"

Change Your Business Path If You Don't Like Your Direction

One of the great advantages of running your own business is that you have some control of the atmosphere and business environment you call home. A consultant friend of mine is very picky about who he brings on as a client. If he feels that a client is unnecessarily crude, harsh, or inappropriate, he phases that client out with the comment, "What's the use of running your own business if you can't throw out the jerks? Life's too short." So, to my boss who thought the unsavory aspects of business would be unpleasant, I say, yes, unsavory behavior by clients, employees, and associates is unpalatable, and so I choose to remove those qualities from my business rather than avoid business ownership. And I encourage all business owners to refuse to put up with poor behavior in any business relationship.

But this principle doesn't have to hold your business back. There is plenty of great business out there with people who make your life richer. After fifteen years of running my own companies, a good portion of my friends are people I met through business. Some started out as customers, some started out as vendors. Many of these friends started out as associates whom I took to lunch to pick their brains about marketing or product development. After the first few years, the unpleasant aspects of business became a smaller and smaller part of my business day. I have found that you can change your business to accommodate your values and preferences. You can take your company down a road that increases the positive aspects and minimizes the negative experiences.

Some entrepreneurs try a number of products and services until they find a mix that works. I've seen network marketers try a variety of product lines until they find the right blend between products and customer base. I've seen retailers who experiment with different types of products until they find the balance between products they can be proud of and a clientele they enjoy. If the mix doesn't seem right at first, play with it until you get it right. When I began a publishing company, I tried a number of magazine products, from newcomer guides to construction-association directories. I finally found success with a magazine titled *Chile Pepper,* which was a food magazine devoted to hot foods.

Part of the success came because I loved the subject matter and its market. The subscribers were extremely enthusiastic about hot foods, and the advertisers were a colorful bunch of food producers who were very passionate about their hot sauces, salsas, grilling glazes, and gumbos. For me, building this magazine was tons more fun than calling on real estate companies, banks, and ad agencies for ads in city publications. You are more likely to be successful if you can find a market with a product or service that you find exciting and stimulating. So work with your business and experiment with different directions until you find the match between your passions and a ripe market.

How Long Are You Willing to Struggle?

You can't determine all of your business moves through logic, calculation, and planning. Sometimes you just have to feel your way through. I was once told that when you are doing what's right for you, the doors will open by themselves. Okay, I also know that sometimes doors give way because you push on them long enough. The difference between your success and someone else's failure is your willingness to lean on the door longer. How much struggle is required to get a business up and going? How long are you willing to struggle? At what point do you give in, accepting the belief that continuing to struggle will not get you where you want to go? We all have to come up with our own answers to these questions.

At different times in our lives, the answers to these questions are different. Each business you attempt will come with its own set of answers. I have owned three companies, and with each company the answers were different. I had one company that required a great deal of struggle, but the more I tried, the better the business performed. I pushed hard on the doors and the doors gave way, albeit slowly. I owned another business that required a great deal of struggle, and the more I struggled, the tighter the doors held. Finally it was too late, and I had no resources to continue the push. Next, I started a business that required almost no struggle. It seemed the doors were already open, waiting for me to walk through.

I don't know what to make of any of this except to say that it's hard to tell if you're in the right business until you get there and begin working to get it up and going. The work may exhaust you, or it may stimulate you. Usually it is a combination: some days exhausting, some days stimulating. If you are excited by your work in the business, you will probably figure out a way to survive and succeed. If it exhausts you and you don't get replenished by the sheer fun of it, you will probably try to find a way to get out of it while you still have breath left. Don't be afraid to switch courses if your efforts seem to bring no positive results.

If you are absolutely determined to own your own business, you will push harder, learn faster, and find the whole effort exciting, even if it's frightening at times. If you are really determined, business failure won't stop you, it will only delay you. I know a western history writer who carved a name for himself by telling the true stories (as opposed to myth) of gunfighters. In talking to a group of would-be writers, he said, "There isn't a person in this room who isn't a better writer than I am. I didn't get fifteen books published because I'm a greater writer. I revise my work ten or fifteen times. I'm here with fifteen books published and you're there listening to me without any books because I outworked you. I guess I just wanted it more."

It was fairly stunning. Certainly the students in this workshop didn't expect those comments, but they were true. The truth is that he was determined to succeed as a writer and didn't let his perceived lack of writing talent stop him from pursuing what he loved. It's the same with your business. When you launch, you will learn a great deal about yourself. The important thing you will learn has little to do with your abilities or talent; it has everything to do with your determination. If you are determined, committed, and persistent, you can develop the abilities you need. If you find that running a company is just not for you, it will come clear over the weeks and months of trying to succeed. If you're determined enough, failure is merely an obstacle.

Expand to a Bigger Arena

You may find that you have a real knack for business. One of the qualities of business ownership is that you don't reach an end to its challenges. If you seem to have a good handle on your local business, perhaps you should try to expand beyond your community. The sky is the limit for business owners. Sometimes success in the home company just gives you a taste for something larger. The home-business movement leaves you with a wide range of choices. In a home business, you can often expand your enterprise without moving out into public quarters. The Internet is especially ripe for home-business expansion, since you can build a very credible presence online without moving to an outside office.

Your opportunities to expand your business while staying in your home setting will only grow with time. The business world no longer marginalizes your work because you do it from home, and your home will continue to provide great overhead savings as you continue to expand and extend your company. Don't let your decision to remain in your home limit your view of how big your business can get or how far it can reach. If you are determined to grow and succeed, and if you are equally determined to keep your company in the den, use your creativity to devise ways to make it happen. Home-business owners all over the country are demonstrating that the home doesn't have to limit your company's possibilities.

Constrict to a Smaller World

Other business owners may find that the larger world of expanding horizons diminishes the charm of a small business with friendly clients. Sometimes the answer to a business that just isn't as fun as it used to be is to gear back down to a small enterprise that is easier on the nerves. Growth is not always positive. I've seen companies reach profitability with revenues of $250,000 per year, only to go back in the red when the owner committed to a larger overhead in an attempt to drive receipts up to $1 million. I have also seen companies grow to greater profitability only to become an unpleasant set of headaches for their owners. If getting bigger takes the fun and profit out of your company, downsize to where it's pleasant and profitable.

This can be fairly easy for the professional practice. Attorneys, architects, marketing consultants, and even landscapers can keep their companies growing while keeping it trim by qualifying their clients and reaching to the top of their markets. An attorney really only needs one client, if it's the right client. It's the same with other professions. Business growth can often be just a matter of continually improving the client base, thinning out the low-paying, slow-paying, and no-paying clients. For non-professionals, there are similar opportunities. For the house-cleaning service, you can concentrate on the larger home; for janitorial services, you can focus on the larger office buildings.

Often a young company will take any business it can get just to launch. Then it's owner spends years and years trying to improve the client base and move up to the more profitable portions of the market. In this case, growth is not a matter of quantity; it's a matter of quality. You stay small, but you improve your customer and client mix to bring higher profits and a more predictable cash flow. Usually you can't start right out capturing the best clients. You have to prove yourself before the most desirable clients will begin to try your services.

Judging your suitability to run a home business is not just a matter of deciding whether business ownership is for you, it is also a process of finding which enterprise is right. Within a few weeks or months, you will have a pretty good idea whether you find business ownership appealing, but it may take quite a bit longer to discover which business is ideal. And the type of business that is right for you may change through the years. I went through a period when I wanted to see how large I could get a business to grow. That was followed by a period when I wanted to see how profitable I could get a business to be. These are different goals. Throughout your career as an entrepreneur, you may create different styles to accommodate different needs and goals.

Judging Yourself as a Business Owner— Points to Consider

1. Business is full of surprises and unexpected turns. Some people thrive on the roller-coaster aspect of being an entrepreneur, while others find it too unsettling. Leave yourself the opportunity to exit if business ownership is just not for you.

2. You may find that growth is so enticing that you are ready to leave the home nest and get bigger, bigger, and bigger. Allow for this possibility in your planning.

3. As your business changes and grows, you may also find you preferred it when it was smaller. Growth is not always good, but it is usually the automatic goal for all companies. Remember, sometimes it's best to gear back down if you find that your growth has made the business either unpleasant to run or less profitable.

Chapter 35

Always Remember the Rewards

It is hard to build wealth when you are an employee. Business ownership is the most common path to financial independence. But for most entrepreneurs, building a business is about more than just making money. Usually the business owner seeks independence and the means to achieve and grow creatively and professionally. Few other jobs offer a continuing challenge to grow, but owning your company is nothing but an opportunity for constant growth. The profits are often the means for measurement and the justification for the endeavor. Profits are the proof that your efforts have been successful.

Owning a business is the heart of the American dream. It's a way to take control of your own destiny, a way to test your stamina, your creativity, and your wits. It is certainly not boring. Quite the opposite—it comes with an intensity that needs to be moderated. Part of the pressure is the knowledge that a lot is at stake (Uncle Carl's nest egg, for example). Often this brings out the best in people. Great achievement is possible when you own your business. The rewards are personal as well as financial. Creating and growing a business is a way to find out just how much you have to give.

Take Breaks and Vacations

As a business owner, you can get so wrapped up in making sure you succeed that the race to profitability gains the quality of a life-or-death dash. Under the pressure and circumstances of a business start-up, the idea of a break or vacation seems ludicrous. But what's really ridiculous is the belief that you can sustain a high level of quality effort without taking breaks and vacations. Lee Iacocca said you are not successful until you can be effective in a forty-hour week—not that he kept his hours down to forty. The idea is sound. If you have to put in eighty hours to make your business successful, you're not there yet.

How far can you run when you hold your breath? How long can you keep going when you sprint all-out, going faster than you have ever run? On the other hand, how far can you run if you keep your breathing steady and stop before you're exhausted, then try again the next day when you're rested? You get my point. Again, marathon training is a good analogy for getting a business going, but the marathon comparison is only for the start-up period.

Once the business is up and going, you can drop the marathon concept and compare your effort to a five-mile morning run five days a week, with a half-marathon thrown in once or twice a year. Find a pace that is comfortable but still a challenge. Running a healthy business is not about constantly pushing the envelope and running on the edge. That style eventually produces burnout and collapse. As a banker friend once remarked, if you make it your style to live on the edge, sooner or later you're going to fall off.

Here's a hint from one who has been there: Even though it seems impossible to take days off and, God forbid, go out of town on a short vacation, the break can be good for your business as well as for you. For one, you need to be replenished by rest and diversion in order to sustain your high level of performance. Two, it can be very hard to see solutions to your company's difficulties when you're up close, thrashing away at the daily chores and tasks. Sometimes the start-up effort can become a blind frenzy; it seems that if you turn away for even a moment, the whole thing will collapse. That's when you need a break the most, when it truly seems that you can't pause.

But something magic happens when you get away (or when your spouse drags you away with a sober ultimatum): You get some perspective. Three days away and you are beginning to breathe more regularly. You begin to think, not hard but casually. And ideas come, creative thoughts about how you can change a few things to make your business more manageable and more successful. It takes a few days away before you can begin to see your inefficiencies and wheel-spinning that are there when you're in a frenzy. Most business owners come back from a vacation stronger and more confident in their ability to tackle the challenges, and they usually walk into the business office with a parcel of new ideas.

Are You Improving Your Life?

Thoreau said that to improve your life, improve the quality of your day. What's your day like? It's understandable if the first year or two of your business produce pressure, burden, challenge, and push. It can be both exhilarating and unpleasant; that's the launch environment. By the time your business is up and going, that desperate period should transition into a time of growth and fulfillment. Owning a business should improve your life, and not just your financial life. Ultimately, owning the business should improve your life in a variety of ways.

List Your Personal Rewards

Don't wait until your business succeeds before you begin to outline the real reasons you want your own business. Listing these reasons can be a touchstone at times. I started a business that was very satisfying for years, but as time wore on, it lost its luster and became unpleasant. The business was prospering and I had developed a staff of twenty, but I was unhappy: I didn't like putting out all the fires; I didn't like the staff conflict; I didn't like the staff meetings; and I really disliked the investor meetings. As I contemplated selling the company to get it off my back, I thought about my disappointment. I had grown the company beyond my expectations and there was plenty of growth left, so I wasn't caught in the "no more horizons" malaise.

Then it dawned on me: I had lost my freedom. I didn't go into business to make a bundle of money and build an organization. I set off on my own for the freedom to follow my own course and do or die with my own inclinations and dreams. But I had found myself tied to investors, tied to a staff, tied to a set course of growth that was bargained and agreed on by investors and staff alike. This was worse than being an employee. I was the leader, bargaining my own freedom away to inspire others, to gain investor confidence, and to build consensus. Well, to hell with consensus. I sold the darn thing and went back to a one-man shop, a tiny home business that left me free to carve my own fate.

If I had done an inventory of my own motivation earlier, I may have been able to chart a different course for the company, one that would have kept my true motivation at the top of the list. Instead, I had let the belief in continual growth and expansion determine the direction of the company. The company had become the antithesis of the environment I really wanted to create for myself. I don't know whether I could have saved myself some unpleasant years or not. The compulsion to see how big I could get the company to grow may have overridden any soul-searching. But at least then it would not have been a surprise to me that I wasn't improving the quality of my day and that's why I was unhappy.

Let Your Goals and Rewards Evolve

We are human beings, so we change. It's in our nature to grow, move forward, and leave some of our past concerns behind. The things that were important to us in our twenties may not be driving our thoughts when we're in our fifties. But if anything, we become more honest with ourselves and more committed to recognizing our strengths and limitations. So as you grow, the reasons for being in business will probably evolve. You may start out to prove that you can do it, only to finally say, "Well, yeah, I did it, and now what?" Your goal then may be to create a business that allows you to participate in a subject you love, such as fly fishing. Perhaps you succeeded with a consulting service, and now it's time to do something closer to your heart.

Going into business is a long-term proposition. You will need to pace yourself. You will likely be tempted to go full throttle until you reach that magic level of profit that makes you feel safe, but you can crash and burn if you push too hard. Remember to move forward at a manageable stride.

Rewarding Yourself—Points to Consider

1. Take breaks and vacations just as if you were working for an employer. Sometimes it doesn't seem practical, but the breaks can reinvigorate you, making you more productive and creative.

2. Make sure business ownership improves your life. Sometimes the point of succeeding can blind you to the reality that business ownership has a negative impact on your life. Remember, the business should serve you, not the other way around.

3. Develop rewards for yourself as you reach individual milestones: a dinner out if you meet the monthly goal, a weekend away if you hit your annual target. You need to remember to motivate and reward yourself.

Part X
Resources

This section will give you all the leads you need to obtain the resources necessary to succeed—from investors and loans to business plans and marketing strategies. Don't be surprised if the area codes in the phone numbers are no longer valid; area codes are changing so rapidly no book can keep up.

Resources

VENTURE CAPITAL AND INVESTORS

Here are some resources so you can locate venture capitalists and other potential investors to help you with launch capital.

National Association of Investment Companies
1111 14th St., NW, #700
Washington, DC 20005
(202) 289-4336
(This is an organization committed to investing in companies with socially or economically disadvantaged owners. A member directory is available.)

National Venture Capital Association
1655 N. Ft. Meyer Dr., #850
Arlington, VA 22209
(703) 524-2549
(It offers a member directory of venture capitalists.)

Pratt's Guide to Venture Capital Sources
SDC Publishing
40 W. 57th St., #802
New York, NY 10019
(212) 765-5311
(This annual reference guide lists hundreds of sources for venture capi-

tal, listed by state, by company, and by industry preference.)

Small Business Investment Companies
Associate Administrator for Investment
Small Business Administration
409 Third St., SW
Washington, DC 20416
(202) 205-7589
www.sba.com
(It provides a free listing of investors licensed by the SBA to offer venture capital to qualifying companies.)

Technology Capital Network
MIT
201 Vassar St., Bldg. W59
Cambridge, MA 02139
(617) 253-7163
(This network provides a database of investors and entrepreneurs seeking funding. It makes matches according to industry and amount of required capital.)

GOVERNMENT AGENCIES

Federal Government Agencies

Copyright Clearance Center
222 Rosewood Dr.
Danvers, MA 01923
(508) 750-8400
www.copyright.com

Copyright Office, Library of Congress
101 Independence Ave.
Washington, DC 20559
(202) 707-3000
www.loc.gov/copyright

Department of Commerce
14th St. and Constitution Ave., NW
Washington, DC 20230
(202) 482-2000
www.doc.gov

Department of Labor
200 Constitution Ave., NW, Room
   S-1004
Washington, DC 20210
(202) 219-6666
www.dol.com

Department of Treasury
Main Treasury Bldg.
1500 Pennsylvania Ave., NW
Washington, DC 20220
(202) 622-6000
www.treas.gov

Export-Import Bank of the United
   States
811 Vermont Ave., NW
Washington, DC 20571
(202) 565-3946
www.exim.gov

Internal Revenue Service
1111 Constitution Ave., NW
Washington, DC 20224
(202) 622-5000
www.ustreas.gov

Patent and Trademark Office
Washington, DC 20231
(800) 786-9199
www.uspto.gov

Small Business Administration

The SBA has a range of services, from loan programs to free consulting, for the home business through the Service Corps of Retired Executives (SCORE), a group of retired executives that helps small companies. Each state office of the SBA can put you in touch with appropriate SCORE consultants.

SBA Main Office

Small Business Administration
409 Third St., SW
Washington, DC 20416
(800) 827-5722
www.sba.gov.

SBA Regional Offices

SBA Region 1
155 Federal St., 9th Floor

Boston, MA 02110
(617) 451-2030

SBA Region 2
26 Federal Plaza, Room 31-08
New York, NY 10278
(212) 264-1450

SBA Region 3
475 Allendale Rd., Suite 201
King of Prussia, PA 19406
(215) 962-3700

SBA Region 4
1375 Peachtree St., NE, Room 502
Atlanta, GA 30367-8102

SBA Region 5
300 S. Riverside Plaza, Room 1975
 S
Chicago, IL 60606-6611
(312) 353-5000

SBA Region 6
8625 King George Dr., Bldg. C
Dallas, TX 75235-3391
(214) 767-7633

SBA Region 7
Federal Office Bldg.
911 Walnut St., 13th Floor
Kansas City, MO 64106
(816) 426-3608

SBA Region 8
999 18th St., Suite 701
Denver, CO 80202
(303) 294-7186

SBA Region 9
71 Stevenson St.
San Francisco, CA 94105
(415) 744-6402

SBA Region 10
2615 4th Ave., Room 440
Seattle, WA 98121
(206) 553-5676

SBA State District Offices

Alabama
2121 Eighth Ave., N, #200
Birmingham, AL 35203-2398
(205) 731-1344

Alaska
222 W. Eighth Ave., Room A36
Anchorage, AK 99513-7559
(907) 271-4022

Arizona
2828 N. Central Ave., #800
Phoenix, AZ 84004-1093
(602) 640-2316

Arkansas
2120 Riverfront Dr., #100
Little Rock, AR 72202
(501) 324-5871

California
2719 N. Air Fresno Dr., #107
Fresno, CA 93727-1547
(209) 487-5189

330 N. Brand Blvd., #1200
Glendale, CA 91203-2304
(818) 552-3210

550 W. C St., #550
San Diego, CA 92101
(619) 557-7252

660 J St., Room 215
Sacramento, CA 95814-2413
(916) 498-6410

200 W. Santa Ana Blvd., #700
Santa Ana, CA 92701
(714) 550-7420

Colorado
721 19th St., #426
Denver, CO 80202-2599
(303) 844-3984

Connecticut
330 Main St., 2nd Floor
Hartford, CT 06106
(860) 240-4700

Delaware
824 N. Market St., #610
Wilmington, DE 19801-3011
(302) 573-6294

District of Columbia
1110 Vermont Ave., NW, #900
Washington, DC 20005
(202) 606-4000

Florida
1320 S. Dixie Highway, #350
Coral Gables, FL 33146-2911
(305) 536-5521

7825 Baymeadows Way,
 #100-B
Jacksonville, FL 32256-7504
(904) 443-1900

Georgia
1720 Peachtree Rd., NW, 6th Floor
Atlanta, GA 30309
(404) 347-4749

Hawaii
300 Ala Moana Blvd., Room 2314
Honolulu, HI 96850-4981
(808) 541-2990

Idaho
1020 Main St., #290
Boise, ID 83702-5745
(208) 334-1696

Illinois
500 W. Madison St., #1250
Chicago, IL 60661-2511
(312) 353-4508

511 W. Capitol Ave., #302
Springfield, IL 62704
(217) 492-4416

Indiana
429 N. Pennsylvania, #100
Indianapolis, IN 46204-1873
(317) 226-7272

Iowa
Mail Code 0736
215 Fourth Ave., SE, #200
The Lattner Building
Cedar Rapids, IA 52401-1806
(319) 362-6405

210 Walnut St., Room 749
Des Moines, IA 50309-2186
(515) 284-4422

Kansas
100 E. English St., #510
Wichita, KS 67202
(316) 269-6616

Kentucky
600 Dr. Martin Luther King, Jr. Pl.,
Room 188
Louisville, KY 40202
(502) 582-5971

Louisiana
365 Canal St., #2250
New Orleans, LA 70130
(504) 589-6685

Maine
40 Western Ave., Room 512
Augusta, ME 04330
(207) 622-8378

Maryland
10 S. Howard St., #6220
Baltimore, MD 21201-2525
(410) 962-4392

Massachusetts
10 Causeway St., Room 265
Boston, MA 02222-1093
(617) 656-5590

Michigan
477 Michigan Ave., Room 515
Detroit, MI 48226
(313) 226-6075

Minnesota
100 N. Sixth St., #610, Buder
Square
Minneapolis, MN 55403-1563
(612) 370-2324

Mississippi
101 W. Capitol St., #400
Jackson, MS 39201
(601) 965-4378

Missouri
323 W. Eighth St., #501
Kansas City, MO 64105
(816) 374-6708

815 Olive St., Room 242
St. Louis, MO 63101
(314) 539-6600

Montana
301 S. Park Ave., Room 334
Helena, MT 59626-0054
(406) 441-1081

Nebraska
11145 Mill Valley Rd.
Omaha, NE 68154
(402) 221-4691

Nevada
301 E. Steward Ave., Room 301
Las Vegas, NV 89101
(702) 388-6611

New Hampshire
143 N. Main St., #202
Concord, NH 03302-1248
(603) 225-1400

New Jersey
2 Gateway Center, 4th Floor
Newark, NJ 07102
(201) 645-2434

New Mexico
625 Silver SW, #320
Albuquerque, NM 87102
(505) 766-1870

New York
26 Federal Plaza, #31-00
New York, NY 10278
(212) 264-2454

100 S. Clinton St., #1071
Syracuse, NY 13260
(315) 448-0423

North Carolina
200 N. College St., Suite A-2015
Charlotte, NC 28202-2137
(704) 344-6563

North Dakota
657 Second Ave. N., Room 219
Fargo, ND 58108-3086
(701) 239-5131

Ohio
1111 Superior Ave., #630
Cleveland, OH 44114-2507
(216) 522-4180

1111 Nationwide Plaza, #1400
Columbus, OH 43215-2542
(614) 469-6860

Oklahoma
210 Park Ave., #1300
Oklahoma, OK 73102
(405) 231-5521

Oregon
1515 S.W. Fifth Ave., #1050
Portland, OR 97201-6695
(503) 326-2682

Pennsylvania
475 Allendale Rd., #201
King of Prussia, PA 19406
(610) 962-3800

1000 Liberty Ave., Room 1128
Pittsburgh, PA 15222-4004
(412) 644-2780

Puerto Rico
252 Ponce de Leon Blvd., Room 201
Hato Rey, PR 00918
(787) 766-5572

Rhode Island
380 Westminister Mall, 5th Floor
Providence, RI 02903
(401) 528-4561

South Carolina
1835 Assembly St., Room 358
Columbia SC 29201
(803) 765-5377

South Dakota
110 S. Phillips Ave., #200
Sioux Falls, SD 57102-1109
(605) 330-4231

Tennessee
50 Vantage Way, #201
Nashville, TN 37228-1500
(615) 736-5881

Texas
4300 Amon Carter Blvd., #114
Ft. Worth, TX 76155
(817) 885-6500

10737 Gateway W., #320
El Paso, TX 79935
(915) 540-5676

9301 Southwest Highway, #550
Houston, TX 77074-1591
(713) 773-6500

222 E. Van Buren St., Room 500
Harlington, TX 78550-6855
(210) 427-8533
1611 10th St., #200
Lubbock, TX 79401-2693
(806) 743-7462
727 E. Durango Blvd., Room
   A-527
San Antonio, TX 78206-1204
(210) 472-5900

Utah
125 S. State St., Room 2229
Salt Lake City, UT 84138-1195
(801) 524-5804

Vermont
87 State St., Room 205
Montpelier, VT 05602
(802) 828-4422

Virginia
1504 Santa Rosa Rd., #200
Richmond, VA 23229
(804) 771-2400

Washington
1200 Sixth Ave., Room 1700
Seattle, WA 98101-1128
(206) 553-7310

W. 601 First Ave., 10th Floor
Spokane, WA 99204-0317
(509) 353-2810

West Virginia
168 W. Main St., 5th Floor
Clarksburg, WV 26301
(304) 623-5631

Wisconsin
212 E. Washington Ave., Room 213
Madison, WI 53703
(608) 264-5261

Wyoming
100 E. B St., Room 4001
Casper, WY 82602-2839
(307) 261-6500

Small Business Development Centers

These centers, which are often set within a university, offer one-stop assistance to small business in counseling, technical assistance, and training. Many small companies work with the SBDC to develop business plans. The centers are sponsored by the Small Business Administration.

National Web site: www.smallbiz.suny.edu/sbdcnet.htm.

Alabama
Alabama Small Business Develop-
   ment Center
University of Alabama
Box 870397
Tuscaloosa, AL 35487
(205) 348-7011

Alaska
UAA Small Business Development
   Center
430 W. Seventh Ave., #110
Anchorage, AK 99501

(907) 274-7232

Arizona
Arizona Small Business Development
Center
2411 W. 14th St., #132
Tempe, AZ 85281
(602) 731-8720

Arkansas
Arkansas Small Business Development Center
100 S. Main, #401

Little Rock, AR 72201
(501) 324-9043

California
California Small Business Development Center
Office of Small Business
801 K St., #1700
Sacramento, CA 95814
(916) 324-5068

Colorado
Colorado Business Assistance Center
1625 Broadway, #805
Denver, CO 80202
(800) 333-7798
(303) 592-5720

Connecticut
Connecticut Small Business Development Center
University of Connecticut
2 Bourn Pl., U-94
Storrs, CT 06269-5094
(860) 486-4135

Delaware
Delaware Small Business Development Center
University of Delaware
102 MBNA America Hall
Newark, DE 19716
(302) 831-2747

District of Columbia
Small Business Development Center
Howard University, School of Business, Room 128
2600 Sixth St., NW
Washington, DC 20059
(202) 806-1550

Florida
Florida Small Business Development Center
19 W. Garden St., #302
Pensacola, FL 32501
(850) 470-4980

Georgia
Business Outreach Services
Small Business Development Center

Chicopee Complex
University of Georgia
1180 E. Broad St.
Athens, GA 30602-5412
(706) 542-6762

Hawaii
University of Hawaii at Hilo
Small Business Development Center Network
200 W. Kawili St.
Hilo, HI 96720-4091
(808) 933-3515

Idaho
Idaho Small Business Development Center
Boise State University
1910 University Dr.
Boise, ID 83725-1655
(208) 385-1640

Illinois
Illinois Greater North Pulaski Small Business Development Center
4054 W. North Ave.
Chicago, IL 60639
(800) 252-2923
(773) 384-2262

Indiana
Indiana Small Business Development Center
1 N. Capitol, #420
Indianapolis, IN 46204
(317) 264-6871

Iowa
Iowa Small Business Development Center
137 Lynn Ave.
Ames, IA 50014
(515) 292-6351

Kansas
Small Business Development Center
1501 S. Joplin
Pittsburg, KS 66762
(316) 235-4920

Kentucky
Kentucky Small Business Development Center
225 Gatton College of Business and Economics
Lexington, KY 40506
(606) 257-7668

Louisiana
Louisiana Small Business Development Center
College of Business Administration
Northeast Louisiana University
Monroe, LA 71209-6435
(318) 342-5506

Maine
University of Southern Maine
96 Falmouth St.
P.O. Box 9300
Portland, ME 04104-9300
(207) 780-4420

Maryland
Maryland Small Business Development Center
7100 E. Baltimore Ave., #401
College Park, MD 20740-3627
(301) 403-8300

Massachusetts
Massachusetts Small Business Development Center
University of Massachusetts
P.O. Box 34935
Amherst, MA 01003
(413) 545-6301

Michigan
Michigan Small Business Development Center
2727 Second Ave., #107
Detroit, MI 48201
(313) 964-1798

Minnesota
Minnesota Small Business Development Center
Department of Trade and Economic Development
500 Metro Square

121 Seventh Pl. E.
St. Paul, MN 55101-2146
(612) 297-5773

Mississippi
Mississippi Small Business Development Center
University of Mississippi
216 Old Chemistry Bldg.
University, MS 38677
(800) 725-7232 (in Mississippi)
(601) 232-5001

Missouri
Missouri Small Business Development Center
1205 University Ave., #300
Columbia, MO 65211
(573) 882-0344

Montana
Small Business Development Center
Department of Commerce
1424 Ninth Ave.
Helena, MT 59620
(406) 444-4780

Nebraska
Nebraska Business Development Center
College of Business Administration
University of Nebraska at Omaha, Room 407
Omaha, NE 68182-0248
(402) 554-2521

Nevada
Nevada Small Business Development Center
University of Nevada at Reno
College of Business Administration
Reno, NV 89557-0100
(702) 784-1717

New Hampshire
New Hampshire Small Business Development Center
100 Elm St., 12th Floor
Manchester, NH 03101
(603) 624-2000

New Jersey
New Jersey Small Business Development Center
49 Bleeker St.
Newark, NJ 07102-1993
(973) 353-5950

New Mexico
New Mexico Small Business Development Center
Santa Fe Community College
6401 S. Richards Ave.
Santa Fe, NM 87505
(800) 281-SBDC
(505) 438-1362

New York
New York Small Business Development Center
SUNY Plaza, S-523
Albany, NY 12246
(800) 732-SBDC (in New York State)
(518) 443-5398

North Carolina
North Carolina Small Business and Technology Development Center
333 Fayetteville Street Mall, #1150
Raleigh, NC 27601
(800) 258-0862 (in North Carolina)
(919) 715-7272

North Dakota
North Dakota Small Business Development Center
University of North Dakota
P.O. Box 7308
Grand Forks, ND 58202
(701) 777-3700

Ohio
Ohio Small Business Development Center
P.O. Box 1001
Columbus, OH 43261-1001
(614) 466-2480

Oklahoma
Oklahoma Small Business Development Center, Station A
P.O. Box 2584
Durant, OK 74701
(405) 924-0277

Oregon
Oregon Small Business Development Center Network
44 W. Broadway, #501
Eugene, OR 97401-3021
(541) 726-2250

Pennsylvania
Pennsylvania Small Business Development Center
University of Pennsylvania, Vance Hall
3733 Spruce St., 4th Floor
Philadelphia, PA 19104
(215) 898-1219

Puerto Rico
The Puerto Rico Small Business Development Center
Union Plaza Building, Suite 701
Ponce de Leon Avenue Hato Rey
Puerto Rico 00918
(787) 763-6875

Rhode Island
Rhode Island Small Business Development Center
Bryant College
1150 Douglas Pike
Smithfield, RI 02917
(401) 232-6111

South Carolina
South Carolina Small Business Development Center
College of Business Administration, Room 652
University of South Carolina
Columbia, SC 29208
(803) 777-4907

South Dakota
South Dakota Small Business Development Center
University of South Dakota, School of Business
414 E. Clark St.
Vermillion, SD 57069-2390
(605) 677-5498

Tennessee
Tennessee Small Business Development Center

University of Memphis, South Campus, Bldg. No. 1
Memphis, TN 38152
(901) 678-2500

Texas
Texas Small Business Development Center
1100 Louisiana, #500
Houston, TX 77002
(713) 752-8400

Utah
Utah Small Business Development Center
1623 S. State St.
Salt Lake City, UT 84115
(801) 957-3840

Vermont
Vermont Small Business Development Center
60 Main St., #103
Burlington, VT 05401
(802) 658-9228

Virginia
Virginia Small Business Development Center
P.O. Box 446
Richmond, VA 23218-0446
(804) 371-8258

Washington
Washington Small Business Development Center
Washington State University
P.O. Box 644851
Pullman, WA 99164-4851
(509) 335-1576

West Virginia
West Virginia Small Business Development Center
950 Kanawha Blvd., #200
Charleston, WV 25301
(304) 558-2960

Wisconsin
University of Wisconsin at Whitewater
Small Business Development Center
Carlson 2000
Whitewater, WI 53190
(414) 472-3217

Wyoming
Wyoming Small Business Development Center
111 W. Second St., #502
Casper, WY 82601
(307) 234-6683

FRANCHISE RESOURCES

Associations for the Franchise and Business-Opportunity Industries

American Association of Franchisees and Dealers
P.O. Box 81887
San Diego, CA 92138-1887
(800) 733-9858
www.gateads.com/aafd

American Franchise Association
53 W. Jackson Blvd., Suite 205
Chicago, IL 60604
(800) 334-4232
(312) 431-0545
www.infonews.com/franchise/afa

Capital Area Franchise Association
1150 18th St., NW, Suite 875

Washington, DC 20036
(202) 331-3444

Federal Communications Commission
Office of Communications Business Opportunities
1919 M. St., NW
Washington, DC 20554
(202) 418-0990
www.fcc.gov

Federal Trade Association
Bureau of Consumer Protection
6th St. and Pennsylvania Ave., NW
Washington, DC 20580
(202) 326-2222
www.fta.gov

Franchise Information Network
1709-B Hillyear Robinson Pkwy.
  South
Oxford, AL 36203
(800) 444-6670

International Franchise Association
1350 New York Ave., NW, Suite 900
Washington, DC 20005-4709
(202) 628-8000

National Business Opportunities Bureau

2064 Peachtree Industrial Ct; Suite
  404
Atlanta, GA 30341
(800) 829-3547

National Federation of Independent
  Business
600 Maryland Ave., Suite 700
Washington, DC 20024
(202) 554-9000

Web Sites with Franchise Information

Better Business Bureau
(Information on fraud and
  complaints)
www.bbb.org

Business and Franchise Opportunity
  Directory
(Listings of franchises)
www.teleport.com/~ryton/BizOpndx

Business Links
(Connections to Web sites related to
  franchises and business opportunities)
www.gnn.com/gnn/wic/wics/bus.74

Business Opportunities
(Listings of business opportunities)
www.webcom.com/cfnet/keywords/
  busopp

Business Opportunities News Home
  Page
(Listings of business opportunities)
www.business-Opps-news.com

Business Opportunity Page
(Listings of business opportunities)
www.galaxy-net.com/bus-Opp

The Entrepreneurs Bookstore
(Books and reports)
www.kwicsys.com/kwicsys/books

Franchise and Investment Expo (Listings of franchise expos around the
  country)
www.betheboss.com

Franchise Handbook Online
(Listings of franchises and general information)
www.execpc.com/franchise1/

Franchise Update Online
(Listings of franchises and detailed
  information)
www.franchise-update.com

FranNet Online
(Commercial site with franchise information)
www.frannet.com

Home Business Magazine Online
(Listings of business opportunities
  and information on home business)
www.homebusinessmag.com

International Franchise Internet Service
(Wide range of international information on franchises)
www.ifis.com

BUSINESS ASSOCIATIONS

Business associations are an excellent place to learn more about the business you plan to launch or one you already run. Associations provide industry information, business-management education, and networking opportunities. For example, if you want to know the future prospects and earning potential of medical transcription, there's no better place to find out than the American Association for Medical Transcription; if it is graphic arts that interests you, try the Graphic Artists Guild.

American Association for Medical
Transcription
P.O. Box 576187
Modeso, CA 95357
(800) 982-2182

American Association of Exporters
and Importers
11 West 42nd St., 30th Floor
New York, NY 10035
(212) 944-2230

American Electronics Association
5201 Great American Pkwy.
Santa Ana, CA 95054
(408) 987-4200

American Management Association
1601 Broadway
New York, NY 10019
(212) 586-8100

American Society of Composers, Au-
thors and Publishers
ASCAP Building
One Lincoln Plaza
New York, NY 10023
(212) 621-6000

American Society of Interior Designers
608 Massachusetts Ave., NE
Washington, DC 20002
(202) 546-3480

American Society of Journalists and
Authors
1501 Broadway, Suite 302
New York, NY 10036
(212) 997-0947

American Society of Magazine Photographers
419 Park Ave. South
New York, NY 10016
(212) 889-9144

American Society of Travel Agents
1101 King St.
Alexandria, VA 22314
(703) 739-2782

American Translators Association
1735 Jefferson Davis Highway, Suite
903
Arlington, VA 22202-3413
(703) 892-1500

Associated Locksmiths of America
3003 Live Oak St.
Dallas, TX 75204
(214) 827-1701

Association of Independent Information Professionals (AIIP)
c/o Burwel Enterprises, Inc.
3724 FM 1960 West, Suite 214
Houston, TX 77068
(713) 537-9051

Association of Management Consultant Firms
230 Park Ave., Suite 544
New York, NY 10169
(212) 697-9693

Association of Venture Clubs
P.O. Box 3358
Salt Lake City, UT 84110-3358
(801) 364-1100

The Authors Guild
330 West 42nd St.
New York, NY 10036-6902
(212) 563-5904

Center for Entrepreneurial Management
180 Varick St., 17th Floor
New York, NY 10014
(212) 633-0060

Direct Marketing Association
11 West 42nd St.
New York, NY 10036-8096
(212) 768-7277

Direct Selling Association
1776 K. St., NW, Suite 600
Washington, DC. 20006
(202) 293-5760

Florists Transworld Delivery Association
29200 Northwestern Highway
Southfield, MI 48034
(313) 355-9300

Graphic Artists Guild
11 West 20th St., 8th Floor
New York, NY 10011-3704
(212) 463-7730

Independent Computer Consultants
Association
933 Gardenview Office Pkwy.
St. Louis, MO 63141
(800) 438-4222
(314) 997-4633

Independent Music Association
317 Skyline Lake Dr.
P.O. Box 609
Ringwood, NJ 07456
(201) 831-1317

Information Industry Association
555 New Jersey Ave., NW, Suite 800
Washington, DC 20001
(202) 639-8262

International Advertising Association
342 Madison Ave., Suite 2000
New York, NY 10173-0073
(212) 557-1133

International Association of Business
Communicators
1 Hallidie Plaza, Suite 600
San Francisco, CA 94012
(800) 776-4222

International Association for Financial Planning
2 Concourse Pkwy., Suite 800
Atlanta, GA 30328
(800) 945-IAFP
(404) 395-1605

International Communications Industry Association
3150 Spring St.
Fairfax, VA 22031
(703) 273-7200

International Online Network
6303 S. Rural Rd., Suite 1
Temple, AZ 85283
(602) 730-8088

International Reciprocal Trade Association
9513 Beach Mill Rd.
Great Falls, VA 22066
(703) 759-1473

Latin American Management Association
419 New Jersey Ave., SE
Washington, DC 20003
(800) 522-6623
(202) 546-3803

Manufacturers Agents Association
23016 Mill Creek Dr.
Laguna Hills, CA 92653
(714) 859-4040

National Association of Secretarial
Services
3637 Fourth St. North, Suite 330
St. Petersburg, FL 33704
(813) 823-3646

National Association of Systems Integrators
P.O. Box 440
560 Dedham St.
Wrentham, MA 02093
(508) 384-5850

National Association of Tole and Decorative Artists
P.O. Box 808
Newton, KS 67114
(316) 283-9665

National Association of Wholesale
Distributors
1725 K St., NW, Suite 710
Washington, DC 20006
(202) 872-0885

National Candy Wholesalers Association
1120 Vermont Ave., NW, Suite 1120
Washington, DC 20005
(202) 463-2124

National Cosmetology Association
3510 Olive St.
St. Louis, MO 63103
(314) 534-7980

National Decorating Products Association
1050 N. Lindbergh Blvd.
St. Louis, MO 63132
(314) 991-3470

National Federation of Independent
   Business
600 Maryland Ave., SW, Suite 700
Washington, DC 20024
(202) 554-9000

National Pest Control Association
8100 Oak St.
Dunn Loring, VA 22027
(703) 573-8330

National Roofing Contractors Association
10255 W. Higgins Rd., Suite 600
Rosemont, IL 60018
(708) 299-9070

National Small Business Network
P.O. Box 223
Centereach, NY 11720
(516) 467-6826

National Small Business United
1155 15th St., NW
Washington, DC 20005
(202) 293-8830

National Speakers Association
3877 N. Seventh St., Suite 350
Phoenix, AZ 85014
(602) 265-1001

National Tour Association
546 E. Main St.
Lexington, KY 40508
(606) 253-1036

Owner-Operator Independent Driver
   Association
311 Mize Rd.
Grain Valley, MO 64029
(816) 229-5791

Professional Photographers of
   America
1090 Executive Way
Des Plaines, IL 60018
(708) 299-8161

Professional Picture Framers Association
4305 Sarellen Rd.
Richmond, VA 23231
(804) 226-0430

Self-Service Storage Association
60 Revere Dr., Suite 500
Northbrook, IL 60062
(708) 480-9627

Small Business Foundation of
   America
1155 15th St., NW
Washington, DC 20005
(202) 223-1103

Society of American Florists
1601 Duke St.
Alexandria, VA 22314
(703) 836-8700

Software Publishers Association
1730 M St., NW, Suite 700
Washington, DC 20036-4510
(202) 452-1600

Specialty Advertising Association International
1404 Walnut Hill Lane
Irving, TX 75038
(214) 580-0404

Trade Show Bureau
1660 Lincoln St., Suite 2080
Denver, CO 80264
(303) 860-7626

Travel Industry Association of
   America
1133 21st St., NW
Washington, DC 20036
(202) 293-1433

Video Software Dealers Association
3 Eves Dr., Suite 307

Marlton, NJ 08053
(609) 596-8500

BUSINESS AND TRADE MAGAZINES

Business and trade magazines provide a wealth of information. Business magazines are designed to help business owners, while trade magazines include information about the industries they cover—from their trade shows and conferences to their trends and marketing. Business magazines are available for an annual subscription rate. Some trade magazines are free to qualified readers while others are available for an annual subscription rate. Most will send along a sample copy at no charge.

Business Start-Ups
2392 Morse Ave.
Irvine, CA 92614
(800) 274-8333

Catalog Age
6 Riverbend Rd.
P.O. Box 4949
Stamford, CT 06907-0949
(203) 358-9900
(For catalog producers)

Direct
6 Riverbend Rd.
P.O. Box 4949
Stamford, CT 06907-0949
(203) 358-9000
(For those involved in direct marketing)

Direct Marketing News
100 Avenue of the Americas
New York, NY 10013
(212) 925-7300
(For those involved in direct marketing)

Entrepreneur
P.O. Box 19787
Irvine, CA 92714-9438
(800) 274-6229
(For business owners)

Entrepreneurial Edge
P.O. Box 8
Cassopolis, MI 49031
(800) 357-LOWE
(616) 445-4200

Franchise Handbook
1020 North Broadway, Suite 111
Milwaukee, WI 53202
(414) 272-9977
(Periodic listings of franchises and business opportunities)

Franchise Times
1350 New York Ave., NW, Suite 900
Washington, DC 20005-4709
(202) 628-8000
(For the franchise industry)

Franchising World
P.O. Box 1020
Sewickley, PA 15143
(800) 543-1039
(For franchisees)

Get Rich at Home
1115 Broadway
New York, NY 10010
(212) 807-7100
(For business owners)

Home Business Magazine
PMB 368 9582 Hamilton Ave.
Huntington Beach, CA 92646
(714) 968-0331
(For business owners)

Home Office
2392 Morse Ave.
Irvine, CA 92614
(714) 261-2325

Home Office Computing
730 Broadway
New York, NY 10003
(212) 505-3580
(For business owners)

How, the Bottomline Design Magazine
1507 Dana Ave.
Cincinnati, OH 45207-1005
(513) 531-2902
(For graphic designers)

iMarketing News
100 Avenue of the Americas
New York, NY 10013
(212) 925-7300
(For those involved in Internet marketing)

Inc.
38 Commercial Wharf
Boston, MA 02110
(617) 248-8000
(For business owners)

The Industry Standard
315 Pacific Ave.
San Francisco, CA 94111-1701
(415) 733-5400
(For those involved in the Internet economy)

Money Maker Monthly
15738 South Bell Rd., Suite 200
Lockport, IL 60441
(708) 429-4444
(For network marketers)

Self-Employed Professional
462 Boston St.
Topsfield, MA 01983-1232
(800) 874-4113
(For business owners)

Selling Power
P.O. Box 5467
Fredericksburg, VA 22403
(800) 752-7355
(For those involved in sales)

Sign Builder Illustrated
4905 Pine Cone Dr., Suite 2
Durham, NC 27707
(919) 489-1416
(For sign makers, painters, and graphic artists)

Small Business Opportunities
1115 Broadway
New York, NY 10010
(212) 807-7100
(For business owners)

Start Your Own Business
1115 Broadway
New York, NY 10010
(212) 807-7100
(For business owners)

Success
733 Third Ave.
New York, NY 10017
(212) 883-7100
(For business owners)

Successful Franchising
1224 Westwind Trail
Berne, IN 46711
(For franchisees)

Today's Business Owner
1151 Dove St., Suite 100
Newport Beach, CA 92660

Today's Photographer International
P.O. Box 777

Lewisville, NC 27023
(336) 945-9867
(For photographers)

Upline: The Journal for Network Marketing Sales Leaders
400 East Jefferson
Charlottesville, VA 22902
(804) 979-7856

Wealth Building
15738 South Bell Rd., Suite 200
Lockport, IL 60441

(708) 429-4444
(For network marketers)

Working at Home
733 Third Ave.
New York, NY 10017
(212) 883-7100
(For business owners)

Writer's Digest
1507 Dana Ave.
Cincinnati, OH 45207-1005
(513) 531-2902
(For freelance writers)

NETWORK-MARKETING (MULTILEVEL MARKETING) RESOURCES

Here are resources specifically for the network-marketing industry. Since there are some questionable companies presenting themselves as legitimate enterprises, we have also included government agencies that can help you verify that the company you are working with is aboveboard.

Associations

Direct Selling Association and Foundation
1666 K St., NW, Suite 1010
Washington, DC 20006-2808
(202) 293-5760

Federal Communications Commission
Office of Communications Business Opportunities
1919 M St., NW
Washington, DC 20554
(202) 418-0990

Federal Trade Commission
Bureau of Consumer Protection
6th St. and Pennsylvania Ave., NW
Washington, DC 20580
(202) 326-2222

Multi-Level Marketing International Association
1101 Dove St., #170
Newport Beach, CA 92660
(714) 622-0300

Internet Resources

Better Business Bureau
www.bbb.org
(Search this site for information on network marketing in general and for any companies that may have complaints registered against them.)

Business Researcher's Interests
www.bint.com

(This site has a wide range of business information, including information on network marketing.)

Home Business Magazine
www.homebusinessmag.com
(This site presents information on network marketing as well as general information on a home business.)

Home Business Resources
www.networkmarketing.com
(It lists a number of network-marketing companies.)

The MLM Advisor
www.mlmads.com
(It presents itself as a network-
marketing magazine.)

Multilevel Marketing and Pyramid
  Schemes
www.bosbbb.org/lit/0003
(This site offers information on how to
tell a legitimate network-marketing
company from a pyramid scheme.)

Multilevel Marketing Government Information
www.usps.gov/websites/depart/
inspec/pyramid
(This site presents information on
pyramid schemes and how they vio-
late postal laws.)

Multilevel Marketing Information
www.cris.com/~sbis/mlm
(This is a commercial site offering information and resources on network
marketing.)

Multilevel Marketing Resources
www.scott.net/~sw-etc/tm/mlm
(This site offers a wide range of information on network-marketing and
MLM companies.)

Multilevel Marketing Yellow Pages
www.bestmall.com/mall
(This is an online directory of network-marketing companies.)

The Network Marketing Emporium
www.cashflow.com/index
(This is an online directory of network-marketing companies.)

Online Index
www.primenet,com/~magarth/test
(This is an index of articles and publications on network-marketing and
MLM companies.)

HOME-BASED BUSINESS RESOURCES

Associations

American Association of Home-Based
  Businesses
P.O. Box 10023
Rockville, MD 20849
(800) 447-9710
(202) 310-3130

Association of Enterprising Mothers
6965 El Camino Rd., Suite 105-612
Carlsbad, CA 92009
(800) 223-9260
(619) 434-9225

Center for Family Business
5682 Mayfield Rd.
Cleveland, OH 44124
(216) 442-0800

Dads at Home
61 Brightwood Ave.
North Andover, MA 01845

(508) 685-7931

Federation of Small Business
407 S. Dearborn, Suite 500
Chicago, IL 60605
(312) 427-0206

Home-Based Working Moms
P.O. Box 500464
Austin, TX 78750
(512) 918-0670

Independent Business Alliance
111 John St., Suite 1210
New York, NY 10038
(212) 513-1446

International Council for Small Business
3674 Lindell Blvd.
St. Louis, MO 63108
(314) 658-3850

Mother's Home Business Network
P.O. Box 423
East Meadow, NY 11590
(516) 997-7394

National Association for the Cottage Industry
P.O. Box 14460
Chicago, IL 60614
(312) 472-8116

National Association for the Self-Employed
United Group Service Center

P.O. Box 1116
Hurst, TX 76053-1116
(800) 232-6273

National Home Office Association
1828 L St., NW, Suite 402
Washington, DC 20036
(800) 664-6462
www.nhoa1.org

Small Office Home Office Association
1767 Business Center Dr.
Reston, VA 22090
(888) SOHOA11
(703) 438-3060

WOMEN-OWNED BUSINESS RESOURCES

Associations

American Business Woman's Association
P.O. Box 8728
Kansas City, MO 64114-0728
(816) 361-6621

Mother's Home Business Network
P.O. Box 423
East Meadow, NY 11554
(516) 997-7394

National Association of Women Business Owners
600 S. Federal St., Suite 400
Chicago, IL 60605
(312) 922-0465

National Association of Women in Construction
99 Bridge Rd.
Hauppauge, NY 11788
(516) 348-0505

SOURCES FOR COMPUTERS AND OFFICE SUPPLIES

These are sources for purchasing home-office supplies and computer equipment.

Hello Direct
5884 Eden Park Pl.
San Jose, CA 95138
(800) 444-3556
(Telephone products)

MacWarehouse and MicroWarehouse
1720 Oak St.
Lakewood, NJ 08701
(800) 255-6227 (Mac)
(800) 367-7080 (PC)
(Extensive hardware, software, and

peripheral catalogs that offer discount prices)

PC Connection and Mac Connection
Mill St.
Marlow, NH 03456
(800) 800-0004 (PC)
(800) 800-0002 (Mac)
(Extensive computer-supplies catalogs)

Quill
100 South Schelter Rd.
Lincolnshire, IL 60069
(846) 634-4800

(800) 789-1331
(Discount office supplies)
Reliable Home Products
P.O. Box 1502
Ottawa, IL 61350
(800) 869-6000
(Discount office supplies)

Viking Office Products
13809 South Figuroa
P.O. Box 61144
Los Angeles, CA 90061
(800) 248-6111
(Discount office supplies)

HOME BUSINESS MAGAZINE

The Home-Based Entrepreneur's Magazine

This is the premier publication for the growing home-based business market. The magazine offers cutting-edge editorials by well-known authorities on:

- Sales and marketing
- Business operations
- Raising of money
- Franchising
- Productivity
- Business opportunities
- Network marketing
- Mail orders

The magazine also presents lists of home-based franchises, business opportunities, and multilevel marketing companies. For a sample issue, contact:

Home Business Magazine
PMB 368 9582 Hamilton Ave.
Huntington Beach, CA 92646
(714) 968-0331

Index

325